VOLUME ONE

DAMN NEAR

THE CODES TO THE SECRECTS TO THE HAPPINESS TO NIRVANA

Copyright year: 2005
Copyright Notice: by Steven Simmons ALL RIGHTS RESERVED
Front and Back cover photos of AUTHOR: by Steven Simmons ALL RIGHTS RESEVRVED
Front and back cover designed by Brandt Hardin @ Dregstudios.com
Book designed by Gikuyu

No part of this book may be reproduced in any form or by any means electronic, Or mechanical, including photocopying, recording, or by any information storage and retrieval system, without permission in writing from the author.

Contact at: gikuyu@gmail.com

Library of Congress Cataloging-in-publication Data
Volume One Damn Near/ The Codes to The Secrets to The Happiness To Nirvana

P. cm.

Includes index
ISBN 978-0-615-19834-7

Published simultaneously worldwide

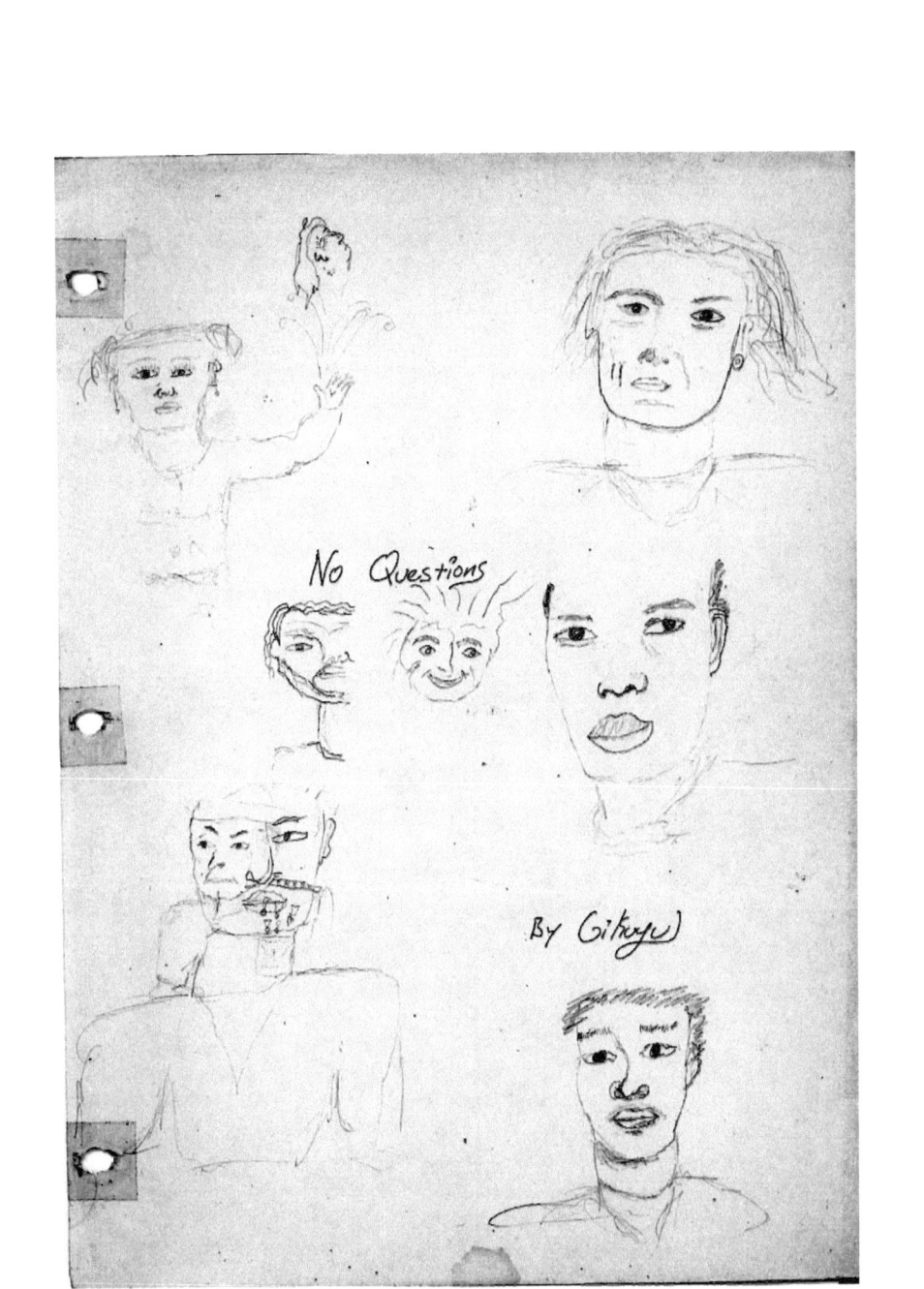

The Introduction

I wrote this Book inside of a huge context and Design. I was going to write One's Introduction, but that would have seem to be apart of this Book. This is Not. This Introduction is Outside of This Book. Though it's inside of The same context. In a different Area.

This book is Numbers oreinated. Oh, Example. Each number at the end of a section Adds up to be 7. And on every 7th Poem Includes the title's of That section. X-cept for The world. The world is All.

I asked a question in the 3rd Poem. My only x-cuse is that I was just getting into This context.

Be care ful when You read this. Though There Are No Questions, Don't take This As Adverse.

REMEMBER THIS IS LIFE!

May 22nd 1989
9:13 am

The Table Of Contents

1.) One's Reality
2.) One's Window
3.) One's Discovery
4.) One's Flower
5.) One's Being
6.) One's Thought
7.) One's Deepenness

8.) One's Style
9.) One's Center
10.) One's Luck
11.) One's Comfort
12.) One's Feelings
13.) One's Ride
14.) One's Extention
15.) One's Day
16.) One's Foundation

17.) One's Holding
18.) One's Awakening
19.) One's Risk
20.) One's Song
21.) One's World
22.) One's Two's
23.) One's Trip
24.) One's ♀
25.) One's Contribution

One's Reality

When one's reality becomes the
      way.
And not just another direction
His friends will say
   And one will refuse
         to take correction.

One's reality
   Starts behind one's eyes
His thoughts Her thoughts
     one's interpretation
One's reality
   Is their reputation
Simply. As a maker's Ideal
   One's Reality

April 1st 1989
3:39 am

One's Window

Outside this clear substance many things
has it's way to happen. This big bright gas shines
and sometimes it's hidden by those things people
titled clouds. Someone judges another and I try
to see the grass as it grows. If you ask anyone
what's outside this clear substance. Would they
answer. The answer. Does anyone knows.
 It's dark inside the window or on the other
side of that window the lights are low. Still
trying to be patient while the grass grows. If
I slow down enough to breath, then the value
will never leave. Just notice what's is said,
and how it's said, advise from the dead.
Live Life. That's what the window reflects

4-1-89
8:01pm
Gilroy

One's Discovery

Wow! No lines in this book
Does that notion get you hooked.
How about the rhyming words
Do you think I don't know
 what I'm saying?
If so. Think Again
 my friend.
Discover my words..for it's yours
I'm not the only 1 ~~one~~ to get wet
 when the rain pours
My little cousin Sinaya is about 3
She can show her feelings
 And if I should die after
She turns 18
 Give my work of 89
Also ~~both~~ on white paper
 to her
The Young Soul. We are together
Discover what's there
 CARE.
In what's or who's even
 Exist.
In what Exist.
 Dig?
If Not Dig Anyway

4-1-04
10:05pm
Gitangeli

One's Flower

The Flowers that exist in the space
  Of Never.
The one I wrote about on X-mas
  of 86.
The sun still shines, the rain still fall
    Around it
    And not on it
    And it still exist.
Some of the whispering words of wisdom
    From the peddles were
      And Are,
My roots are planted
    In the Soul of God!
It's all I need to exist!
The flower I titled LOVE!

April 3 1989
3:35 Am
Gilroy

One's Being

Sometimes there exist the substance
of one's soul.
The Particals that's tangible to the mind
that can be consciously grasped
    And managed
            But not controled.
Is one's Being.

Manage out of the context of
        Commitment.
I was mistaken in what I said
                    Before.
The existance of the substance of
one's Soul,...
        Is All The time.
Even when the shinbay is drained
    of Energy.
One's Being can exist in others.
    As one sees People
        Every day.

                4-4-89
                I am
                Gitayul

One's Thought

A single sentence that
      One latches on to.
Entangled in with others
      and anyone else
One chooses.
The element that triggers
      Feelings or Emotions
      As if they both are the same.
I remember one time I thought
      It ended up being a poem
      Made out of a lesson.
My thoughts are often that.
      Thought...
Anything with insight!

April 7th 1987
Around 3pm
Gilroy

One's Deeperness

When one see's Reality.
It's like some¹ has opened the Window
And One's Discovery
    is the fresh Air.
Which Allows the Flower to Grow.
When One is Being with that
    The thought
Could only widen
        One's Deeperness
    Into Life.

April 8th 1989
1:10 Am

One's Style

The way of expression by the reality that he puts in front of himself. A flame by the book shelf. It allows one to see the titles in the dark.
The Being not the same and also at the same time Being the same but different.
The way of seeing and not reacting out of just pure opinion.

One's style isn't based upon his or her's perception without contious flow of others input.

The way of expressing or sometimes covering one's innerself

The way one goes when 1 forms certain standards in that area

April 8th
3pm 1989

One's Center

The Place of energy
The choice of having to give it free
Or no choice of giving it away
    Because of Being Cool
    Discovering what to say
    Instead of repeating
        Yourself.
    Of course it's Inside
    And That's where You can't hide
People's Perception of their Participation is
    Vague to little to none.
One's center doesn't require thoughts to
        Exist.
    Though many doesn't know the Existence of
        with out Thoughts.
    One's center is Yourself

April 11 1989
4:47am

1's Luck

Yesterday she called him back
Over 365 days ago him called her
Now who would have luck like that?
   She moved in town
Wow what a lucky Guy
   He knew he was lucky
Being underneath the same blue sky

   One's luck
Last time they spoke
            was a year ago
She moved in town
         And called to let him know
He never stopped loving this girl
      Because he knew
They lived on the same world.

4-11-89
7:28 pm

One's Comfort

That's hER ↑
That's not it.
She came walking in my dreams
And expanded my mind.
Taking it as a lesson
With wild theories there to find.
Like running away until yesterday
She was my comfort
The girl who was her name
And Reality dictated the whole
Answere without reasons
        for them.
We were it.
    She was "Her."
  Comfort
That's hER ↑

April 13th or 14th
I haven't checked
  the Calender..
with Her
    we counted life's
        2gether.
11:41pm
      or 11:94am
      who knows
      this to tell

One's Feelings

The Perplexrity of this context
I just speak about myself
We'll see what comes next
Then sea what's left.
She said "What's going on?"
    You Don't sound Yourself.
I told her my situation.
She said BE CAREFUL!
    While you're on the Edge of "insanity!"
SURE. I said at least until I'm Dead.
This world is "IS." Opportunity's and choices
She shares that view.
Every so often I have one finger
    Porpasty Purpose'ly
Hanging on the edge.
            Notice that C spelled Sea?
And Popularity is wild So wild.
Well... Atleast That's My Feelingg.

April 17th 1989
80 SAM
G.Truge

One's Ride

That night I was leaving.
We spent five hours together.
It was cool just Be living -
Slipping and Sliding in the snowy weather.
  We drove up to this community
       on A mountain Peak.
The vibes was so Loud
       You could Almost hear them Yelk!
  We parked on this hill facing the
town. The street lights were like stars and
the snow made the scenery look like the
                Milky Way

 I remember Being in the car
         as she drove.
Remember seeing A person who's walked
Remember seeing the on the edge for over a year
              smile.
       She said "Thanx for being here

                            4-20-89
                            Lithuyu

One's Extention

To write this piece and to give it a style,
I remove this page from the center of this Book.
It's Just Luck that this is written with Deepness.
The way Comfort sings. Extended all levels of the Soul
And the way the determinations brewing feelings without reason
While I am taken for a ride with a simple word Puzzle
the writing before the word and after the words is the word's Extention

Did I mention. I wrote a book in a day
To Extend the foundations

April 23 1989
9:18 pm
Gikuyu

One's Day

One's day consists of
    The sun rising.
Paying immediate attention
    To the opinions
        That fills one's mind.
One's day consists of
    Being conscious
remembering memories
    Because they're there.
Giving and taking lessons
    Which of course
        one should share.
One's day provides the way
    For the sun to set.

April 26 1989
5:55 am

One's Foundation

The way we see things are the way to be. Beside the next way to find out what has us... to be grounded. The world is at the not knowing — which is the Being — soleness of which can be explained by not knowing the outcoming of that that is the reality that you choose to recognize. Stating what you say is yours. I don't know but I just may be missing sense. Sense the world is ones. And belongs to us. And not them. I'm speaking a pure opinion now but not now? Think that one's foundation is life.

April 27th 1989
9:38 pm
Cikoyn

One's Holding

Truth isn't true or false
　Nor either between
Hold that
　　　Any way you wish.
The world is the cause
　There exist "No good or mean"
　The difference between A
　　bussiness man and A Hunger kid.
The way the Hold
　　　Their meal's dish.
The way These words A written
　As if they have A holding
　　in what I say
That is
　　I U wish to hold it that
　　　　　way

April 30th 1989
9:39pm
[signature]

One's Awakening

It has become clear to me that now, more than ever, the choice in life has to be to live it, only on the edge. One's life not lived on the edge, on the uncomfortability that on the edgeness brings. Is just saying this is a pratice run. Which we all know it's not. Eventhough there's past life's and furture life's. The one lived now is a solid step. And not a sliding board.

Yes. It's true I had that dream. And many had that dream also. I admit. Atleast 75% of them I forget, or they get tangled up in life, so it's sometimes hard to differentiatt the two. I bring them out and live that also. It's a pleasure worth no treasure. The treasure will bee here long after I'm gone. I have my soul, though. The life lived here "As U can" is no pratice run.

May 3rd 1989
1:46 AM
Gilroy

One's Risk

I keep putting myself out there to be broken up. To return not the same. This sometimes happens every moment. This sometimes happens every now and then. My sanity is what I put at stake when I put myself out there.

I often don't have time to check in with myself to see how I'm feeling. That's risking my integrity and my commitment to stay on the "To do it right" path. Sometimes when I'm out there. Breakthroughs are caused by any means neccessary.

"Now" is all you really have. What "was" and "will be" isn't there unless you choose to bring it present.

It's my pleasure, and it's a pleasure to be out there inside the not knowing but getting it done!! As I'm young at the age of 22. I know that this risk is something I choose to take for the rest of my life!

May 3 1989
6:54 pm
Gibey

ONC's Song

The Chorus {
Oh yea That sunshine
Bring it on, let's do
    Until time is gone
Yea Darling, You'll Never Be Alone

We held hands and felt the sunrise
We smiled into eachothers eyes
   The rare #A-Tee was a pararty
of a couple in love
Watching the clouds above.
      sometimes below
We watched the sun grow, watched it grow

{the Chorus}

We walked through that
     make shift Graveyard
We saw the kid who's life
     is forever scarred!
Hunger blew up his belly
     She shedded a tear
There seems to be no sunshine here
Was it a dream it didn't happen in "Time"
Like she's really here in this heart
    of mine

{the chorus}

next page

We often broke styles
 And existed with the two of us
The world we are in begin
 Will this time begin
Together we can win. We can win
 Forever you be here
   And I'll be near
      By your side
Holding Your hand when you don't hide

    Oh yes
      That sunshine
       Bring it ON
    Let's Do
       Until time is gone
    Yes Darling
       You'll Never Be Alone!

                May 7th 1989
                  9:04 pm
                G/Kuyu

One's World

My World is full of Discovery. The Reality of Being a flower in the desert. I rarely ride my feelings, because of the Deepeneness of thought that exists in my Style. That Extention alone gets me to the center providing an Awakening that's some of the many elements of my foundation.

My world has been sometimes described as a window. Holding it in that context, Allows a life to be a contribution. Luck is a Basis you have to take. With comfort which I called her luck. One's Perception of the world Becomes two's view of the Possibility.

My world is the song I choose to sing. My world is involved in the party of what I choose to Bring.

My world is a TRIP.

May 9th 1989
5:20pm
Gitoy

1's 2's

I need shoes
My belly's Empty
And I'm feeling the Blues

3's 4's
And the tear pours
And you don't cry
I wondered why

5's 6's
Can it be fixed
Can love and Action
Get mixed

7's 8's
I stand before these Golden Gates
I die of Hunger
Yea I've wondered

A 9 and A ten
~~~~ save my friend
Support him
Before his life ends

MAY 10 1989
2:08 AM
Gikuyu

One's

God is
KUool for
you

May 12th 1989
7:42pm

One's Life

Oh that Girl, was Comfort's friend
She knew me to never end.
Having that fun smiling and being wild
Life said to me "I Love You Child"

She didn't see herself
                    As being different
She characterize herself   And unique

        As Being what you speak.

Babe.. was so cool, smooth, and sometimes
                unknown to me.
Life was the kind that Gave You Life
                             for free
with no response expected
                But Always Given
That Girl
    Made Sure You was living

                    May 17th 1989
                    11:57 pm

One's Contribution

I was walking thru Central Park, with Andrew and Sherri. We was discussing the world, and how hard it is to contribute. We was walking along a path where people rode horses. 10 feet in front of us there was this bridge with just the steel structure. The cement wasn't poured yet. The half finished bridge was crossing over the path.

This jogger came up to the edge of the bridge, and stopped. She was about to go around. When we saw her about to give up and go around, we supported her in getting across. Andrew ran up the hill to the other side of the bridge and held his hand out, while me and Sherri stayed down on the ground below.
- We was telling her "You can do it. Don't be afraid. You can do it." The lady trusted us. 3 strangers who had faith in her. She made it across. She jumped for joy and hugged Andrew and thanked us. And went on her way.

May 20th 1989
3:46 AM Githa

I may be dead when I'm able to say "I was once a writer."

Gilroy

If one forgets the past and remembers the future. Does the now exists as real?

April 1991
Gilroy

I refuse to see the sky without Trees.

Gilroy

Because in this book there will not be what was. Or, what will be, which will then become what is.

Being in Life is being Alive. Living is Life Being in You.

Gilroy

Gilroy

One not immobilized by the Somedays. Yet it's the mobility that one's Being - existence depends.

Gilroy

Why should you know my name.
I know who I am.

Gilroy

chapter two

Only I

35

Speech Given To Life in April

People have always believed that there's nothing new under the sun. So if you are not enlightened by the context of this speech, I'll take it that you are a part of that crowd.

My name is Gikuyu; I'm a few years and 9 months old, I'm a writer. At this moment I'm a great unknown writer. It is not necessary for me to go into details about my books and plays that I've written. For if this you've read some of my work, unless you're one of the few that's around during the writing of this speech, and this book, which this speech is the first piece of.

It's hard for me to accept sometimes that I put my life at stake. I put my sanity at risk. All for the cause. The cause of being a writer. Over the years it could be said that I've acquired some wisdom, which by the way, I don't see it as the same as knowledge. Even with the wisdom, I've come upon situations where I had the choice to play it safe or not, or to once again put myself at risk. I choose almost all the time to put myself at risk. Although the wiser part of me tells me to not, I do it anyway, for it always ends up to be the Outcome that in order for me to be there I must forget all if not most of what I've learned, and be present to what's apart of the here and now. So I ask you, not that I need an answer, but for you to maybe inquire into this. Is it wise to put one's wisdom at risk, or to chose to lose all that is wise in order to receive a much more profound way of being?

Even though I say sometimes it is hard for me to accept it when I risk my sanity, and put my life at risk, what I realize is, it's the only way for me to live. During the period of denying the thought that I choose the right action, I process myself. I look and see where I'm at inside the outcome, and I look and see if this is really it. Of course when I look at the later "is this it." I come to the only conclusion that's there. "This is it." So I accept it. It has taken from a brief moment, to quite a while to accept responsibility for my actions, and deal with where I'm at in the present time. If I've made it seem difficult for me when I'm deciding whether or not I've done the right thing. It's not. It only makes it difficult to beat myself up, so I can justify it, if I'm in what may appear to be the wrong outcome. It's actually easy to accept because I have 100% faith in God, and I know that where I'm at is where God put me.

Although the saying "Feast or Famine" has been around a long time, and I've heard it before, I didn't think about it as in terms of me. For it is often used to describe a writer's life. Not until recently I inquire into the saying as it pertains to me. To break it down, I'll say this; it doesn't pertain to me at all. Feast is a onetime occasion of celebration. Famine is an ongoing experience of suffering. It said you can't have the good without the bad, as for the saying "Feast or Famine"

I feel that the good and the bad must balance each other out. When one uses that saying to refer to their life or way of living, it is obvious that they are knowingly or unknowingly saying that they suffer more than they are in life with joy. And as I get older my "being" becomes more solidly grounded within an universal foundation. It's like this. Say one acquires wisdom for the first time. That wisdom makes a space within his being. Then when one let's go of that wisdom it leaves an open space. Then when one acquires new wisdom, that wisdom fills up the first space, and makes more space. Then let's that newly acquired wisdom go, the next newly acquired wisdom fills the first two spaces and makes a third, and so on and so on. This means that each time the wisdom is acquired it is received with a more profound impact than the previous times. That's how it is for me. Even though one may receive wisdom that's more than required in order to live out the rest of one's life. I've had that quality wisdom countless times. So why would I put it at risk again and again? That's what it takes to be a writer. There's no guarantee that wisdom will return. For that matter neither is there a guarantee for one's sanity to be saved or life to continue if one puts it at risk or at stake. For me in order to have wisdom to return and life to continue, I must be whole heartily committed and have {as I do} 100% faith and trust in God... I'm not really all that concerned about my sanity, for if I was I wouldn't be a writer.

I tried really really hard once to go insane. And I still don't know if I did or not. Because what the hell is the difference... I don't fit in the norm, but yet it is normal for a "True" writer to not fit in the normal. So if I'm normal to me, and seem un-normal to others am I insane? I really consider it blessed.

What is it that makes life "Life" in this fourth month of this year. I leave you with that question.

Stay beautiful

Post speech remarks.

I wanted to have this speech to be at least 5 pages, but it seemed complete, or I completed it. Since there's no introduction to this book I'll pause here to introduce it.

This book will be whatever it turns out to be. As you can see the style of the first piece usually sets up what the whole book will contain. If so I'm convinced that's going to be a very interesting journey.

DEAR WORLD

Hi. How long has it been? I don't exactly remember myself. Thought I'll write one of these N-Touch-2-Touch letters to ya, so that you and I will know that everything is cool.

One reason for this letter is to have an excuse to once again announce to you -YOU- that I'm in jail. And this time I think I got what I "wanted" at least six months. But as you and I both know, that's a blink of an eye to the "Most High."

I'm wondering what will be the outcome of my writings if it's not just to get me out, like the others were before. You see I have been sentenced to six months, straight up and no chaser. Dig? There's no early release. So my writing in this stagnant world will impact out there in ways I'm not sure of yet, and will not find out until the end of the year when I'm released.

I'm going to only express my situation of incarceration only in this letter. {maybe} or I may just write you a letter every month or so things and to keep in touch.

I've somewhat started practicing the many talents I've put away when I started this vacation almost two years ago. I must say I'm a little rusty. The few times I've been "Being" it looks like only when there's no distractions can something be created. But the something has to be big. I've only created or helped another create one big something for himself. Only a few times have I tried without success to pick another's thought. But hay I have about 5 more months left to remaster that style again. I had some photographs sent to me. 45 in all. All of them taken within a span of 3 or 4 years. When I was entering all the way, and year before I decided to take a vacation. The visual; images allows me to sort-of supports me in reminding my Being and what it was about my Being that had all the ladies go wild over me. It's like I could go back over my poetry and rediscover who I was and find out the source to that, and integrate that with my present source of Being, and have a totally new outcome. I'm using the photographs in the capacity of the poetry.

It's interesting to say the least that I'm truly writing with no immediate goal in mind.... Just that statement alone opened up a "Can of insights" if you will. First, I can't count the times when I've said I'm not living for myself, only for you. And yet I realize the power of writing. I've used it time and time again. Yet the first statement of that paragraph suggested, if only for that fleeting moment until I caught myself, That I only write to impact my reality, which in turn write for myself, which in turn ,Live for myself, which all of that is only an interpretation.

If there is such a thing as a "catch 22" or anything to the saying "You can't win for losing" which there will only be if your interpretation are leaning that direction,.....Pause.....I just realize that I'm about to repeat myself. Not in this book but I've written it before. But what the hell, you might not have read it before.

What I write is a gift to the Universe, therefore the world, and in return the Universe gives me a gift. Something that I'll like in the near future. But since I know that I'll Be here for sure for the next six months. {I'll be incarcerated for the next six months} Then when I said immediate goal, I found it interesting that there wasn't none. First let me point out,... did you see that my interpretation was that maybe you would interpret that way.   Second, it's also interesting how I just discovered that I was writing interpet like "interpret", which only let me conclude that these past two years on vacation in Georgia is affecting my language.   Now I'll continue on, with the possibility came out that insight. I can choose to do on of two things. One I could have an immediate goal not pertain to me. Or I could stack up all these "Points" and when I'm released "EXPLODE" onto you.{remember this letter is to the world.} I choose the later for it will have a bigger impact, for I'll be there, with a smile.

                      Until then   the next time
                                    Peace and Love

Another Pause

In all the times like these, one has to consider that Life is truly a gift from God. The Most High. The times for me are seen as trail and tribulation. Only life can provide such obstacles. Death only boredom. So why choose death?

I've been weary of writing on this style which is so to speak off top of my head. For all of my major projects this size has been this way and one would think it's the only way I know how to complete such a major concept.

Two things.. First that's my interpretation. Second "major" isn't the correct way which I would describe this since it's only outlined to be 45 pages. I think the "Largeness" is not in the length but in the depth of the context. As of now I have yet to title this particular book. Also the context of a book isn't in the length but also in the depths of the context. The same is with a novel.

Through all the conversations I've had, I haven't come upon some new discovery or insight. It has been more information of confirmation of previous discoveries and insights, which by providing a firmer foundation is good, but I yearn for some discoveries. And yet although that is true, I continue to write and think. Maybe not everyday {writing that is} the insights and discoveries, when they come will be more profound I'm sure.

Sure for me, I would love to share with you some of the conversations that has firmed the existing foundation, But I won't because I feel it'll just take up space, which will lead me to misleading interpretations about what this project is all about.

This is why there will be no more loosely written pieces like this in this project. For I will only later look upon this and remember that it is not suppose to be here as I originally planned it. {If you can see it that way, for I cannot.} What I am willing to repeat, and always be willing to repeat is that Nothing I write is purposeless and not needed. It is just as important as the 20 intermissions or the various pauses. It provides the reader to relax but not stop.

For when one ceases to move, it is sometimes difficult to get moving again. Now let's continue. Speaking of continuing I'm going to. It has occurred to me that one of the main causes of my lack of writing is due to the fact that I'm reading a lot. This has captured most of my creative mind. For I understand what it is that makes writers write. But I'm choosey about what I read.

Recently I've narrowed my fiction down to one or two, and on my list of books to read I have 6 others that are nonfiction of various subjects from the occult to management, theory and application. Those are due to be finished by the 20th of next month.

So I conclude that I will by then be spending more time writing. Even though you may notice a gap between pieces only by looking at the dates, I will still make a needless request to be present.

Of course along with all the books I'm reading, I will everyday for as long as I live in this period of trail and tribulations continue to read the bible.

As I continue to read the bible I come to a clearer understanding of what IT IS "for me" Notice I didn't only say what "it is" But also added for me.

Also over the years I've learned that even though when I start a project just as this{controlled but yet open} I can only go with the flow, knowing that in the end, This book will be what it is……

Now let's continue.

The *ShowDown*

As I was leaning back in the driver's seat with my arms folded, flying over a field. I read the speedometer; it read I was cruising at 190 knots. Although it didn't actually say knots, that's what I thought. Mitch who was in the passenger seat pointed to the highway that was 50 yards at 3 o'clock, we was cruising at an altitude at about 100 meters. I pushed a few buttons and we were soon in the traffic on the highway. Not only were there transport vehicles like ours on the freeway {or hovering the freeway.} But there were also old fashion 4 wheeled cars. For some reason we needed to be in the traffic in order to reach our destination.

Below, in front of us, this kid in the back seat of a vintage Mercedes rag top, waved at us. Our waving back got the attention of the lady who was driving, which I assumed was his mother. Mitch caught her attention by just smiling and thinking and asked her to pull off so he could talk to her.

Apparently they {the lady, her son, and a female passenger.} were going to the next exit anyway. Because Mitch said "Let's go to the service station point 64 North East." I programmed the board. Even though we rose above them and went over trees, they were pulling up at the same time as we were landing. Because there were a lot of trees I had to manually land. I had difficulty landing, which came as no surprise to me or Mitch.

The two doors opened with an air lock kind of swishing sound, and we hopped out and met them as they came from around the station where they had drove their car in the garage in the back.

As Mitch went up to actually speak with her, her son ran past us to check out our transporter. Only within the past few years have there been transporters like mine. As I watched her son gawk at our vehicle, I thought to myself how closer and closer those transporter people are getting to have these vehicles look like the ones in the Jetsons cartoon.

She invited Mitch to the T.O.D.D. machine. Me and her friend just stood back. Our eye's met. I thought to her "He flirts all the time but not this deep. " She smiled yes and said "Yea Tracey has the same habit." I held my hand out for the shake and said "Hi, my name is Gikuyu." She shook my hand with a strong grip, and replied "Vanessa Bealer. Are you the 'Gikuyu'?" "Just one of the few." I said with a smile. We didn't get too wrapped up into each other because we weren't each other's style or something. We were just cool with each other.

Mitch on the other hand was crazy about Tracey; at least that was how he was acting. I knew otherwise. I didn't understand why he would join Tracey at the T.O.D.D. Machine. He never did that before. We both knew people who have been killed because they played that game. I thought to myself "If this game is lost there's certain death for him, and if it was him, it was for me too. Because no one or nothing fucks with him and gets away with it."

A few years earlier a school teacher discovered a way to teach anyone telephony. Now everyone is able to think to another. Whether it is a crowd or one person. Rarely one could read you thoughts unless you were caught off guard, or you allowed the too. Like giving total access to a family member or spouse. Except for the T.O.D.D. machine.

The machine was designed for couples who seriously wished to get married. In this day and age, society has set regulations on marriage certificates. Along with the blood test, the male had to pass the T.O.D.D. Machine. A devise made up and put into use by a female President a few years back, because her husband decided to deceive her. She felt that her husband knew or was just not aware of the fact that he wasn't truly in love with her, and used her to help him get prestige. She vowed that with the help of the machine, no woman would be put through that again.

She used the acronym Todd in memory of her ex-husband. It worked like this; the man would be in one seat, and face the lady seated in another chair across the table. He would put his finger in a slot in the table; she can ask him any questions she wished too. The first time a man lied, a steel strap would bind his hand and cut his finger off with a laser. That way his stub of a finger would heal then and there, and they would continue on. The man could choose whether to continue or not after the first lie. Since he knew if he lied again he would forfeit his life. This brought down the marriage rate.

Even the birth rate since a woman couldn't have a baby unless she was married. This method also made the divorce rate become almost nonexistent. A woman now days only lost her husband or vice versa through Death.

Mitch and I got into long debates about the "Truth Or Dare Death" machine. We covered everything. Like, what about the ladies, what if you met a girl and got her pregnant, would you have to marry her? Try answering that one, for my son's mother was crazy and of course I was crazier. Luckily the machine didn't exist in the early 2 zeros.

Mitch had always said that one day he was going to challenge the machine. One of these days he was really going to do it. We both knew it was crazy. There's this short window of time when the machine releases you after it has caught you lying. Released you so you could say good-bye with hugs or something before the lasers comes from the sky and kills you. Even if you use the time to escape the scene, it didn't matter. Because of the prones. Because the prones would search everywhere for you. The cities on land, the cities in the ocean, everywhere. I remember the prones found this one guy on one of those space stations just a few days after he failed the test. So for sure to challenge the machine would be crazy, and even though Mitch was insane in society terms, I was still crazier. And if he decided to go for it, he knew I'll be right there because I had his back.

And here he is. They just turned off the machine and he comes walking up to me holding up his left hand smiling and yelling "Look man four fingers and a thumb." But there had been a defect with the finger laser. Tracey was sobbingly telling Mitch how sorry she was. Mitch just smile and asked her in a comforting voice "How did you know I was going to lie about my age?" She just shook her back and forth knowing his fate. Because there was a malfunction with the finger laser the machine just upped it a notch (The only next notch.) and decided to straight up kill Mitch. I was thinking about how Mitch was a crazy Crazy motherf***ker.

I yelled at Mitch "Come on Hero!" We were both slightly running to the transporter. Mitch said to her "What's you full name, maybe we can go out in a week or two." I shouted "Wishful thinking! Wishful thinking! Come on!" She replied "Tracey Ka-Shish." I hopped in first and started the engines and flipping the switches, while looking skyward at the same time.

Mitch jumped in as the doors swished closed and I mastered the dance with the many trees real quick.. We hit 400 knots like nothing was wrong.

Since the transporter engines were solar powered, I decided to just ride the sun's shine for a while. So we just started coasting the upper atmosphere while keeping up with the earth's rotation. Mitch shared with me what he had found out about Tracey.

Tracey's husband died in a car crash a month after their son Immanuel was born. She never played the T.O.D.D. Machine since they were married before the law was passed. To have guys leave her alone she would flirt with them, and then offer to play the machine. Knowing that no one, at least no sane person would actually play.

She didn't understand why Mitch would not only play the game, but would actually lie to her to boot. At first she became distraught at the thought that she would be the cause of his death. But when Mitch smiled at her, she rationalized that he had a suicidal personality.

Mitch also found out that she was traveling to the city to run in the annual marathon that next day. He said it was the perfect forum for the Showdown. Tracey was starting at the beginning of the pact, so that draws a lot of cameras and with that exposure we could show the world how to defeat the prones, and the lasers from the sky. I agreed.

As we were flying with the rotation of the earth we took turns sleeping. Neither one of us could sleep more than an hour or so. I would think about the lasers in the sky, whether or not the prones had anti radar shields, which they probably did. We got back around to the city; we landed on the out skirts and made our way downtown for the Showdown.

We sat on a sofa in a display window of a furniture store, facing the street and crowd. We had bought a can of beer from the store next door. I told Mitch if we were going to die we might as well be mellow. I gave the manger of the store a 50 spot and told him we wanted to watch the end of the race in style. There was a sign across the street that read "finish line ¼ mile away." There was a news van with a guy standing on top shading his eyes from the sun looking for the racers.

I was downing the last gulp of beer when Mitch elbowed me and pointed to the guy atop the news van. He was focusing his camera that was attached to a tripod. The crowd started cheering and we knew they were coming. The first runner came jogging down the avenue. We figured that Tracey would be turning the corner soon. We picked this spot for a few reasons; one is that it was close to the finish line and we figured as the race went on, more people would be watching the ending more than the start, We had decided to join and run with Tracey and we didn't want to start at the beginning because we wanted to save all of our energy for the prones, {which by the way we hadn't a clue how to defeat.} We was both used to being put on the spot. Grace under pressure is the best way to describe our style. A few guys passed, and then we saw Tracey. She was very easy to see. One could see her bouncing breasts a mile away.

I looked at Mitch and smiled. We rushed out the store, through the crowd and joined Tracey as she passed by. ...She was surprised to see us to say the least. Mitch said in a Shakespearian voice "My dear, I've come for you. You'll witness my destruction or victory, whichever way it turns out; will you marry me?" Maybe from the fatigue and stunned at seeing us, tears started to roll down her face and over her smile. She started shouting "Yes! Yes! I will marry you!"

Before any of us could really get into the enjoyment of the moment, we heard a buzzing above us and we looked up to saw a drone hovering 10 feet above, in front of us matching our pace.

It was a round gold disc, about two meters in diameter, and about six centimeters thick. The prone job was to locate the Being to be destroyed and either destroy the Being itself, or send the coordinates to the lasers in the sky. I wasn't sure how it decided which to do. Didn't care either, because one would be killed either way. Because each person is different and yet the same, the prones would probe the brain until they found the right person. It'll search their memories and thoughts for their identity. When a person is hearing your mind, it feels like a caress. I knew the prone was probing because of the scratching sensation. I knew from the incident with Mitch that the machine was fallible, yet I couldn't think of what to do. I knew we only had moments to spare before it found out who was who. The ideal came. I thought to Mitch "Hey Gikuyu, it got me." Mitch thought back "Gikuyu what the hell are you talking about?"...

Then he caught on. "Wait a minute, I'm Mitch Washington!!" He loudly thought. "No! I'm Mitch Washington!" I loudly thoughtfully replied.

The stall tactic was working. The prone hovered in front of him then in front of me. It went back and forth only three times when it produced a high pitch beeping sound. I thought it had found Mitch out and was generating its laser or notifying the other ones in the sky or something. To our surprise it was summoning four more prones. They came quickly buzzing in. I almost tripped over Tracey looking up at all of them. My mind was really being scratched now. I just hoped that Mitch appreciated this shit.

I heard somewhere that sometimes the probing caused brain damage and I needed every bit of my already damage brain. I shouted to Mitch "Remember my teen-age years. "

Mitch and I met under strange circumstance when I was about 16 yrs. Old. (That castle in the sky thang.) We knew everything about each other. As I was thinking his memories he was thinking mine. I hoped he was thinking mine. He was doing something because that scratching sensation became worse. We started slowing up and Tracy showed more than a little concern for us. We was sweating and breathing hard. Mitch told her to keep going, after all it was a race, plus he didn't want her in the line of fire. She moved a little ways ahead of us and I and Mitch jogged on damn near hip to hip. A realization and insight occurred simultaneously. I realized the prones didn't hear me when I spoke out loud to Mitch; they were solely mind machines. The machine had us thinking hard and that was it. That's where the answers lay. In one thoughts.

Since the prones operated and decided on thoughts, it was the thoughts of the victim that essentially energized them. The more the victim thought the more powerful the prones became. Literally and figuratively. It was the thoughts deriving from a victim. Thoughts derived from fear. So fear is the source of its power. I whispered to Mitch (I was getting to weak to speak louder.) "Don't think about them, don't acknowledge their existence, matter of fact don't even look at them." I was gambling that it wouldn't acknowledge the existence of someone who doesn't acknowledge its. The prones started drifting away toward the sky without a buzz to be heard..

We turned a corner and saw the finish line a couple of blocks ahead of us. I thought to my self that this has been one hell of a ¼ mile. I started hearing the crowd lining the street. They had seen us defeat the prones. So either they was cheering for that or the race I didn't care. My legs felt like melted rubber, my lungs were burning, and I just knew I was going to puke in front of a world wide audience.

We fell about ten feet from the finish line right on our face. Skinned up everything. The law was rendered useless since everybody knew how to defeat the prones. The old fashion way of dating someone came back into vogue. Leaving marriage up to human instinct and not a woman made machine. Mitch married Tracey 13 months later. It took so long because he wanted to make sure that she was the one.

As for me I'm still single and only now realized that I'm dreaming. Oops. Because I've realized it. I'm waking up.

52

OnLy I

    I only see one sky at night, and one in the daytime none of the stars exist in the same place after darkness has arrived again. These onlyness of my dreams do not come from my reality. For I willingly dream of her, when she's of the many that I've chosen from the few. Next to the thought I have is the realization leaning leisurely as if by realizing my death is comforting enough to allow myself to believe that one of those stars in the one sky of night is the place from which she resides.

    I only love all for the none does not exist for me. If You are a part from some and exist within others in stead of within all, then it's not correct if you assume I do not speak of you. You are included in my all. If my brain tells me what my reality is, But the reality that's the interpertation of my mind is different, From my mind which is the creative source of who I am and my brain the somewhat careful source of who I am which you think I pay attention to. That's the all my mind says you are so I take that not with a grain of salt. But with a ton of Love.

    I only walk along some avenue of rose bushes in the coldness of winter to see the harsh sticks with surviving thorns, to be reminded of the gift of one's relationship with the most high God. In some cases the thornless sticks would seem unlike a bush that could flourish with the change of a season, Like a heart with just the change of a reason.

    I only ask a simple question of life and receive with the answer a response that brings forth further questions. That in itself allows me to widen the scope of my "Mind's" reality. This comes from (for me) questions that are simplistic by nature, and not by design. I only ask a simple request that not necessary made to be granted, only most of them asked, in order to provide a space-place for a possibility. And which possibility that is to occur is for me to ultimately to choose, for if one is freed from the restraints that shows up around one's "brain's" reality then one understands the true power and gift of a request.

I only Think, when I do. Although often I think when I don't realize it. Or thinking Has been for me some what as a habit, which I've purposely encouraged to develop within my mind. For if I perceive correctly, The brain is the source of thoughts and yet it is one's mind that by dancing with thoughts, thinking occurs. The only really thoughts that are acted on purely without referring with my mind are only those of which is to provide a contribution to all.

I only Believe in one God. The mother of all living and once lived existence. I've often referred to God as she. Which not as of yet May cause concern to those who have believed that God is a He. I say She in order to have you stop and realize that God is neither and God is Both. Dig? I only Believe in one God. For those who are out there in the world whom doesn't believe in God, God exist. That's all I can say to that.

I only fear nothing. But it is that for which I strive for. For with nothing comes a state of uncomfortability that only one survives by being authentic to the nothingness and facing it head on. And creating what it is to become. I'm cool when I got something going on. I have a few ideals I'm working on. Some in my head(mind) some actually out hear in the physical world.(universe) But as you should know, I'm for being uncomfortable so with this something I destroy the boundaries which allows it to exist as nothing . With nothing freedom is. With freedom, True freedom of one's being coexist life and death and as a human being I fear death {my brains does.} So I only fear nothing. I as if I'm speaking to the source of who I am. At least in this context I am. I haven't done so before and will let you know if I do it again within this piece. A cloudless sky is a shade of blue, with out without sunshine, yet although that may seem true to you, consider that the sky is never cloudless and is out the sun shone upon it... It is that assumption that prevails in most peoples ideals of how reality is. For they've never been with nothing, thinking that having Nothing isn't valuable. That's just like thinking that no one can touch the sky Again consider there's no such thing as a sky. Only a concept of a image titled sky. Really somebody made it up. Made it up from nothing. True or false that's for you to choose. Also again consider there's nothing true and there is nothing that is false. Considering that, how would decide. For me {the source of who I am} I only fear nothing.

I only laugh at myself. Just before I cry. Then after wards I...... Laughter can be for me a smile to giggling to a physical reaction to a humorous situation or thought. I rarely, well let me say I remember only twice I've laughed at cartoons, for even though I'm a being with no bounds, I relate to cartoons as myself. Though the dialogue is not meant for me in a sense. I did find humor two instances. Can one laugh at one's on sorrow, Escapism is meant as a safe haven. In a life threatening situation do you; would you laugh at death? I would and I have. I only laugh at myself.

I only know that knowledge without wisdom is useless. There are many facts in this world. "True" True as an opinion not as truth. One has to not judge one's life by that that has been taught, for what is learned is not always true. Truth is. Dig? "TRUTH IS" its existence cannot be questioned. For if one truly knows then its truth, not true. I've known for many years about my purpose in life. It wasn't something I learned. It became something I began to know, and over a period it was known.

I only write as a participant, not as a spectator. At times I participate as a spectator when I'm writing; the latter is by choosing not by accident. Sometimes when I'm writing I catch a thought when I'm writing a word, about how the ink is flowing out this pen and making marks on a piece of paper which the marks could be translated into language. It still amazes me how this simple little transaction could cause some of the most profound contributions. Yea I only write.

I only change what is changeable. Of course that's almost everything. But some things cannot be changed. There are things the existence of "IS" And can not be something else. It's either all it can become, or all of what it once was. I once thought that I could change my mind. Then I realized that I did no such thing... I moved on, or retreated to various thoughts. I choose to react differently to the decisions I made, but it was clear that there was no changing occurring. My mind; during any given moment of "now" is all that it ever was ands all it can ever be. Only through the continuation of my being's existence does my mind grow... Well let me "Change" that what I just said. My mind doesn't grow, Growing is a concept of change. Only through the continuation of my Being's existence, from which strengthens my mind with the capability to create the various realities needed to provide the contributions within the moments of now, that long ago I made up my mind to do.

I only praise how she felt. How her appearance in my dream impacted me. It was a showing up that made miracles seem like ordinary occurrences. {Which they are.} She made her presence known so authentically. I felt her authenticity which was everything she was. Yes, although she was in my dreams, She was, "is", a separate entity. Yet we was and also is one. It wasn't her feelings that I only praise. Dig? It's how she felt. Pure sunshine, without protection can dissolve the matter of the human body. Yet we were spirits existing in that realm, so the energy she gave off was wild and powerful. She came, she left, she will return, all in all I only praise how she felt.

I only live as a myth. As a concept, unstructured contexts. For my life is to represent what could be. To represent a vision in existence. An opinion less runned existence. Living; doesn't come from being safe. Being safe is asking life to do it to you. It never ceases to astound me how "crazy" my life gets, and how I somehow manage to survive. Sure there was times when I could have literally died, and I'm here now, not because of life, but because of living. What is living large? As oppose to living small? I suppose. It's cool if one chooses to live at one extreme while another lives at the other. Only if one truly understands that Living isn't being in life.

I only cry after I laugh, then afterwards I...... Once I wrote tears of joy, tears of Pain, whatever the tears the tears do rain." A poem titled loneliness. Written when I was once younger, it captured my understanding of crying that I've come to know. Sadness, Madness, Gladness, all are emotions. Emotions a triggered by a thought, that could be about something, or a thought triggered by something. Never-the-less a thought. When I was once younger although I never actually cried, I did know that if tears from joy or Pain did occur it would not be withheld due to any macho-ism. That's what the poem represented. I've recently felt sadness of a profound nature in a dream, although I knew it was a dream and could have changed the outcome; I decided to go with the drama. To experience that emotion so rarely on the spot "felt" any given situation could be sad one or a glad one. Being authentic allows the tears to rain.

I only understand that which is made clear to me by the Grace Of God. If I understood something that later would have me to be safe, then I would prefer not to even comprehend. Though that has never been the case, for I truly understand that that is a gift from God. I wonder by my writings, how much of my tomorrows am I taking away. My wonderment is twofold, for my writings are also. Concerning the latter. It's a nice way to say it, but what's the message. Concerning the wonderments, One is when I write. I'm using up the space of an era, so when a project is complete, I move on onto the next. Also by doing that I wonder about the velocity of the peace in which my tomorrows are meeting my yesterdays, Bring the now's closer to non-existence. Understanding that what I am is the force of the cost; tomorrow meeting yesterday, squeezing out now. "I have to whole heartily accept it, for there's no freer freedom than truly understanding one's being."

I only wish that after all has been said about me, after all has been taught, after all the rumors has been out to rest after all the few tears has been shed at my funeral, that you will not go astray and accept nothing more than an empowering interpretation of who I am. Not who I've been, but who I am for as long as these words are here so am I. It'll be interesting for some one to read all that I've written, which they will not be able to do, for there are some pieces like the poem I wrote Susie Rode, who attended Russell Sage College years ago, that she only has a copy of. If you only read this page. I only wish you understand.

I only advise you to not eat the menu of life.. Advice I'm sure has been given before. I'm a part of that crowd. Although some may not request that so loud, I do. Yea do not get filled with the many possibilities and be satisfied to the degree that nothing is worth going for except for creating new possibilities. Possibilities are great when their a goal of which one is in action to obtain. They are of irrelevant use {maybe.} when one only daydreams of the infinite numbers and does nothing but enjoy the fantasy.

I only assert that chasing comfort in ones life is vanity. Again that's nothing newly known.... Unless Comfort is the babe in 'The Week Of Crying' for some she may be all of one's life. My many possibilities, {dreams, wish's} is to have a love as if she's my whole life. That is only possible after I'm a writer. Which will be after I laugh and after I cry. When I speak of one's life I speak of mine.

I only stand on this mountain top waiting to return no more, I'm here. This mountain top is the context which I stand. Only when you acknowledge that I am you and you~I, will you understand that I have never returned, for I have never left. You have left me. Look at that…….I only stand here on this pedestal, for you have only leaped off. Yet you think I'm special. NO. It's not like that. There are others on this pedestal. This pedestal called Earth.

I. only stand for one thing, and that's me. Individually. apart from you. Yet "I" am never apart from anything. I am Infused. Joined together by the same source of Life that created us. I only stand for you

I only Die…. It was when I was once younger when I wrote, I laugh before I cry, I cry before I die. Dying Like Beauty is in the eye of the beholder. With whom's eyes do one perceive from. It is not true that with you I'm alive now. But am I around. Does being around becomes a requirement for being alive. Does being alive become one for being around. I only Die. Yet what is done s done with that knowledge. And that knowledge exist not as useless as some knowledge does. Yea I only die.

I only am OnLY I

Speech Given to Life in May

In my last speech I stated an assertion that generally is not true. I said "People have always believed that there's nothing new under the sun." People. As we know people to be may have always believed that. But people as we know not of them to be, for example, People of another land, People of the deep past, Children, Open minded people, they may not believe that. I have come to that conclusion.

One drawback that comes from me not reviewing what I've recently written is the unknowing of whether or not I have out into words my thinkings. Sometimes I do and when I do put them down they still linger as if I've left something unsaid. A "thinking" could be a brief statement, but that statement could be a title of a piece or book, or trilogy, or even a Novel. Yet often it's such a brief statement that has occurred in the midst of a vast amount of thoughts. I do not go and search for it to see if I did or did not write it down. Instead I let the thinks hover over and be there while others occur. I let it be there like sunshine until it sets.

That context of which is hovered over that context which is written. The latter has {for me} to be authentic. Has to be original. Not an original copy. The former is separate from that which is written, and is contextualized by me to be like sunshine.... I can only conclude that there is something new, always under the sun.

Although many dates have been given about the last day of my vacation. They were unknowingly given blindly. Given only from the point of view of the external circumstances. My circumstances dictated the date. Since I'm not "runned" by my circumstances, the date arrived and passed without the ending of myself imposed vacation.

With that... I've decided that my vacation will be over at 11:59 P.M. E.S.T. August 4th 1991. That will be two years to the day plus or minus a day or two that I began my self imposed 2nd 2 year vacation. The first reentry from vacation I rode a bicycle one hundred and ten miles with a dollar and ten cents in my pocket. That's what I saw what was needed to be done at the time. This reentry will be different. You see the last time I needed something to reawaken my creativity because during my 1st two year vacation I did very little writing. Also I was clear about what I was taking a break from and it was easy to explain and show others. The difference now is although I know and understand what I've been taking a break from, It's hard to explain,{*or I make it seem that way.*} because it's difficult to believe, and it's hard to show{*or I also make it that way.*} because you have to be by my see and see it for yourself.

There was a lot I choose to ignore, because I knew I was going on vacation. That I will not this go round. Without going into details just yet, I'm coming to grips with the next 5 or 6 years before my next vacation. {next 5 or 6 years if God's willing.}

Often in my pre-vacation ERA, the future existed as I wished, for my commitment would have it to be, no matter how the circumstances were. That only occurred in a mild way during this vacation because, because...well it's obvious. When I found myself in tonight spots I created the future. For example, when I went to prison camp and I wanted to get out of there fast. I looked and seen what was an appropriate time to spend there for the crime I did and I decided to not stay any longer. True to form, I didn't stay longer that I had "*written*" about. As a matter of fact I was released two weeks earlier.

You may think I'm arrogant to even suggest such a thing. It may even be arrogant to think that I'm of the humblest of employees of the universe, and I do nothing that doesn't fit into my coexistence with God. As an employee I was given a vacation. A vacation from publicly being seen or recognized as one. Not from being one. I'm sure once I return; the impact upon myself will be one of intensity.

Yo' Life This speech is given to you and it seems that I and {*I assume the reader also*} thinks I'm talking to you as if you're some entity. Something That I can visualize. Well I'll say this, for you {*the reader*} as well as for me. Life is a concept, unseen, untasted, unheard, and yet felt within the innermost areas of one's soul. When I speak of one I speak of me. This speech is one of many thinks which is given as a gift.

When I speak of the future; it's not in the context of tomorrow. For tomorrow is now. I speak of the times yet to come. My sense of the way of light isn't confined to just brightness. The dark is also a light, and each can blind me with just as much power. When blinded by either I must guide myself with my inner self which source is from that if the light that is Brightest.

These many speeches is my acknowledgement to the~~~

Continuance of the existence of life that which I'm a part of. And as long as the word written by me is read I will always be in life, as opposed to Life always being in me, which has me to live.

Yo' Life, Thank You, Thank You, Thanx.

61
AgeLess

Soon I will be a year older. That would not be unusual for anyone to accept, except for me. I've been sure of the fact that I'll be expiring from this skin bag at a relativity young age. I've been sure of that for quite a while. Every since I was once younger. I remember when I was in m teens telling babes that in order to discourage them from chasing me. It wasn't for its dramatic effect, although my sharing that particular belief did have one.

What's not so unusual about my age is that I'm totally aware of the fact that I'm not that young anyway. I mean it in the context of age, not a in a context like ohh I'm getting on up there in the years. You dig? A context like years in a skin bag is a blink of an eye for a 1000 year old soul.

When I was once younger I didn't see myself living beyond the age 21. Yet I'm 25. One could take that two ways. The first way which isn't obvious to those who haven't had the pleasure, "Bout" time I turned 21 the 'I' I spoke of was dead. Another way of looking at is a new vision came to me and it depicted my going age to be 43... Still another way to look at this is I'm here going on one hundred and twenty which makes me younger than I expected and a view of life which broaden my horizons if you will.

If you knew if you were going to live to old age would you do everything you ever wanted to do, or since you feel that there's very little time in life, do you choose carefully what you do in Life. That's the most profound catch 22 I've ever come across. What you consider old age, young age, age period is just a blink of the eye of the most high.

Now what if one's "BEING"….. You ever wondered what was the "BEING" in "Human Being".. Now what if that being wasn't like our skin bag. Meaning it did grow with time. But it's like already in existence whole and complete and life is provided for us in our sin bag in order for us to uncover more of what was once covered by us previously or to continue to uncover until our being is known to be whole and complete to us. What if one's BEING doesn't grow in a sense of upness, but outwardness and one has the choice to being able to exist on any area of being that has been revealed up to now.

I thought about that for a while, because even though I know not what people think about, I'm always remembering things. Not because of any certain incident that makes me flash back, but because the moment exist as real for me now as it does for me back then. I could be writing about something philosophical and then boom I begin picturing leaning on the car fender in Shamida's car port while Kim does a little cheerleader act, thinking to myself "What A Life."

If the possibility of the outwardness theory could and it does exist. Then I'm saying that, "Who we've considered ourselves to be, meaning 19 years old, 60 years old and all of that, and going about life underneath that consideration is not the correct concept to be perceiving who we are as we do go through life. The context of time of which one's being exist is ever lasting, So there's is no quote "age" One's BEING was created from beyond the beginning to continue pass the ending as we know it. So we are **AgeLess**……

It was after morning Just before noon
Chinganji sat on the edge of the conduit
Of the upper pool on Fuller Field Road
Knowing not whom he sits and waits
Yet being there to clear the space

Kezia, enjoying the late morning sunshine
On one of her many recently walks
She saw Chinganji {chin-gan-ji} and smile hello
There was a brightness about him, by the way the pool shone
He was by himself yet she knew he wasn't alone
As he sat there wondering how much longer
He smiled at the presence of joy
Seeing her he knew it was her who he felt.
Seeing her he also knew she was the one
Standing to greet, then their togetherness begun

He was the only she met on this road
Yet she was aware that he has met many
He wasn't a stranger to these parts
She knew he's never been here before
Maybe he was the one who could open her mind's door

This story will not be completed in this book. Maybe it'll continue on, I haven't decided on it yet. I had difficulties figuring out what it was all about. Along the physical reaction to the beginning of a new month, plus a decided dead line for this book {which by the way has passed.} Taking all of that into consideration I decided to continue and return to the tale of Fuller Field Road at a later date.

It's imperative that I complete a project within a reasonable proximity of the dead line. I felt that the weeks it would have took to decipher the tale would definitely have me not to reach my schedule.

This page and the previous will not be included in the table of contents. An Idea not yet complete.

AUTHOR'Z NOTE

      If I was here I would clearly say in a smooth sort of way say to you Thanx.

      Thanx to you whom have given support in wayz that'z sometimez from the outside the box state of mind.

PEACE AND LOVE

The Opening Ending

The completion of Day Sky Dreams is the last of the 10 projects I've written in the 12 months I've been incarcerated. The 12 months which I've gone through a county jail, to another institution, and finally to a work camp.

Again, unless you want to read my handwriting and want to understand me, then you will. I don't write just for you to skim through this. Just like I don't talk just to waste my voice.

The completion of Day Sky Dream. Is good.

Peace and Love
Cathy

The Table Of Contents

1) 3 to 4 P.O.P.
2) Day Sky Dreams
3) Speech Given To Life in January
4) A Note
5) The Matter
6) Day Sky Dreams Again
7) A Talk
8) Speech Given To Life In February
9) A Letter
10) Speech Given To Life On My Last Days

3 to 4 ▲ P.O.P.

The otherday I was walking back and forth in front of a house. The only house on this dirt road. I don't remember what I was thinking, I just know I was deep in thought. I hear my name called and I turn around and see that it's Chambers who's calling me. The detail officer that had just ~~got though~~ finished talking to him walks past me and heads toward the bus. Which by the way is about a block further up the road. I joking~~ting~~ly tell Chambers, with whom I'm working with, that the officer just ignores the fuck out of me. And tells you what's needs to be done, for you to tell me. "You just walk away" he replies. I asked him what time it is, and he tells me 3 o'clock.
    Our job that day [Me and Chambers] was to walk down the dirt road ahead of the bus and pick up dead wood and bushes that had been cut, and place them along the road so that others can put it in the chopping machine, hooked to the back of the bus and make wood chips that it would spit out back along side the road. The officer told Chambers that we ~~was essentia~~ essentially ~~we~~ was doing too good of a job. That we didn't need to pick up every little bush and stick. Told us to take it easy. We was about two blocks away from the end of the road and quiting time was about 4 so he couldn't have told us at a better time, except for at the begining ~~at~~ of the day.
    Having not much more work to do, we had the oppertunity to conversate. I told Chambers how incridable it was to meet a guy who's been locked up for nine and a half years and who

68

is still locked up. I asked him about different things he's seen. We touched on a few subjects, but the one that pertains to this piece on peace is when he shared with me his experience he had last year.

He was at a work camp and there was this lady who worked in the kitchen. He called her Janet Jackson because she wore a baseball cap and her hair had a pony tail in the back like Janet wore in one of her music videos. He told me how she would flirt with him, and they could talk about anything. She was sexy with a nice body. Untill one day she was killed.

There was this guy who worked in the butcher shop who was serving time for killing his wife and another lady. And one day he snuck up behind her and slit her throat. Chambers didn't actual see it but he heard how she was fighting back and put up a hell of a struggle untill she lost too much blood and couldn't fight no more. How the guards was scared to go in and stop him. How the guy butchered her. How he was sent to another prison and the inmates of that prison took turns kicking his ass.

I told him that I remember seeing that on the news. And I remember thinking how ironic life really is. We contived to to pick up the sticks, [being very selective.] we got about 15 feet from the stop sign that was at the dirt road cross roads and I seen head stones that was about 5 feet from the side of the road.

It was a small graveyard. It consisted of about 10 graves. I went and read one and the date on it was 1889 or something like that. I read another and it was around 1861. At the edge of the graveyard stood this big grey headstone. I knelt closer so I could read the inscription. It was the grave of Susie C. Butler. Born March 22 1857, died October 24 1884. The words underneath the dates stated that she was a wonderful wife and an affectionate mother. For a brief moment there was total silence as I reflected upon this lost of life. I counted the years of her life, and she was 27. I yelled over to Chambers "Hey man this babe was only 27 when she died." He didn't respond, because he wasn't interested. Knowing that he wasn't interested I still pointed out that it said she was a wonderful wife and an affecuate mother and he replied "She's not down here helping us pick up these sticks so I don't give a shit who she was." I laughed at that and joined him finishing up the job.

The diagram shows a main road and the single line is the dirt road. The spot mark is where we was standing and the X is where the graveyard is. We was standing there rolling up a cigarette and he said "Damn is that a girl? That is a girl!" Of course I couldn't see her, and after I spent a few moments rushing and fumbling with my glasses to put them on she was gone, and I had missed the only sighting of a female all day.

We stood at the crossroads and waited for the bus, hoping to see maybe a female driving by on the main road. We was standing there shooting the shit, and I was thinking about how we must look. two guys dressed in prison strips with prison blue jean jackets on, and army boots on, standing at on the corner with no officer in sight. Soon after this thought a school bus that was driving up the main road veered off to the right and headed straight toward us. I thought to myself "Well, here we go folks."

Looking at the buss head on it looked empty. I was disappointed and relieved at the same time. The bus made a wide right turn then I saw a few heads. They was sitting on the opposite side of the bus that was facing us. A young girl about 12 or 13 years old stood up and walk to the side we was on. Actually she ran to the side or jumped to the side because the bus was moving swiftly. I thought she was going to wave, but instead she gave us the Peace sign. And I returned it. I turned away and observed the acknowledgement and when I turned back the bus had made it's turn and another young girl about the same age. And there were others to but she was the one I saw. She also waved the peace sign and once again I returned it. Then the bus moved on out of sight.

I reflected on that seance for a moment and noticed how the first wave of peace was cool but the second on seemed artificial. It felt like she was doing it because the first girl did it, and I just waved back because she waved at me. But I waved back at the first girl with a peace sign because it was an authentic acknowledgement. After that quick reflection I turned to Chambers and asked him what time it was and said " 4 o'clock."

I decided that day to write about what occured between 3 and 4 pm. And the title automatically came up. The reason I say P.O.P. Is because this is a Piece of Peace and in a deeper way is a Piece on Peace. Although it may appear that the first subject about the young women who got murdered isn't about peace yet in the end that's what she received. Dig?

5

She received peace just like Susie received it. Peace of mind if only for a brief moment is what I experienced while standing in front of Susie's head stone, standing on top of her grave. Those kids surprised me. Not at the moment when we acknowledge each other but later on when I was reflecting on this. Out of all the things they could have done they wished us peace.

Oh yes before I go, I'll give you an insight of what's with inbetween. The reason I wrote this now and not a couple of days ago is because I wanted this piece of/on Peace to start off "The Otherday"

Day Sky Dreams

A few times during the previous week I've woken up at 3 A.M. This morning after spending a few moments reflecting on the dreams I've had I did what I usually did. I went back to sleep. Only this morning I thought about something other than the dreams. I thought about the statement that came to my mind which is "Is this the beginning of my day?" Then I asked myself "if so, should I go back to sleep?" From thinking about that statement I realized the difference between "days" here in prison, and days at home.

The days of the week are known by what the news announcer says it is. It's not a day that you must wake up and go to work because you have bills to pay. One goes to work because hopefully you'll look good enough in order to get an early release. That's what the big picture is. Personally I realized that there was very little difference in the way I operated while in prison and when I was at home or wherever I should be. I've still kept to my own agenda. It had me to reflect upon how did I write when I was at home. Since it's been a few days shy of 10 months since I've been home, it was hard to remember my old ways. I do remember that I had no certain schedule, and I still got volumes of work done. Just like now there's no certain schedule and I'm getting work done. I'm working on 3 different projects now simultaneously.

This morning when I woke up again I was really into thinking about the "days" concept. Thinking of the correct context to put it in, so I could write about it. So it was it

73

7

really a suprise, when I ~~walked~~ walked outside this morning I was in awe with the sky.

This morning I was wide open, as far as my state of mind is concerned. I was exicited that I'm well into my poetry book as to be comfortable about the way it's turning out. Also comfortable with chapter one of my 2nd Novel, and I've begun this project and it's starting out great. Also this morning is around 7:30 when it was time to be called out for detail {work.} I was sitting by the door looking at what I could do to not go out today. My only attempt was to promise the universe that if I didn't go out, I would write 5 pages in this book before I went to sleep. Yet deeper in my mind I was thinking that I would sleep first, then realizing that I would break my promise, I thought if I did go out, I wouldn't write, Then I realize that that was false also, When my name was called I accepted with grace. The distinction of "Prison days" still lingered in my state of mind. You could say that in order for me to draw a distinction that would be clear enough to share I had to be in the moment. While being in the moment I stepped outside. I looked to my right and the sun was just rising. The sky had atleast 7 shades of blue with 3 different shades of gray from the storm clouds that was bejining to "gather." I thought the question if there's a difference between a prisoners' sky and a free mans' sky. This morning I didn't dwell on the question. Now {which is evening.} I feel that for me it's not an answerable question for the question doesn't apply to me. I'm always a free man. Just now I remember that in my book "The Wisdom of A Man" written in 1987, on a page I stated something like the sky down south is much larger than the sky up north. The impact that the sunrise made on me will remain forever. Everytime I reread this passage I will remember. It may be unfair of me to not go into graphic detailish description, yet it's the concept that I want to get across. It's the question that I would like to leave you with as I finish this paragraph. "Can the sky appear or be the same as the sky of one who is not incarcerated?"

The insights about the days and skys occured for me right when this piece needed to be written. I thought that I was just going to write about my dreams. Eventhough it would've only been about a page and a half, which I atleast wanted each piece in this project to be a few pages. One of my dreams last night, for the first time in a few months had a sky in it. I mean I actually looked out at the sky. A sky could have been in other dreams but I mustn't have paid attention.

The latest series of dreams I've contemplated seriously about writing down, yet I felt that I shouldn't. Not because of anything secretish about them. They were more than dreams. They were for me, [one who have documented many dreams,] they were new. For example I dreamed about Shelia Garnest. A babe I went to elementary school with. I haven't thought about her for years. Soon After I dreamed of Martha Graham whom I also went to elementary school with. I dreamed of ⎯ Deborah whom I've thought about and still think about a lot.

What these dreams have in common is that the scene all occurs in the future. I've had many more dreams recently that also occurs in the future. The only thing that I've written from those series of dreams has been "Whitney Houston 1893 The Message." I wrote that down without clarifying what I mean. ~~And I'm not going to do it now.~~ I feel that with my knowledge on the power of writing, that if I were to write down what I've dreamed, in one way or another it might come to be. I remember the awful news Martha told me, I remember ~~som~~ seeing Deborah, I remember ~~the~~ talking with Shelia but I don't remember what we spoke about.

Another ~~con~~ insight that occured for me today while designing this piece is that it was just possible that I was a part of a world that existed simonatronlsy. Yet even with that insight, I couldn't wholeheartedly accept it, so I still unwilling to share my recent dreams with you.

It's funny. Although I'm really finish with this piece I'm going to contive in my "Withinbetween" style and share with you this. All day I knew what I was going to write about in this piece. Dreams, Days, and Skys. For the concepts came in that order. As I was thinking of a title it hit me when I realized that I was day dreaming while ~~watch~~ watching the sky. I just smiled for I had a title.

Gikuy

Speech Given To Life in January

The reality often gets mixed up with the reasons, which in turn just so happens to appear as real stable and factual, but the truth about these reasons are that they are meaningless. So that leaves the reality without foundation. Although this is not the type of all reality this is the type majority of the time.

Last night I was looking at news and they had a segement about how some black college students was acknowledgeing Martin Luther King Jr. Birthday. These kids was marching around to different sites where people were murdered and showing stop the violence. This one female student said that black people needed to understand their heritage and learn to love one another. Although that is true, she stated it as if that was all of her reality. And that's the kind of reality I speak of that's apart of the majority.

I asked this fellow inmate what he thought about how society celebrated the King B-day, and in his opinion, Society treated it like a joke. I could dig where he was coming from, like at least on news one only hears occasionally about people getting together for peace. Then when one race celebrate Mr. King's birthday by speaking for one race, It's obvious that they didn't get what Mr. King was talking about. Although I could go further in expressing my opinion about this subject I feel what I've said already is enough.

What these protesters are doing in my opinion is symbolically taking a stand. Yet a flare of showing off is present. Belive me I'm one who can notice unathenticness. The otherday I refused to go outside to work because it was cold. That's exactly what I told the officiers. I didn't tell him I was sick or any other lie. I knew that the consequences were that I'll be put in lockdown, get wrote up, and that'll delay my parole. Yet I took a stand, while others went out there when it was 24 degrees. A guy came up to me and said "Simmo why don't you want to go out?" I told him "First of all it's 24 degrees, the gloves don't protect your hands, the hat don't protect your ears, I don't have a thermo T-shirt, and I refuse to work in this cold." I was telling this while I was packing my stuff which the officier told me to. Because I was on my way to "the hole." He told me "You're gonna go to the hole." I told him it's just another room in prision." Anyway this guy told the officiar I had no thermo underwear and the officier decided not to put me in the hole. I didn't go out. Because I took a stand no matter what the cost. I didn't do it symbolically like say I didn't want to go out, and when they threaten me with the hole I went outside. I was willing to do the next 2 years of my time in the hole if that is what was called for. I think those protesters even tonight which is friday night, will be partying and not even pay attention to the homeless people they pass on the street. Or listen to those screams of desperation of the members of the community that their college campus is located. Like I say every once and a while they give this candle light vigeral, but what the hell can a flame do in the winter time do, unless it's in your heart, and that flame turns into a fire that burns your soul, and have you get off your ass, and have you committed your life to making a difference in the world, other than giving ~~lip~~ talk. All that's bullshit. I guess that's what I'm saying about the realities of those protesters. You don't believe me? Yea well I bet when they get paid they go out and ~~b~~ buy the latest fashion no matter what's the cost. Instead of buying durable stuff that's cheaper and ~~spendy~~ giving the ~~rest~~ rest of that money ~~of~~ to donations to organizations that's up there with the causes that Dr. Martin Luther King Jr. gave his life for. You think my opinion is wrong? Are you a part of Society?

Thank you Thank you Thanks. I speak here before you because you've allowed me with your humble existence to ~~she~~ Be cool.

A Note

Dear World

What's going on? I mean what's really going on? I was attempting to get intouch with your trees the otherdays and I belive that the winter time does something to them. It's like they're hiding thier conscious. Maybe it's me. But I put out 100% and all I recievee is just a small hint of existance. That sky of yours though is beginning to have new meaning for me. I wrote about that earlier in this book. I find it's interesting that if it ain't one thing it's another that I discover about you.

Yo' World you might belive this but there's some people that devides you up into two seperate contexts, like free world and the unfree world. Do you think I should let them know that there's only one world?

I don't pretend to be wise, smart, intellegent. I don't even act like I know how to spell my words correctly. Eventhough I'm a writer. It's odd to contive to see my death, that exists right before my eyes. Not my eyes actually but more like my mind's eye.

I met this young woman name Kricket. I was getting off a bus at my old high school. She was infront of me. I just had to get to know her, yet I couldn't because there seemed some kind of invisible wall built around her. I lingered in her background. I begin to feel her. She walked up to a guy and told him her name was Kricket. K-R-I-C-K-E-T. She spelled it. And that was just after I had thought about asking her name. I looked over and I saw her glancing at me. A small whisper of a smile adorned her eyes. I began to really feel her.

Alot of visual stuff happened in this dream, after her eyes smiled at me. A few places was visited. For example the clouds from the center developed a hole the perfect size of a rectangle. The point is, Bricket at the end of the dream was telling me by singing a song how she was hooked to images. I guess it was ironic that she was saying this, because of the various sciences I had just witnessed. Yet what she was saying was that my body didn't fit her image and since she was hooked she had to say good-by but it was nice meeting me. Dear World will you ever be a witness for me when I placed on trail for being insane?

The funniest things happens that seems life threatening. I laugh at the wild and crazy occurrences as if they're everyday happenings. One time I was walking home through the park and a guy stops his car and gets out and puts a gun to my face and says "Motherfucker, why you do it." or I'm walking though the path at the back of this house and a guy runs up to me with a bigger gun than the last guy and says "Give me all your money or I'll blow your brains out, and I says "My sister lives in this house." while pointing to the bedroom windows at the back of the house and smiling while looking at the hole the bullet will come from. Dear World, In times like these will you let me know when it's time to become sane?

15

Being a believer in the possibilities of all things being possible, I've come to know that perfection is just one of the many ways of life that has death as a style.

While walking with Angie to the devil spot, I knew that she was beautiful, and knew we would be friends and also knew we would say good-by although she thought I couldn't talk. Even today, or up until now there still has not been an experience of speechless love that can match the power of those moments. Moments spent so long ago. Moments that comes back to me time and time again. Back to me in ways of energy; that impacts me in a style of empowerment. Dear World will you make a note of this note to remind you that growth is expansion of context?

G. Burg

The Matter

For the matter to be resolved one must listen to the unreasonable requests that's dictated to one by a voice that at times, times that has no sequence of occurance, could be wrong. And will be wrong if one chooses to see it that way. The matters are in themselves a happening that's a choice.

I realize that in all of the disturbance of a state of mind, I've remained alive. That's not a hell of a realization in the normal sense of the context. It's for me an insight. One that hasn't occured just naturally. I was thinking about all I had gone through in my life time, and I had thought about what it was that made me choose to go through that. The state of mind at the time I concluded had something to do with that. Disturbance is of one's own interpertation. That's the one I choose now. I was attempting to sum up my existance to one reason. And after narrowing it down to a few, and fewer still it came to me. The reason I've survived everything is to be alive and live.

By just having one ideal when I was a kid, my life began to unfold as a choice of many choices. The discovery of the power of words provided the necessary force to produce the ideal. I at times marval at that discovery. It's so simple yet so hard to grasp. How am I expected to just simply accept with no questions the purpose in life that has occurred from this unfolding of life. Tell me how am I? Can you answer that. No need to. I've already have. The answer is easy..... "Just do."

17

For the matter to be seen as I see it, one must be free of all the inhibitions that runs one's life. Although I'm not that free of all of them. But I'm close. One of them is being free. Being free leaves me with a choice to decide what I want to do. So I have to go looking for death, so to speak, for life is death in the begining. The "Looking" runs my life. And that's the matter. The matter when one asks "What's the matter?"

The matter at hand is Life that's taken as a stand. A stand of purpose. The purpose to serve the commitement that's the context of the path. The path that's chosen for one from the one most high. The one most high? Yea I speak of God. The secret to Life is to do God's will. That may not be a happy journey, but it will be a fulfilling one.

Peace And Love
Gilroy

Day Sky Dreams Again

A few days ago I went outside to work for two days straight. The first day I relooked at the trees. Because I think I mentioned earlier in a note that I wasn't receiving any vibes from them or something like that. So I began being with them intensely to discover or I should say rediscover for myself who are the trees for me now. The insight that occurred for me came when I was walking along this country road and looking at the forest behind this pasture for the cows. These particular trees was leafless and I noticed that there was no trees that really stood out from the rest. They all was the same height I estimated within 3 feet. And the limbs of the trees were in total harmony with each other. Meaning if one limb took up this space another limb "allowed" that to be and took up another space. Also the limbs of one tree, those limbs grew with each other. That provided a pear shape for the tree top. I discovered that first day that I was looking for complexity the last time and it's really in the simplicity.

The next day I went out with the purpose to do further inquiry into this simplicity. Because it was like once that insight of simplicity occurred for me, that's all there was that day. That's all I could see. So the next day after a night's contemplation I wanted to get deeper into the insight. So with this purpose I went out.

During the lunch breaks we usually park on a dirt road and eat. And we did this this day. It's wild. The other images spent that hour or so, to hang out and talk shit, and I spent the time being with the trees. This was a more close up examination of the branches and the trees itself. What I discovered was that on the limbs that appears in perfect sync far off is actually thousands of little branches connected to a bigger branch extending from the trunk of the tree. I discovered with the evergreen trees that if it's let's say 100 feet the first 80 feet there's no branches with pine needles on them. As a matter of fact the branches seems like they've been sawed off. At first I thought it was ridiculous that someone would come out here in the forest every few years and saw off the branches. Then I realized that what was actually happening is that the top of the forest blocked the sunshine so that it depletes the necessary source needed for the growth of the branches. I went looking for a line of ants on various tree trunks and discovered none, but it did allow me to see the complexity of layers on the bark. I saw a branch tree that was growing downward. I noticed that the end of it that was out by the road appeared dead. I broke off a 3 feet piece with a simple snap. At the breakage point in the center there was a hole where a long ago termite was feasting.

If anyone would have asked me why I was so interested in these trees I would have told them that a friend of mine was a botomonist. I doubt if they would have bought that I was discovering a consciousness in these trees. Which is how I spent the day.

I was standing there in the middle of the dirt road looking up at the trees, and then it hit me, of what's beyond the treetops. The sky. Clouds moving across the sky. I noticed an odd thing. The clouds what was "below the sun" could be clearly seen moving, but the ones in the further parts of the sky "away from the sun" seemed to be moving slower. I know that it was an optical illusion, but it was my first time noticing that. Later on that day I said to another inmate like it was a passing comment. I said "Damn. The sky never ceases to amaze me." He didn't hear me, or perhaps he didn't respond. I meant it though. In that moment I realized that there's really no sky. I mean on a cloudless night is there a sky? no! I'm saying when I'm in an airplane I don't see a sky. Yet there's blueness all around. But no sky.

Just like the one before, I was looking for something to write, and the trees, which is about how I spent my days, the sky which is the insight that occurred that day and the next paragraph which is a report somewhat about my latest dreams.

I was getting fed up with having precognition dreams. Then I had a dream a week ago about 3 airplane hijackers, and the plane was one of those old ones with propellers. Something happened like the plane crashed or landed I'm not sure but the plane was on the ground and police and emergency crews was arriving and they needed to get out of there quick. So one guy came up with an idea and changed in to miniature clothes and told his other two partners to come on out when they see him with a bundle of wire over his shoulder. That'll be the signal that he had a viechle to get away when he left the plane I woke up. I was satisfied that I had that dream, not for any other reason other than it was a dream, and not a vision to choose from. Dig? That period of time when I had those visionary dreams I feel that they are possible futures to choose from.

I had another dream. I was with 4 other people somewhere I don't remember now the specifics of the surroundings and all that. I do remember the core of the dream. There was a guy with us, a simple guy, a a little too simple. He bought refrigerated food because he didn't have a refrigerator he thought that there was no need for that, because it was already taken care of. He said that those people in the space ships knew him. They knew about all of us, but knew him because he knew himself, and wasn't lost among the ego and personalities or acts. The funny thing about this dream is that when I woke up I could still hear him talking, in my head.

The other night I dreamed of Kathina. Looked a little bit like Amy Z. I hope I have those kind of dreams again.

A TALK

You know this is nothing new?
Yea I know that. I just felt like talking with myself any way. Or should I say have a dialogue with my self.
The reader might not know who I am?
You are me as I am you.
So what is it you want to talk about?
I don't know exactly. This morning when I decided to write this piece I had a clear idea about what I wanted to be the topics of conversation, but now all I can remember is a few things such as I usually don't write in this style, meaning that I use the whole line on the page unless I'm writing a poem, but what the hell this is different. How would you have felt if I would have made you Mrs. R.
I think that you should first let the reader know that Miss R. or Mrs. R. is the lady reporter of the interview you created for the introduction to your 1st book "Gihyu 19." Well I think that the reappearance of here would have been historical, but this is more historical, dig? For she has already happen. And maybe you should bring her out when you write Gihyu 29".
So who the hell idea was this anyway. I mean really, was it mine or yours disguising as mine.
I think it was the both of ours. You had the thought and I agreed with it and formed it into an idea. One thing you could tell me is what is it about within between that has you so riled up.

Well the book is one of my most difficult because I have to interpret the meaning of each line in the poems. right now I haven't written anything in that book because of one line. In the poem the line makes sense but when alone, I have to dive into it and bring out what it's meant to mean. It's wild because even though a poem may take only moments to create, what's with in between can take as long as weeks to put down.
I don't mean to change subjects so quickly but have you not noticed your hand writing.
Yea, I've explained the different ways I write already many times I don't feel like doing it now. This chicken scratch is nothing new.
What is it that this piece is to accomplish.
I know what you was thinking about asking. You was about to ask is hope to accomplish. But you checked your language and knew that hope is out of the question. Hope is even out of town she's been gone for more than 5 years but that's another story. I use the term, clearing the cobwebbs. Yet in this instance it's not exactly that there hasn't been anything blocking my way to write, more like I've just been thinking a lot about the statement in the poem and even though an reasonable interpretation has occurred. I'll hold on to it for a while to see if anything else needs to be added. Also the 1st chapter of my second novel is almost complete. I have the different scences already in mind, well that's not true, I have the next scence for sure already in mind, but I don't have the dailouge to fill the scence yet. That'll come in due time I'm sure

So what is the purpose of this piece?
I think that there is no certain purpose per-say that I can put a name or title too. I'll just continue writing and talking and conversating until I've said what's needs to be said then I'll complete this piece, by then the purpose will be served, and be known, even if the purpose is only fill up a few pages with mind clearing thoughts.
What is it that's on your mind that you feel needs to be cleared?
I can't exactly say, There's dreams that I've wrote down that I want to put into this, There's just different points I want to make, such as, I'm working on this and two other projects at the same time and I'm about at the same page on each, and it looks like I'm going to finish them around the same time. Which'll be cool because I don't think I've finished 3 projects within 5 days of each other before. Before you ask, let me just say that the dreams I wrote down wasn't in complete detail just outlinesh like.dig?
Let's talk a little bit about the effect this prison term is having on you.
Nope. Let's not talk about it.
Come on I'm sure the reader is interested.
If so. Let the reader read my work.
That wouldn't be a fair thing, given that your work is only moments in the 10½ prison term you've served already. After all you started this dallogye this after

noon around 2:30, Now it's about 1:30 AM and this is only the 4th page, but the reader wouldn't know that unless the reader was informed. What happened to you between those hours. What was you doing?
You know what the hell I was doing.
Sure I know but the reader doesn't.
Well that's true. I played chess, I read the beginning to a novel, And I looked at televisions You know that at any given moment I could sit down and write, but I chose not too.
If that is so why is it taking you "so long" with these projects. —
I don't consider this as a long time. As I get on in years, I've come to understand more about the quality of on foresight. I've learned to keep it, turn it around in my mind for a while, look at it, and then write it, that is what takes up the time.
Who's Chrystal?
Who?
Chrystal?
Why you ask that, I thought we was talking about how much time it took to write a projects.
Well, she just popped up in your mind, therefore my mind, And since you don't want to talk about prison maybe you would like to talk about her.
Nope.
Well what the hell do you want to talk about.?

92

Do I have some sort of frustration?
You might, You tell me. There's some things that you want to talk about and some things you don't want to talk about. Who's to say that the subjects you don't want to talk about isn't the most important?
I've in my time withheld things that are important to put down in writing. Sometimes for good reasons, sometimes for no reason at all... I tell you what, Since I really don't want to have this dailouge to finish this book, because I have 3 more pieces to write after this one, You can ask me one question that you feel is important, I'll answer it, then we'll close up. Deal?
Deal.
Okay what's your question.
This question isn't only important for me to know the answer to, it's also I feel important for you to write down before you're released from prison. Did you try to attempt suicide?
No.
Why did you cut your wrist
Good question. First of all let me say that I never try to do anything. As you know, I either do it or don't do it. I cut my wrist so I could kill the life in this skin bag so I could move on. I had just got arrested and I didn't feel like spending time in prison. Also I was mad because the action that got me arrested was done by a writer. I didn't want to be a writer any more, so I thought I

could leave. After all if I'm not a writer, I'm dead anyhow. I started cutting vertically my left wrist, but I only got a couple of inches and it started hurting so I stopped, and started cutting my right one. I cut about an inch line and that started hurting so I stopped. Then I felt wild with bleeding wrists that hurt like hell, knowing that I wasn't going to die. So I decided to wait and see what happens if I don't write. That lasted about two weeks and that's that. Here I am, here you are.
Are you saying that could happen again?
You mean cutting my wrist?
No. I know that's not going to happen again, I mean are you going to kill yourself successfully in the future?
I'm sure I am, one way or the other.
What do you mean.
Either by choice or natural cause which is one in the same to me. I tell you one thing, I'm not going to leave any books unfinished. If I should die right in the middle of a sentence then that's the end of the book or the piece whichever the case may be.
Would you have written what you just wrote if I haven't have asked you?
I don't think so. I probably would have saved it for my autobiography. Which by the way I've started in already. I probably get more into detail when I put it down in there than I've done in here.
You know, so many people are going to have the opportunity

to read that about you cutting your wrist, but so few will really read it, is that why you chose to answer my question.
No, I answered it because you asked. You may not remember that twice I eluded to the cuts on my wrist in the past 10½ months.
Oh I don't remember, when did you?
The first time was about a month or so after, in a piece in the book "Yours Truly Steven" when I say something like glossy gashes that's not glamorous. something like that, I know I say glossy because the cuts was shiny pink. Another time is in the book "Thinkings" in a piece I think I titled "The Children." When I was in a Majic Market tell this girl how great life was and her little brother thought to me if life was so great how come the cuts on your wrist? So you see I didn't exactly hide it, I just didn't discuss it.
That's true. You know there's so much we could discuss in this piece, and so much left unfinished, like what are those dreams you wrote down, or something not mentioned like the sword, the Flower, and the ink pen with 7 drops of ink leaking from the lead of it, that you have tattooed over the scar on your left wrist, what's that all about. And who is Chystral?
Well the dreams, and tattoo and stuff, I'll leave that for another time. I will tell you that Chrystal is a Beautiful woman, who fascinates me to the

95

Max. I love her. She's my distant cousin from North California. I'm seeing her again for the 3'd time in 5 years in July. If God's willing.
You know what?
What?
You still don't know how to spell, I mean all those hundreds of novels you've read, and still can't spell.
I probably don't have my grammar correct either, but who gives a fuck. Writing is like life, it's a state of mind.
I can dig that.
Hay dude this is it, we have to get out of here so I can write my speech and my other two pieces and declare this book completed.
Yea, okay. See ya later.
Yea. Peace.
Peace.

G.Burg
G.Burg

Hay?
What?
Did you title this "A Talk" because you couldn't spell Dailouge?
Yea, so what?
Just asking. I can't spell it either.
I noticed.

Speech Given In Febuary Of 1992

Months ago, I don't remember exactly when, I discovered myself in the midst of a game. That's wasn't usual. What was, was that it was a game that I had started, and got lost within. An easy title for the game is "Call me Steven." The insight that occured from that discovery was that I was being trapped by the identy Steven, Even when I was Gikuyu. You see, I was only Gikuyu on paper in my writings and not Gikuyu Known as Steven, I was Steven, which was the trap because I'm Gikuyu. Dig? I decided to contine playing the game. There was no chance of being trapped again.

Now months later I'm still playing and I've been allowed the opportunity to observe who Steven shows up to be, by others who only knows Steven. Different people at different times has nicknamed me Professore. Some still see me as a weakling, I was about to say none, but it's really only a few respect me like I'm Gikuyu. The otherd.

The otherday I was explaining to a guy the powers of the mind and he excused himself to go get a cup of water. That's when it struck me that he only knows me as Steven, and didn't even consider that what he did was disrespectful. You may not even consider that either. The point is, I took time out to share with this person knowledge in a atomsphere where knowledge is seemed a waste of time and he didn't share my interpretation of the importance of my actions. Just that lead me to thinking.

I thought about why am I playing this game. One excuse popped up right away.... I'm playing this game because I'm hiding behind Steven, Because if I insisted on being known as Gikuyu, then It would overwhelm the space of this simple atmosphere and cause to much friction. Then I realized that the ideal of Gikuyu is much larger than Steven, It would be like trying to hide a full grown Red Oak Tree behind a watermelon seed. It's impossible. Well not impossible unlikely done with a societalized effect dmm'd.

Then I considered the excuse, that I'm playing this game because it has thoughts provoked that wouldn't be otherwise, because of the nature of this space. Then again I realized that As Gikuyu I've played many games ~~in many~~ strange spaces that has provoked thoughts.

A few more excuses came, but they so breif that I forgot them. Finally the answer came. I'm playing this game "Call Me Steven" for the simple fact, that I decided to. It's not a reason, It's a fact, and that's that. Dig?

Breif speech. Quick point. Great Insight. That's my review, What about you? Thank you Thank you Thank. I appreciate the opportunity of being allowed to be.

Peace and Love
Gikuyu

I have been incarcerated for 11 months. Never in my time did I imagine being locked up for so long, And I'm talking about an imagination that dreamed of a great love like the one I share with Debbie Ingerman, so you see that's no small imagination.

Last night I finished chapter one of my 2nd novel, I woke up the next morning with a splitting head ache. It left me to wonder which side is the creative side. I forget. My head ache was in the front left part of my brain, which I concluded to mean that I prematurely changed it for the last 5 or 6 pages of the story. I also wrote a page or two in this other book I'm working on. So now I'm working on two books instead of 3. This one and this other one I previously mentioned. I think that I wanted to just write in this book to make sure it doesn't feel left out, Although I have nothing to say.

One can actual say that this is a sort of "I still know you're here" page. Because the only purpose it's serving is to be a reminder, which I feel is very important.

Thanks
Pearl

A Letter

Dearest Universe

    I forget the last time I've written you, but I believe it hasn't been to long ago. Once again I'm just checking in. Well actually that's not exactly the truth. What I'm doing here in this letter is having your presence occur. for me once more. Or to say to have your presence show up more profound. Because you see lately I've been concerned about what's been going on outside of me rather than inside. Or you can say I've only been paying a little attention to what's going on around me on the otherside. That's sound more clear.

    For the past day or so, ever since I wrote the previous page, I been thinking about what to put in this letter, and even though I haven't thought of anything I still write you. Since when did having nothing to say ever stop me from writing. What I did decide to do is to just write until I fell asleep or until I've reached my prospective go of the number of pages I wish to have this be.

    As I mentioned in the previous page, I've been incarcerated for 11 months. When I first got arrested I knew that I would be serving atleast 12 months in jail. or in the prison system. What I want to bring up now is the hint of doubt that it'll only be twelve months. It could be longer but of course that's up to you. And of course that's why I'm writing you this letter.

I'll try to write a little clearer so you'll understand me quicker, but you know what happens when I get rolling. I not for the first time am lost for words as to what would be ~~appropi~~ appropriate to say. This lost for words is in a different context than "the having nothing to say" that I mentioned earlier. I feel like although I've been writing there should be some kind of shift felt or seen that would indicate my reentering. Two things... First this the obvious, since I haven't been paying attention to what's been happening around me on the otherside, the shift could have easily been unnoticed. Second, I feel that eventhough I've written 8 projects to complete perfection and on the 2 that I'm working on now, I'm only less than 15 pages from the end on both, there's still a feeling that there's one more project left to be done. The thing about that is I always have that feeling. Pluse given the time allotted to complete these 2 projects which is in 2 months time I don't see that other project forming. But I know that in a week's time these 2 projects could be complete. So what I'm saying is I should design a final project and complete it, but my concern is it will not be finished on the date that I requested from you to be released which is the sixth of March 1992. As you know the average time of my projects has ~~po~~ been atleast 2 months and the sixth of March is about 2 weeks away. Inside this dwelling on the decision is the ~~do~~ ~~the~~ hint of doubt. Could it be that I should write the project and be rereleased weeks after its completion or finished these projects and wait till March sixth and

35

See what happens?

I just realized that in my own way I've communicated to you the two things that's been on my mind. The doubt and the request. Actually as you know the request came from a dream I had. The dream if you don't remember is when I dreamt that I was looking at my release papers and the date said "The 6th of" and it was left up to me to fill in the blanks. Obviously my first rational thought was April of 92. Then I looked at the calendar and noted that the 6th of March was the first Friday and I wanted to go to that poetry reading, so being irrational in my request I made it March.

If again I remember correctly I made a request of you to go to Florida and sure enough you granted that request. My promise to you then was to become famous. Forgive me but I don't remember if I said Famous in a social kind of way. I probably did. You yourself have to admit I did that. Did I say any thing about taking my books to publishers? I don't remember, but as you know I did that also. Each promise was made and kept with my own interpretation. I remake those promises and I tell you know that I won't seek as much control of the outcome as I did. I will leave it to you. Yet I will do what comes natural, well maybe not what comes natural, I will not sabotage it to allow me to remain safe but uncomfortable. Dig? If this request is granted I will go full out 100% until my next vacation. I will even

36

shave 6 or 7 months off to repay for this extra time you've provided me to be able to crease the ground work for my 2nd novel. Which by the way I thank you.

I think or I should say I know now that I can work amongst society now. I understand my plan. I will of course be a writer first and a societilite second, but not like before when went out there twice and didn't suceed. The main difference now is I'll be working to fund my projects which in turn will allow me to be a more profound writer. One thing you should know I will never set-up something just in case I should need to have something to fall back on. If my writing is societyly SUCCESSFUL. For other than being a writer the only thing I have to fall back on is Death. Death of this shimbay shotsso.

You know I bought a new ink pen weeks ago. Figuring that this one was going to run out since I've written one project with it and writting two other projects with it, but it seems this pen isn't going to run out of Ink. It would be a shame to leave here without using it to write atlerst one project. That ofcourse means I would have to kick ass. It's not like I haven't done it before. Remember on my birthday a few years ago I wrote to back page projects 4's pages each in about 5 days. A weeks or two on one project should be interesting. But what would the insight be. What would the ..... I was about to ask what will be the contribution be, Then it dawned on me the project itself will be the contribution.

103

37

The little things I do now which when I was writing lingering thoughts I would have wrote down, I don't write down now. Meaning, when I shared about the guy masking his stupidity with intelligence. What intelligence is that. Well here I've come up some interesting incidents that leaves me in amazement at the state of minds of some of these males. but I don't say so myself I should share this because these pages are becoming few and it's "Known" that my time is getting short, So I write what is needed. A thought occurred for me while I was just writing that, Other than the thoughts like "man you've read hundreds N-novels in the past eleven months and you still haven't learned how to spell," or "What's up with this handwriting?" The main overriding thought that occurred was that, what I just said could be a clear sign of the shift.

So, Universe check this out, I am going to pay more attention to what's going on around me on the other side. I wish I could say that in a shorter way, I just can't think of none write now. And I'm going to serious consider writing another project. Maybe it'll be a drailogy. If I ever learn how to spell that correctly. I know this hand writing may make it difficult for you to understand what I'm saying swiftly, but take your time. You got until March 6th. Thank you thank you Thank Peace and LOVE

Cthy

Speech Given To Life On My Last Days

Started 2-25-02

Thank you! Stop clapping. (The reader pause for a moment for the people to stop clapping.) This is my last day and I have some things to say. I only have a few pages time to say these things. First of all I'll like to address the context of "Last Day". What is meant by that? Well one thing and everything. This like no other time is written because this is my last day.

It is interesting to say the most, that my humble acceptance of this fact comes to me so calmly and occurs for me as easily as if it's just another cloud in the afternoon sky. When I first realized that I was going to be writing this speech my first decision was to not attempt anything classic. For in the past, the pieces that I've considered classics come when I knew that some time in the future I would be looking back on this and smile and say "Damn, that's a classic." Do you see, that decision was natural? Because there will be no looking back on this.

I was flabbergasted to say the most, to notice my actions at the moment the realization that my last day was coming, occurred for me. All of a sudden I began to comb my hair. As before I was never concerned about my hair because there was no need to. Where was I going? On a date? Of course not. My hair was just another exterior thing that needed not to be worried about. But now I know that I'm going to be moving on. Moving on to my next Era. I know that this next Era will have people who se very much concerned about how one looks. I've been there before

Originally I was writing this speech as if it was the last day of my life. But I decided that this isn't the right time to do that, yet the context will somewhat remain the same. I just a moment ago added a "s" to the title. I will not change anything on the first page. You see I just officially got the word yesterday that I am to be released on March 4th which is in about 8 days. So you see my request was somewhat granted. Yet the decision was made a day before I made the request. I thought about what meaning that had for me as far as my promises were concerned since they was made the day after. Then I realized that the promises were made authentically because I did not know of the parol board's decision, so the promises will be kept.

I'm currently finishing up my project "Within between" which is one of the most extensive poetry books I've ever written. I believe that along with continuing my novel when I get out, I will continue that also. Which means that with the "Potrait/story book", the series "The One Door Man" and the novel turned short stories, I'll be working on 5 projects when I get out. Which undoubtly I'll be trying others soon. Oh yea, I've also started my autobiography. So I will be one busy writer.

Lately though it's been difficult to read. I've currently given up on continuing to read and finishing a 600 page novel, of which I've read 183 pages. During the time it took me to read those pages I read two other paper back novels. One about 600 pages, the other about 300 pages. It's like all my attention is on being home again after almost 12 months. But of course I don't find it difficult to finish this speech for where writing is concerned

Last night I was dreaming, and I knew it. In the dream
was reading an artical about how the owner of two major black
ip clubs had a condo, although he wasn't living there. Another
y who was, had a room where one could pay to have a live
rated act performed and videod. Then the dream slipped
to another space and I was reading an artical which had
picture of this female and her name, and the town she was
in. Now I wanted to see if this was real. So I decided to
rise up only slightly and grab a pen and while still seeing
is in my dream, I wanted to write this down. I've done
before when I was writing my book "Thinkings." Actually,
was doing a form of what I intended to do. For then
was between sleep and awake and I wrote down the trea
I wanted to write down something specific in the dream
I lay there for a moment and calm myself. I wake up
I know that if I move to get my ink pen, the physical /
tion would have me lose my dream. Yet I do it anyway
sure enough I lose it. Yet I'm still floating around in th
of the space where that dream came from. So everything is
lost.

o now I'm exploring the space, knowing that my pen and
is by my right hand. I shift my view to get a larger
of being in this space and I catch myself. I realize
I was dreaming that I woke up from dreaming. Which
re to also realize that that artical was 3-deep, and
condo scene was even deeper. Deeper in space, 3 or 4 lays
d reality as we know it. You understand what I'm saying?

no matter where I'm at, I'm at home. Because as you know the source of my writing isn't my physicality more like my spirituality. Dig?

With each passing line, my page time is closer to becoming complete. And the nearer I reach that completion, the simpler I become about what it is I'm gonna say.

That new ink pen, well it's being used to write some of this speech then it'll be given away, for there will be no state if mind it'll need to contive once this project is complete.

I told someone in a dream that I had a short while back that in his state of mind when he percieve in my poetry as simple may be complex to another with the same state of mind, because the other may have a different reality. Yet that does not mean that my poetry is reality based more than state of mind based. As I thought about this, I decided to once again share with you that my writings is universally based. Therefore it's beyond the state of mind and most defintly one's reality.

I as I've said before am thinking a lot about my next era. Although that's nothing new, what is new is that what I'm visualizing isn't the later part, but the beginning. Ofcourse I've always known that there could be no later without the begining, but the begining was only seen as the no thrills part so it was never dwelled upon. Not untill now. One thing I remember is considering the possibility of not seeing my "friends" for another two years. For reasons stated before. The only thing that is need to be known about that is that I'm still considering that. It won't fit in with the no thrills part of the next era.

Last night I was dreaming, and I knew it. In the dream I was reading an artical about how the owner of two major black strip clubs had a condo, although he wasn't living there. Another guy who was, had a room where one could pay to have a live x-rated act performed and videoed. Then the dream slipped into another space and I was reading an artical which had a picture of this female and her name, and the town she was from. Now I wanted to see if this was real. So I decided to wake up only slightly and grab a pen and while still seeing this in my dream, I wanted to write this down. I've done this before when I was writing my book "Thinkings." Actually, I was doing a form of what I intended to do. For then I was between sleep and awake and I wrote down the tea. Now I wanted to write down something specific in the dream. So I lay there for a moment and calm myself. I wake up and I know that if I move to get my ink pen, the physical exertion would have me lose my dream. Yet I do it anyway and sure enough I lose it. Yet I'm still floating around in the area of the space where that dream came from, so everything is not lost.

So now I'm exploring the space, knowing that my pen and paper is by my right hand. I shift my view to get a larger area of being in this space and I catch myself. I realize that I was dreaming that I woke up from dreaming. Which had me to also realize that that artical was 3-deep, and the condo scene was deeper. Deeper in space, 3 or 4 layers behind reality as we know it. You understand what I'm saying?

So I decided to totally wake-up. I did right there on the spot without any warning to anything. When I totally woke up I felt a sinking sensation within my Abdomen. My first thought was picturing the shakras, and realizing that the area where that sensation was coming from was right where one of my shakras is located. Also had me to think of shakras is the sensation traveled upward in a straight line. I point this out about shakras because I believe for myself I have discovered an important avenue to journey when I'm dealing with dreams.

You know I remember when every now and then when I wrote about something happening in the future I would think "If God's Willing." Sometimes at rare moments I would even write it. Now I've come to know that if I see it I write it, and I wouldn't see it unless God is willing for it to be seen. Dig? ...{pause for a moment of digging}

Yesterday I decided to see what my reaction would be when I saw the scence of the Prision as I arrived from the detail, knowing it'll be the last time I saw the scence. On the way back I got to thinking about the begining of my next ERA. I might have mentioned it, if not I know I thought about how I was going to be a maniacc with the women. I reflected how before that would be improbable because there were so few out there who knew themselves as they really are. That was of course my opinion. Another thing was they was in public and I rarely if at all talked to females in public. After reflecting on that

I realized that I won't be a manic as much as I thought I would. Then I started picturing the being of the first female that I would talk to. Who she'll have to be and all of that. I got so caught up in picturing or I should say visualizing how she would feel. Spiritually ofcourse, I missed the science.

I have now 3 days and a wake-up to go before the beginning of my next Era. How time flies when it's real. I have in the past 12 months experienced forced relaxation. And contary to what is percieved, my vacation started almost 3 years ago. I calculated it and it'll be 31 months. That's 7 months over. So that's 7 months that'll be taken away from my next vacation in 6 or 7 years. I've decided that at the end of six years, if all is accomplished I will then take my vacation. If by reality that another year is seen needed I will delay my vacation till then. I'm even willing, at least right now I'm willing to work through my vacation and go straight for 14 years then take 4 years even, not take that 7 months, included it as a bonus for skipping a vacation. But I thinks that that's just a passing thought.

Today is February 29th, I haven't given an significance to this date before, I'm going to in one way or another now. It's a leap day and to my knowledge I haven't completed a project on this date. I'll see what I can do about that.

My last days, my last days, what is there to say. One thing is that when I've said that the thing to do is forgive some one for their ignorances, I meant it. I know that what

I'm about to say may sound arrogant, it's not. I'm saying this humbly. Do not forgive me for anything I've done or said. Writing is also saying. For everything is done or said with a commitment to contribute or to strengthen the source of the contribution. If anyone feels that I've wronged them and any way, do not forgive me, I request that you look at my actions in another way. In a way that will empower you instead of robbing of you of your power. And if it empowers you to feel that I've wronged you then in a real sense that is my contribution to you. Dig? {Pause for digging.}

In my lifetime I've tottered on the edge of insanity. There's been times when I've actually been there. Even when I've managed to return, I come back with the wisdom of the state of mind of insanity lingering within my mind. Eventually it stops lingering and incorporates itself with my everyday thinking. Which has me to dance along the edge with more of a purpose and design my own moment to choose to step over, when it'll be best for me.

Well folks, I have about a page's time left. There will always be something else to say. Another project that needs to be written, an ideal that needs to be enhanced. Yet for me there will never be anything that I need to rewrite and put another way. Meaning that I need to change the context of something I wrote.

Day Sky Dreams has become for me to be a larger context of just day dreaming. It's a form of vision creating. Just as each project is. Just as each moment is. What else is there to say in my last days?

This speech is given to life. Which means you. I've often say that without you there is no life. Which you should know that I don't me without you there's no me. Understand? [pause. Allow time to understand.] Essentially I'm saying that these words has no meaning without you. There are just lines on paper or ~~said sounds~~ sounds coming out of my mouth. You are what gives them life. You are what gives them meaning. It's your choice.

On my last day what is there to say? I'm not going to say things that refers to past loves, now and back then, found, and lost. I'm not going to single out any individual that has impacted me the most. I'm not going to say that my last request is peace on earth and all of that mushy stuff. The only thing there is to say has been said. The only thing to say is Nothing.

Peace and love.

Oh one ~~more~~ thing. Just to follow tradition. Thank you, Thank you, Thank. For Allowing me to be here and now

Peace and Love

G. Thuyet

I've reread my last 10 projects. Well 9 of them. I haven't read my 1st chapter. There's two things I will like to get straight.

First I said that I began an era a few months ago. And I said I'm beginning one tomorrow. I didn't declare that I was in one that began after my official vacation. I've decided that I am in an era withing my extended vacation that began Aug 3t 5th And will end to morrow March 4 which will also be the end of my vacation and Dig?

Second is that there's a third time other than the glossy gashs, and In Timbings. But I mentioned the time I got the tattoo the moment of Sandy. I cryptly mentioned it in "the Wave" in the book "withinbetween"

All in All I'm satisfied with my projects, or I should say with your projects.

Peace And Love
Ciky

CHAPTER FOUR

FRESH FROM THERE

FORWARD

This project was penned over a period of years. It's a combine effort of books. This is not "the best of" collection. This is only what's needed now. I would like to thank Dan Marshall, and Brandt Hardin. They kept the hand written script safe while I was on that 2-year walk about. True Friends...True Family.

Peace

The Favor

He had five children. He hugged his five year old daughter. She vaporized in to a small ball of shiny light, and started to float around his head. The lady that was the "Him" asked what was going on. He said "I'll explain later." Two of his sons that were age seven and eight ran up to him crying. They hugged him and before he hugged them back he asked them to tell Héllèn that he loves her. Just like his daughter before them, when he hugged them they also vaporized into two small balls of shiny lights and started floating around his head. The oldest son and daughter were crying asking why they had to go back. It was a favor he replied, and the favor was over. Yet don't worry I'll be with you someday.

They ran up to hug him. Before his daughter reached him the woman grabbed her and demanded to know what was going on. He explained "My wife promised that I'll see them again. I didn't know when that time would be, it's here now, but if you don't let her go she'll be late then I'll die right now." He reached his hand out and she let go. His daughter ran to him and he hugged them both. He started whispering "Someday, Someday." They all were crying when the kids vaporized into the same small shiny balls of light. The five-baseball size lights were floating around his head, then they left going toward the sky. Before they got above the trees they disappeared. With tears running down his face he whispered "I'll see you later..." Then he started walking down the sidewalk, leaving the lady very confused.

Trapped

I woke up in a small grey room. I found myself watching a blank television, with two females. At the time I knew them. One was tall and obese; the other was short and slim. We were having a conversation of sorts. Joking around and all.

The television came on, and it was a news cast showing a picture of a city that I've never seen before. A big ball of pure light was dropped on the city, and the reporter said "The bomb has been dropped. The dinosaurs have been destroyed. The city is safe. We will now start beaming people back to the city now." My friend who was sitting on my left {the short, slim one, let's call her Tracy. She reminds me of this girl I know name Tracy.} She said "That's great! Let's go back now." When she said that we sort-of slid into another scene. We were on what looked like the 30th floor of a 60 story building. It frightened me a little seeing the height of a building while being in an office of that building at the same time. That's when I realized this was a weird dream. Since it was a dream and I realized it before I woke up, I wanted to have some fun. I looked up at Tracy and she got this wild eyed look on her face, then she ran to the window and started screaming "They lied! They lied!" The other young lady {who reminds me of Tonya from Tate who rushed out to talk to me in the snow with no socks} ran to the window and started lamenting "Oh no! **OH God** No!" I began wanting to wake up.

I ran to the window to see what was going on. On the streets below there were Dinosaurs, as far as I could see. From in the horizon they were slowly coming toward us. Some how I ran through the building, literally through it. The walls, elevator shafts, and walls again. I wanted to get a look from the other side, and the view was the same. It was like we were in the middle of the city, and all of the dinosaurs were coming straight for us. I ran back through the building to the room to tell Tracy and Tonya "Good-Bye."

I tried and tried but I couldn't wake up. Then Tonya shouted franticly for me to shut and lock the door. She said she was mostly scared of those special dinosaurs that can shrink to six feet, and they can come in and get us. Locking at least four latches and a deadbolt, I joined them in the middle of the room. There was a white marble card table where I stood on one side and they stood on the other. I shouted to Tracy to slap me because I wanted to wake up. She drew her hand back, far back. She slapped the $#*t out me. But I didn't wake up.

As we jabbered in the irate debate we came to the conclusion that someone was dreaming and it wasn't me. I said "Hey Tracy sorry but you have to wake up." I drew my hand way back. She put her hands up and protested it wasn't her. I shrugged my shoulder and she put her hands down, and put her face out. Asking for forgiveness as my hand smacked her face with a reverberating POW! She screamed and her face turned redder while tears started rolling down her face. First we heard the ding from the elevator.

Then the stomping of the beast coming down the hallway. I turned to Tonya said something like "Sorry you know, we gots to go." She just smiled as I drew my hand back and began to strike. I got about a half of a hair's width from her face then I woke up.

I woke straight up, no early morning fogginess or anything like that. It was so early in the morning I didn't feel like thinking about it. So I just chalked it up as being another wild experience. When I went back to sleep, I woke up in the same small grey room, I was sitting in the only chair. There was no television this time. Suddenly Tracey appeared and said "Tonya apologized for having you trapped in her dream, but she was scared of having the past catch up with her." Then I woke up... No I was awoken.

Close and Different

She thought about knitting her afghan blanket. Then thought about me pulling her legs open passionately. The first time I heard her think that, I said, "Okay I'll do it." She just smiled as if it was no surprise I heard her thinking. The second time she thought that, we were in a restaurant and I did thrust her legs open. She sweated with passion and so did I, yet that was a far as we got.

The third time was Valentine's Day. We were in a café. She received a poem written on a napkin. I heard her read it to herself silently It read "I've decided to stay so will you go out with me. I'm at the end of the table." Then she was thinking that thought again as she was looking around the café for the writer of the poem. I had one hand on her knee; she found the writer, composed herself as if in shock and knocked my hand away. I turned around and there was a lady smiling. (The scene was first a man was there, in the back of the café, and then she was looking down at his stomach before she looked up in his eyes but to the side she saw a hand waving from side to side as if to get her attention. That's what shocked her. Then she looked up.)

Another point is she taught ballet. I was watching her teach about five children a dance sequence in Spanish. One kid had his little guitar and she had a stopwatch timing them.

The inquiry this dream put me in was how a person can get so close to the other person that they share each other's thoughts

Mother's Love

I was driving and my friend was riding in this pickup truck down a street. This lady waved us down. She jumped in and said, "I'm with the C.I.A. you got to help me find my kids. I said "Sure where are they?"

She pointed to this huge apartment complex that was just up the street. We drove in the driveway; I let my friend out at the front of the complex while me and her continued on to the end of the driveway. There was many turn off driveways on the main one we was on. I asked her how we'll pick the right one. She said she'd just know. As we drove along I asked her to explain her situation. She said she had two kids a few years ago and gave them up for adoption. Her brother and sister-in law were willing to take care of them now. Then she pulled out a map of the apartment grounds the ones where there are roads and squares drawn on them that symbolize the apartment buildings. We got to the end of the driveway and she didn't choose any of the turn off's.

I asked her "What do we do now?" She looked at the map and pointed to where we were at. All of a sudden a square that was on the map turned into a child's face that started to scream "Help me! Help me!" According to the map they were at the first turn off and we were all the way at the end. I quickly turned the truck around and put the pedal to the metal. We were doing at least fifty around the corners and up hills, dodging cars, people with their dogs and everything.

There was a 18 wheeler moving van hugging the whole driveway about ten feet from the entrance of the turn off where the kid's apartment was located, headed straight toward us. I said, "Hold on baby!" We sped up and turned in the driveway inches before the truck hit us. My friend was there pointing to a couple on the upstairs balcony with two kids. The lady screamed, "Those are my babies! My kids! Get them! Get them!" She was very frantic. My friend ran up the stairs to get the kids

A security guard came calmly walking out the building next door. I ask her for her C.I.A. badge so I could con him by putting my thumb over her photo and say I was with the agency. (I saw it in a movie or something.) She gave me her purse and I searched for her I.D. She got out the truck and was sort of hesitantly pacing back and fourth, like she couldn't decide to run to her kids or stay close to the get away truck. I found her wallet and to my surprise she wasn't with the C.I.A. my first thought was "Oh shit, we're going to get charged with kidnapping." My friend came running out the apartment with a kid under each arm. The lady started screaming and crying tears of joy. It was a very emotional moment. The guard walked up to her and said "Your brother and sister-in law were killed in a car accident." Then he turned and calmly walked away.

One could almost see the changing of the tears from gladness, to sadness, then to madness. I jumped out the truck and ran up to the guard and yelled something like how could he just tell her that with no compassion, with no sensitivity, you fucking asshole.

My friend put the kids down, and they ran back upstairs. She was crying. My friend pulled me away from the guard just in time. I was so angry for his insensitivity I was going to punch him in the face. My friend also called him an asshole. She was just crying. I put my arm around her shoulder; we all got back in the truck, and started driving out of the apartment complex. I asked her why? She said "Because............"

        Then I woke up.

The Lake Guy

He was in his room with a friend having a wild conversation. I say it was wild because of the high level of emotion I remember them having. He has these white 3 ring binders with clear plastic covers so you could put pictures or articles on the front. He picked up one of his notebooks and showed him a picture he took a few years ago. It was a picture of a man sticking his chest out and flexing his muscles out. There was this girl in the picture standing a little to the side of the man. He remembers taking the picture and also remembers that the girl just happened to be passing by. Yet she posed too. In the corner of the photo it was written "The May Remembrance."

He told his friend that the guy in the photo was in that new play opening in the theater. His friend asked him "you mean the one everyone is striking?" he said "Yea." His friend thought he was lying, so his friend said "Prove it." The guy said "Okay." The guy went to the theater and asked to speak to the man. The man came from the backstage area and said "Hey dude how's it been?" The guy said "life man life." They reminisced for awhile and this is what I remembered from their conversation.

The man - "Do you remember that picture you took of me
          a few years ago
The guy- "Yea, that's what had me to come here."
The man - "Remember the chick?"
The guy - "I didn't know her."
The man -"Nether did I. But when you gave me the picture
          I saw her in it, and I wanted to see her again.
          So I searched for her and I found her. She's
          now my wife and we're in this play together.
The guy- "yea?.. This play?"
The man- "Do you know why this is?" (He says while
          pointing in the distance.)" I mean those people
          over the hill has no other reason. Unless you
          know of one.
The guy-"I really don't know."

    All of a sudden over the hill they saw people coming. The way the scenery switched from being the backstage of a theater to being in the middle of an open stadium. The bottom of the hill was at the entrance to the stadium. About a hundred people with his friend in front came walking toward them. By this time the guy and the man was joined by the girl. (his wife.) They sat. The crowd sat.

They sat facing each other. The crowd was upset that the play was being held in their town. The guy said something wonderful. I don't remember what he said, but when he got finished talking, everyone was satisfied. The man said "You know you've always had a way with making peace." The girl wanted the guy to take another picture of them. The guy agreed. The guy suggested that since it was spring a good picture would be with the lake in the background. They agreed. The next scene is at the lake with a white life guard tower standing on the edge of the shore. The guy, the man, the lady, and The guy's friend, were the only ones there. The guy told the man, and the lady to stand on the top of the tower so they could be against the sky.

They climbed up onto the platform, as the guy was focusing on them, his friend was some how up there with them. They smiled and the guy took the picture. As they was climbing down the ladder the man asked the guy if he'd heard about the monster in the lake. The guy answered" No." The man said "Yea dude, legend has it; there's a monster that only comes out in the fall and spring season. He skips summer and winter. The guy asked" Why do they call him a monster?"

"He's not really a monster," the girl continued "but people haven't seen anything like him before so people call him a monster. The funny thing is, he doesn't know he's a monster. He spends all of his time contributing and making peace. The guy said "What makes you tell me this?" The man said" Because I wouldn't be surprised if you was the legend they talked about. If I remember, I only saw you in the season of spring. Never saw you in fall, or the other seasons.

The guys' friend said" You see this person doesn't know he's what other people call monster. They say monster for the reason like she said. They don't know anything, and also they are the ones who don't want to be contributed too. But the real title is hero. This person doesn't know who he is until it's too late. Then he knows for a minute and forgets when he returns. I don't know why that is, but that's the way it is."

They finished climbing down the ladder, all but the guy. Then the ladder fell into the lake. Catapulting the guy toward the middle of the lake they said while on the bank of the lake "We'll see you in the fall, and thanx."

Then all I remember is hitting the lake and sinking to the bottom with my hands crossed at my chest and I woke up in that position.

Reunion

I'm sitting at a table with about five other people my age. There's this beautiful female sitting next to me. I somehow know it's a family reunion, and I know her. I also know that I'm in a dream. But I can't control it like I want to. So I just let it be. I told her" you know this is the first time in a while that I've been involved in a dream and I actually know your name. She smiled and said "I know." (I don't remember her name now but "then" I did.) We talked for a while. She pulled out a photo of her and her boyfriend. She said "Yea we're going to the Bahamas." I said that's funny I'm looking at going to Vermont University also." She said "I said the Bahamas not Vermont University." "Oops" I replied.

Before long the dinner was over. We walked toward the elevators. The line for the elevators was long and it seemed that everyone wanted to get on at once. I, this girl and a couple of more friends or family was congregating about ten feet from the doors of the elevator. There were three sets of doors for the three elevators. There were three lines for each elevator. Behind us there was a line for water. The line was long and she wanted to get in it. I said sure what the hell. We was in line for a minute or two, I decided to show off. It being my dream and all.

To the side of us there was a pitcher of water. I reached in my pocket and put 5 quarters and a couple nickels on the table next to the pitcher of water. I asked her to get a few cups. She went up front, got some cups and came back with them. She asked "Why you want these cups?" I said "Want some milk and cookies?" she said "Sure." I touched the pitcher of water and the water turn to cold milk. I waved my hand over the coins and they became cookies. She was impressed to say the least. She grabbed a couple of cookies, and then all of a sudden her mother or older sister called her to the elevator, saying I got room for one more. She ran to the elevator and said back to me "Meet me downstairs!" I nodded my yes to her. Soon after. Maybe a second after the waiting area was empty. It was just me and this dude waiting for the elevator. The elevator came with the elevator operator who said" Going down!"

    We got on and to my surprise it was glass elevator. I'm talking a glass one. No cables were attached. It only had a floor, a back wall, and a left wall, going down fast. We must've been on the eleventh floor or something. When we got to the lobby, we went around along the side of the walls. I was tripping to say the least. I said "Hey dude this elevator is going side ways." He said "Yup. Sure is. Don't worry we'll be stopping momentary." As we were riding around the lobby we were two floors up going around like a whirlwind to the ground floor. I was looking around and noticed the posh setting.

Marble floors, golden handrails, and all of that stuff. Somehow I thought that this is where I need to be to meet up with this girl. The lobby I mean. When we stopped; me and my friend looked around, we were in awe. My friend stepped off first. Then as I was stepping off the elevator, I remember blinking and it only took a split second to blink. Yet within that split second instead of the lobby, I stepped into a hallway of some building.

I started walking down the hall and to my amazement it was a high school. I walked past classrooms and I remembered some of the teachers from way back. I followed the exit signs and went out the fire escape doors. I went one flight down and the doors exited me right out into the lobby of a police station. A bunch of things were happening at once. The cops were tussling with this one guy; another cop was booking this lady; fingerprinting and everything. This other person was getting his mug shot taken. There was a row of chairs where bums and hookers, and other citizens were sitting. I walked through the lobby looking around at all the activities and noticed the doorway to a gym. There were a few high school students in there playing basketball. As I continued to walk two kids came running up to me saying" We're lost, could you help us?" I said "Sure son"

We started walking deeper into the Police station. I turned my back for a second and the two kids got in line for something. I said" Yo come over here!" They quickly went and sat on a bench filled with citizens. The oldest one said "I guess we'll sit down in these seats and wait for our mother." I was a little hesitant to leave them there; after all they were no older than eight. But I thought there was a bunch of cops around so what the hell. I left them and started back toward the gym.

I eventually got to another lobby. It atrium was 2 stories high. This guy who I somehow knew ran up to me and said" Yo man come and take this picture with me." So we went outside to the yard of the next building. There were at least a hundred students in graduation gowns walking in the building.. The guy said here. He gave me the camera to take the picture of him. I said "I thought you said take it with you."

He said" That's what you're doing, I'll just be in the picture and you'll be behind the camera." I smiled" okay" I didn't want to take a picture with all those students in the background so I told him to face the crowd while I take the picture. I had the crowd behind me; I put the camera to my eye, focused and took the picture. When I brought the camera down I saw this tall hotel in the background. Again I somehow know that that's where I suppose to meet the girl. I gave the camera to my friend and instead of walking through the building I walked around it to get to Main Avenue to the hotel.

As I was walking to the corner, so I could take a right and continue on about three or four blocks to the hotel. When I walked past this café I noticed this kid by the window. He was about 13 yrs. of age. He looked mean so I looked mean. All I was trying to do was to scare him for some odd reason. When I turned the corner I noticed him still watching me. Then somehow he threw a knife at me through the window pane. I watched the knife pass behind me and land by the curb. I walked through the mud to get the knife. I walked back around the corner and in the front door of the café. The kid was sitting at a stool by the counter. I screamed "Come here little man!"

Then from the corner of the café to my right where I couldn't see came a man whom I knew from way back. He said" Hey brother let met talk to you for a minute." He gently grabbed me by the elbow and walked me back outside. I said "Hey brother how's it been going?" He said "Great." He pulled out a few bucks. Then I said" I was just going to scare the boy. He said" Good I was going tell you to lighten up!"

Then I woke up.

WELCOMING THE SHOW

Shoot me I welcome the show. Evette and Kit trying to flirt. Getting a ride home. Six and getting three in return. Getting a ride to the hotel not home. We're walking up the stairs and Kit asking the femmes " What's your room number?" The two femmes come upstairs in a sec. and ask "Were you serious about your invitation?" I say "Sure." I offer them some beer, and then some kids appear.

One kid is on the table; his chin reaches to the top of the glass. Don't forget the photo of the famous tennis player when she was young. Say didn't we see her at the Sheraton?" Kit says. No holiday Inn. And I said don't get the photo mixed up with the femmes. Because they have the same photo. 3 before she said something and I said what she said I had to make sure it was okay with S.U.L. 'stat. she said "sweet unique Lucy. I said "Shew I thought you was one of those religious types. Back to Evette for a moment. She wouldn't talk to Kit because her boyfriend drove a beamer. When I was sitting on the curb he drove toward me then swerved quickly to not hit me. Then Evette's brother ran up to the window and whispered something. I thought he was saying cops or something like here comes momma. I quickly went across the street and tripped over a downed wire while crossing. I sat on a short wall so I could see the beamer. The guy's leaning on the fence on the otherside of his car. From up the street her mother drove in a driveway and jumped out the car limping with a umbrella in her hand. She started whipping Evette up to the car and Evette got in and drove them both home.

Before we got in the car to go I asked how was Evette. Her brother said"20 and she needed to be congratulated because she returned home last night. Back to the restaurant. I pulled the kid from the back of his pants and told him he wasn't old enough to drink beer. Earlier the kid was telling another" Come on it's just like milk." The girls were turning into teenagers then 12 yrs. old then without warning the scene changed…. I was sitting facing Kit. And behind him was the fire escape looking doors.

There was loud music and this dude behind me was sitting like his feet was in the seat and he was sitting on the back of the booth just moving and moving like dancing. He was elbowing me in back of the neck. And it seemed like it was on purpose. I looked to my right at the mirror, I saw him and his partner behind me and I noticed my strange hair cut. Wondering how the hell I got that.

{maybe also mention the guy who ass you kicked because farting on me. He pull me to him and farted. Seeing Julie riding down the street and waving at her.}

I leaned to the right, looked over my shoulder and pulled the guy back to threaten him to stop hitting me in the back of the neck, or I'm going to kick his ass. {The farting guy started because I told him with enough room I can kick anyone's ass. Even the big fat china man in the corner. Room like just the size of the small house we was in.}

As the guy was falling back he reached in his white jacket (like the one I have at home.) as if he was going for a gun. Then I quickly returned him to the straight up position, and took my hand away and quickly apologized. He fooled around in his jacket for a second, as if he was putting his gun back in the holster.

I told him you were poking me in the fucking neck. The dude said sorry man. Then the security Guard said to the dude "Son you wouldn't want to do that because you'll lose." The dude said "Right." Then another guard appeared and the dude got up with his partner and said come outside. The guards were blocking the doors up there behind Kit so they went down the isle to the doors on the left. Then they walked out the fire escape doors and the security guards locked or closed the doors behind them.

Me and Kit got up just as they was walking out, just in case there was a shoot out. When the doors closed behind dude I told Kit come on man let's go get a beer. When we were coming backing back, one dude opened the door and threatens a guard. Saying come on out. I'll shoot you. That sort of thing went on for a few seconds causing a lot of commotion. Then when me and Kit got back to our tables, there was one security guard at the doors. Both of the two doors on the right end opened and the other two sets of doors were closed.

One dude stood in the doorway and the guard stood in the middle doorway. There's this fool I remembered from high school walked up to the dude and said "Shoot me I welcome the show." The dude pulled out his gun and pointed down at his shoulder, and shot. Then started shooting at the people in the crowd. I and Kit started heading up for those door quickly.

Then I either felt myself get shot or I felt the bullet when he shot the guy in the shoulder because my right shoulder was in pain. When I and kit got about five feet from the top of the stairs, the fool that had just been shot had a gun, pointing and aiming at us.

{Within those seconds of the fool getting shot and running for the stairs, I looked around to see where the dude was aiming next, because I had already been shot once. I saw the security guard struggle with him for a sec. and he pulled out his gun and shot dude in the head. }

The fool appeared when we turned the corner, and was close to the top of the stairs. There was now about a 100 people in front of us. And we were on the 2nd floor. When I and Kit saw the fool with the gun we both dove off the side of the stairs. While hearing bullets wiz past my head, I woke up.

The Mixture

I was telling the employees in the school cafeteria, how that between the age of 16 and 25 there was a big difference in my concept of school and my understanding of how the grown-ups that works here now are committed to making a difference in the kid's life… The woman asked me if I've learned anything, and I answered "That first there's answers, then once they're here, there's questions, and once one put those together, insights occur. It depends what one does with the insights that makes wisdom." Then I woke up.

Sure you can learn all you want to. What good is knowledge when you don't know how to think.

The Response

He was walking with her to her house. He told her that his family had come to accept and like the map for over 300 years now. A woman standing with her friend in a yard on a hill next to the side walk for which he and she was walking commented;

"Isn't it amazing that you can even read a map?" and he replied "Isn't it amazing that you hate so much?" She replied "I guess I walked into that." "No." He replied "You have walked into dookie." She said something about Rachel and walked into her house first.

As he was walking her up to the porch, an elderly couple with a baby in their hands came walking up from behind them and said "Rachel died a horrible death." He just smiled as he heard her tell the couple that he was Rachel's son. The woman replied "oh my." And rushed past them to let them in. He held the baby and noticed the total lack of hate. The baby smiled as he held him.

As he was closing the door behind him to go into the house, he glanced next door where the woman and her friend were standing. She stood slantingly with her hands on her hips and shaking her head

The Kiss

There was a ghost at a gathering being held in the upstairs parlor. There were 16 people. 7 people who didn't know about the ghost. The ghost himself, who was also the host and the remaining eight who knew about their host. But for those who knew about the gathering and didn't know, they would have only seen 15 people.

At the end of the party the host greeted them good-bye. The 7 as they were leaving suddenly felt a force grab their hand and felt a sudden warmness. Some felt a sudden warmness on their check. He kissed their hands to symbolize that they had somehow given him a helping hand, their cheek to symbolize they've been sweet with their love. He always kissed one or the other.

The remaining eight as they were leaving either held out their hand or presented their cheek for a kiss, for they knew how they helped him. At the end of the line there this elderly woman who was kissed on her the first time, so she held out her hand this time. He smiled and as she was about to descend the stairs she felt a sudden warmness upon her cheek.

The Thoughts

    I knelt down about 15 feet in front of the mirror. I was about to get executed. As the executioner stood behind me with his gun he decided on his on to blindfold me. He placed a napkin over my eyes. I pulled it off. Due to the perspiration on my face some pieces of the napkin stuck to my face. And I thought "I'm going to die with paper stuck to my face." I wasn't thinking about anything pitiful, just it was great that this long life was over. I had just been in a war and the side I was on won, but I was captured. As I knelt there smiling at myself in the mirror, the executioner asked me if I wanted my glasses, I said no. I thought I ought not to put them on just in case the bullet breaks the lens, then I wouldn't be able to wear them at my funeral, {if I had one.} As I heard the gun shot, I woke up.

The Children's **Effect**

After floating to the store I stepped in and briefly met the manger as he was going to the back to the back. He left his oldest daughter in charge of the store and her two younger sisters and one younger brother. I asked her to show me where the beer was. She showed me and we were drinking. She told me how strict her father was. I told her about Zuwena and Kinaya, how their father was strict. But now one lives in Paris and the other is happily married. I was telling her how wonderful Life and the world is. Her younger brother cut his finger on something. So I unwrapped a bandage that was around my wrist and wrapped his finger with it. He thought to me "If life is so great, Why the cuts on your wrist?"

I disregard his thought, then she decided to escape for a better world. She ran and hopped on motorcycle and started off. I became concerned for her younger sisters and brother, because they were each holding on to a rope that was tied to the back of her motorcycle. She tried to shake them loose as she rode through a field of tall grass, but they would not let go. Finally at the bottom of a hill she stopped and got off. They let go of the rope and stood up and dusted themselves off. She went back to them and started back toward the store. I waved good bye to them in the field of tall grass. After I waved good bye to them in the field of tall grass I continued up this hill.

At the top of the hill a man stood with a live baby's head at his feet. The baby was crying. The tears made the soil around his feet grayish. I thought to myself, "Damn this is some wild special effects Then "Wham"

He put a machete right through the baby's skull, and the baby stopped crying. After I knelt down because of pure shock, he did some kind of ritual where a branch of a tree with a bucket containing something at the end of it swung in a circle around my head and he said "You must praise God after one has past. You must Praise God Immediately. "

The Explorer

There were 5 people at the party in the Victorian style house. I was one of them. Thru the skylight on the 2nd floor came a parachutist. He dropped in saying that this was his assignment.

As I lit up a cigarette and drew smoke, something strange happened; everyone except for the soldier appeared different. They seemed like they've been hit by a bomb. They was pale, skinny and sickly looking. I had an opportunity to look at me through the soldier's eyes, and I appeared the same way. Only when I put the cigarette out, did everyone appear their same attractive selves.

Then it came to me. The soldier was an explorer, whose assignment was to report on those people who constantly escaped and only when faced with death or doing something that brought death quicker was they able to see beyond the facade they placed about themselves.

The Sign

I doubled headed her six year old son the rest of the way up the path from the car. We stopped in front of a house with tall weeds in the front yard that obscured the sidewalk leading to the house. I asked him "You don't really live here? Do you?" He shook his head no, and got off the bike and went to a shack on the other side of the path in front of the house. He removed a white water heater that was blocking the door and lead me inside. There inside on a couch which sat his 13 old sister, holding her 3 month old baby, beside her sat their younger 3 yr. old sister. They were watching a 21' black and white T.V. that was on a milk crate. To her right and to my left there was another black and white TV. that was not on, facing a chair that sat in front of a window. Though the sun shined thru the window, the room was still grayish, The walls was of a dingy grey color, and the air smelt like old wood because of the wood burning stove.

Then and there the thought came to me "I must publish as soon as possible if only to help this family out." As I looked out the window I saw their mother walking up the pathway with my friend, and I knew she didn't want us to know where she really lived. The house with the tall weeds in the front yard; although it was a wreck, it was an elegant mansion compared to this one.

So I hurried the kid outside and put the water heater back in front of the door. We rushed to the side of the house to play it off. Just in time too. They were at the front of the house. Me and her son acted like we didn't see them. But I knew they was going to come where we was at to see what we was up to.

So I pointed out to her son how the branches of the trees were intertwine so complexly, that a sight like that is rarely found in this part of the world. Then I really got into it. Because I was no longer really concerned about his mother or my friend. The scene was beginning to fascinate me. There was a pond there in the back yard. It looked like glass. Although frogs was swimming around {and only frogs, there was nothing else living in that pond.} there was no waves being made. And on the other side of the pond the trees at the forest was huge and the further back the forest went the darker it got. I looked up and the branches were more like vines now. They weaved a pattern like it was a fancy ceiling of a hallway.

His family began thinking of a polite way to get rid of us, before we discovered where she really lived. Her son knowing this. grabbed my friend by the hand and lead him to a raft that he wanted him to take to the pond with him.

My friend recognized everything. He knew that her son wanted us to stay so that his mom would relieved of her burden of her secret. He knew that his mother did realize how much of a burden her secret was. He knew that I knew her secret. He looked at me and as he did; the sun switched off and on twice. Then I got it. Then my friend posted a sign to the front side of the shack. The sign read:

"A place considered to be one's residence, no matter how shabby, no matter how pristine, must always be considered "It" Like in "This Is It." and respected because it is after all one's shelter."

The Lucky Ones

As I was walking with her, from behind I noticed how huge, pudgy, and ugly her feet were. They were badly scared up. Then as I stepped up along side of her I remembered who she was and where we were going. She turned and smiled at me and her face was also scared up with boils and busted boils and her teeth were rotten. She said "It was just around the corner." She held her hand out to me for support. Her hands were webbed at the fingers and on the inside of her palms there was also warts and boils. I gladly accepted her hand for I realized who she was and where she was taking me.

We walked through a ghetto and after we turned the corner we stopped a few houses in the block, and there on the porch were her students. There were 20 or so students. At first I saw them as I expected to see them: sad looking. There were some who have been neglected and rejected. They were leapers. There was one kid near the front with sores and busted sores on his face. He had no body; his head was connected with his feet. I could see the dried up tears tracks as he smiled at me. I smiled back to let him know that he was cool.

It hard to describe how rough they looked. The air reeked with the smell of solid waste. Some still wore cloth diapers that looked and smelled like they haven't been changed for a week. In the back row to my left I spotted a normal appearing boy. Then I spotted what appeared to be his sister on the other side. My first reaction was one of surprise.

Then she just looked up at me while she was standing up and waved her arm out and asked "Why do people live like this? I was put in a drug program, but they made a mistake and sent me and my brother here. I'm not going anywhere until I find out why people live like this." My first thought was that she spoke about why people chose to be reincarnated in this form of human being; Then I knew she was asking why they continue to live in a society that knowingly or unknowingly deprive them of their basic services. I answered the only answer that came to mind. "To show love, To teach Love, To be Loved." She kept asking over and over as if in the state of shock "Why? Why?"

I then realized that I had had this dream before. But for some reason I didn't write it down. As I thought that, I felt the question was directed toward me, and the answer I knew not.

The Guardian

I was leaning in the doorway to the kitchen, they was in the living room. I announced to them that I would be returning back to school. Each of them looked up and smiled. They were obviously pleased with my decision.

As I was walking to school I was thinking of the many possible ways I could apologize to my teacher, and also request to come back at the same time. The ideal of a sign occurred. I thought it didn't matter what the sign said as long as I was holding it. It could say sorry and request my request, along with breaking the ice.

I stood in the hallway along with the others students moments before the classes were to start. When the time came the teacher open the door, and smoothly said" Good-day." to the leaving and arriving students. I stood ten feet in front of him, he looked over the student's heads and read the sign I was holding up. Which read; Can I Pleze come in when the class begin" He smiled and nodded his approval.

I was one of the last students entering the class room, when I got to him, we conversant for a moment. I told him I was serious about coming back, but I couldn't today because I had one more place to go, yet I'll be back tomorrow. He believed me and said that was okay, Then he was distracted by someone or something behind me. I turned around and saw two guys. Each holding a sign. One read" When the class begins,"

The other one read "Can we come in. Pleze" I turned back to see the teacher angrily shaking his head "NO!" He left me and went to talk to them. After a few moments he walked past me into the classroom. Then the thought occurred. It's not the sign but who's holding the sign.

I walked in the spring sunshine on this path in the middle of a field of tall grass. I thought about when I had seen this scene before, but I couldn't remember. When I reached the end of the path I heard someone whistling so I turned around and saw two guys on horseback. They began charging down the path.

I was standing on the left side of the path when I first saw them; I crossed over to the right side, which was only six feet across. The reason I say it was the end of the path is because the tall grass abruptly was cut to a corner right there. I went around the corner to look at the field and to look at them coming. One guy who was on my side was wearing a sheik's turban of red that was waving through the air. I put on my glasses to see more clearly and reached out with my mind's eye to touch them and feel them. Although I could clearly see them, I felt neither danger nor comfort. That is until it was too late.   I first realized I was in danger when I saw the one wearing the red turban waving his arm up about around his head with a rope in his hand, like he was a cowboy. I remembered them as the two guys from the school.

My first thought was" these boys want to lynch somebody. "ME!" I said "Shitttt not the kid!" I ran up through the tall grass. Red turban man and the other one stopped their horses. Red turban man came down the path and hit a left then hit another one to follow me. I then decided it was useless and hit a left toward the path. When I got to the path I was in front the guy with the red turban and I began running down the path. The other guy stood in the clearing ahead of me. Behind him there was a hill and atop of the hill there stood a tree with a branch sticking out like an arm, and I again wonder for a moment that this place seemed familiar.

The Red turban man came riding pass me on my right. He got about ten feet in front of me and while still moving forward somehow lashed his rope back at me. When I saw the noose and how big it was, I just put my hands in front of my face. The noose went around my neck and wrists. He started and continued on and I was swept off my feet. Thinking quickly I figured my hands would be better used untangled from the rope. So I wiggled the free. As soon as I did the guy began to swing me around in a circle. My arm was waving to the side. I felt like a fucking kite.

About the third time around I glanced behind them and saw this beautiful babe kneeling in the field of tall grass. She had a loin cloth covering her breast and private area. She had a bow and pouch strapped around her which she carried arrows. I closed my eyes and thought to myself;

My guardian angel
Sending arrows thru the air
Striking down my attacker
And his mare

I woke up leaning back facing the sky, tied to a pole, which was tied down by a rope. I looked to my right and there was the other guy holding a sword. He told me that when he cuts the rope I'll be flung through the air toward the forest, and if I survived I could go on where ever. But if I died, Tough Shit.

I looked down in front of me and the forest were quite a distance away. I looked to my left and there she was, about ten feet away. She was flipping a gold coin in the air with her right hand and letting it land on the back of her left hand, as if deciding which way she wanted to save me. She looked at me and smiled a comforting smile.

Each toss of the coin, or to say each time the coin landed on the back of her hand it became louder and louder, with a certain rhythm to it. I closed my eyes and concentrated on the rhythm. The rhythm started to sound like water dripping. Then I recognized the sound as being from the shower head that was dripping before I went to sleep. And as I was waking up I thought to myself "So this is how she's going to save me."

The One Within

We were waiting for the bus at the top of the hill of some apartments. Jonathan fooling around with me started playing wrestle and I pushed him away in the street. When sun got in his eyes, I rushed him and grabbed him by his shirt and fell back. We flipped each other on down the hill. We were like a gymnastics team the way we were rolling over and under each other. My date yelled at us to get out of the street because there were cars coming. Plus we were bouncing on asphalt. I didn't feel the asphalt and Jonathan was laughing so I assumed he didn't either. But she did have a point about the cars.

So we stepped on the sidewalk. We were at the bottom of the hill facing each other, the sun was setting to my right, and our dates {Val and Dee Dee} were at the top of the hill to my left. I crouched down to defend myself, Jonathan smiled and charged. I again grabbed him by his shirt and with his momentum I fell back and flipped him in the air. This time he landed flat on his back. But he didn't immediately get up. As I lay on my back, I looked to my left to look at his shadow on the wall to see if he was moving or not. I saw that his knees were bent; I also noticed that his head was arched at a funny angle.

I jumped up and noticed that his head had fallen in an open water meter. His head had hit the steel surrounding the opening and his blood was clotting at the bottom of the hole.

I grabbed the back of his head and leaned him up to a position so I could lift him. The way he straddled me was awkward. I know it must have looked crazy. He had his legs around my hips and my right hand was under his bottom, while my left hand was underneath his right arm supporting the back of his head. He was unconscious. As I started up the hill I felt blood running through my fingers down my arm. As I was struggling to run up the hill, I leaned him back and shouted his name a few times, but he was out cold.

I screamed, "Help! Help!" to our dates, but they didn't react because for one it seemed they couldn't hear me, and like I said they must have thought that we was playing piggy back backwards. I kept yelling, "Help!" I waved my left hand panicky, it was particularly red from his blood, I screamed twice for them to call an ambulance. I screamed his name trying to revive him.

He woke up for just a moment; spoke in a kid's voice then went unconscious again. I had almost made it to them when I noticed that Dee Dee had fainted. Val was totally seated and kneeling at the same time with Dee Dee's head resting on her knees. Val was waving a white hanky over Dee Dee's face to cool her off. Val looked up at me then she pointed to an apartment on the corner to my left. I looked and a dude had the back door open waving me in.

Before I went in and as I was headed toward the stairs I noticed to my left on the other side of the driveway the other residents of the apartments was laughing at the way we looked. A grown man carrying another grown man like a baby or something. Since this dude didn't have a phone, Dee Dee had fainted, and the residents thought we was bullshitting, no one called an ambulance. Graceful under pressure was the only choice of actions I had to undertake. I jumped the steps as if I was floating. We entered the kitchen where I placed Jonathan on the floor.

After I placed him on the floor, I brought him up straight so I could get a good look at the cut. There was a shaven part of his head where the cut had occurred, like a doctor was preparing to put a few stitches in. There was a long vein running down the back of his head. And blood was squirting out with each beat of his heart. {The reason I said running down is because the pulsating beats along his skull was going downward.} While I was holding him in position, the dude was taping the cut. Jonathan began to wake up. I asked him if he was okay. And he said "Yea." But his voice was like a kid. I asked him his name and he said Steve. He jumped up like a flash and ran to the door for an apron. He began making a noose with the strap and he placed it around his neck. And the knot came undone because his knot wasn't tied right. Me and the dude {after a moment of shock} dashed toward him and subdued him. I had him in the middle of the floor while dude tried the phone, {which I thought he didn't have.} but it didn't work. Steve wasn't only different from Jonathan in personality but also in size. He had shrunk to fit the character of a kid.

I was holding him down when he seemed only to seizure up a little bit. The next thing I knew I was thrown awkwardly against the wall by the door. Steve dashed to the kitchen drawer and pulled out two butter knives. He started playing drums on the kitchen walls and cabinets. It was like he was saying "Do you really want to see how fast I am?"

The dude was standing there looking stunned with the receiver in his hand when Steve quicker than an eyes blink turned the knives around to the dull edges and chopped the receiver up to tiny pieces. Then he started drumming back around the kitchen toward me. He started along the walls, then stove, then sink, and then got to me. He started playing drums in the air, stopping about a quarter of an inch from my face. Briefly to my left out the corner of my eye I saw Dee Dee walk in. Steve went back toward the pots and pans that were next to the sink. He started beating on this little mixing stainless steel bowl.

As he was dinging off the sounds, Dee Dee sat down next to dude along the wall behind Steve. Val stepped in and sat on the floor next to me, she leaned back against the wall and also watched in amazement. While Val was wiping the sweat from my forward, Dee Dee screamed so she could be heard over the noise. "Boy your hands sure are fast." Steve stopped beating and the bowl fell to the floor about a foot from me. He placed the knives in the sink. He turned around, smiled and replied "Yes maam." It surprised me how Steve respected her. She smiled back and asked him his name. He told her and she said something else but I didn't hear her because my attention was drawn to the melting stainless steel bowl in front of me. First it was getting holes, then it started melting in a white plastically form along the floor by my leg.

The white stuff oozed its way right to my pants and started sizzling a hole toward my leg. I gave a little yelp as I jump stood up. Val grabbed the apron with the undone knot, and started balling it up, I guess to wipe up the remainder of the white melting stuff, I looked at Steve and said "You wanna see fast? Watch how fast I get these slacks. For some reason I not only wanted to get of those slacks quickly, I also wanted to empress him. So I decided to do a flip and take off my pants before my feet hit the floor. As I was mid air I felt just enough heat from that white stuff getting closer to my leg that it broke my concentration. I straighten my legs a bit too early and started coming down horizontally. Val seeing this slid the rolled up apron along the floor I guess so my butt would be cushioned. She just pushed too hard. So my feet landed on them. There I lay, my pants around my ankles, my feet about twelve inches apart and propped up on a balled up apron , I'm on my butt in my underwear leaning back on my elbows. Val is close behind me to my left sniggering. To my right there's Steve smile laughing, in front of me, dude and Dee Dee are just laughing away. Dee Dee grabs a metallic shaded string attached to a red balloon that was just floating along the ceiling. She hands it to Steve and asks "What can you do with this?" Steve takes the balloon and looks at it for a moment; he turns and smiles down at me.

He tied the string to my right thigh. He bounced the balloon of my leg with one hand and as it was rising back in the air he missed it a couple of times because he wasn't going fast enough. Dee Dee said "So there are things you can't work with."

I gave her a warning glance and she just winked at me with the expression "I know what I'm doing." Steve obviously seeing our little interaction started to pat the balloon from one hand to the other. He swooped between my legs and around my leg so the string went around twice. All I saw was a red whoosh at the end of a metallic color streak. The he did it again, yet this time I just heard a swoosh. He was moving so fast he seemed to have no arms.

Floating in front of me were a lot of different color balls of lights, like red, yellow, blue, green, orange, all kinds of colors. These balls of light started to solidify and they started falling to the floor. They became pieces of candy. Then they formed to be pieces of dry fruits. With pieces of dried pineapple, banana slices, walnuts, and raisins. Steve leaned his face in closer to mine and smiled. I sort of saw it "All" in his eyes.

Steve stopped, reached in the pile and started eating the mix. After a few moments of stun ness, I grabbed a hand full and ate some. They tasted good. Pointing between my legs I asked" Any one wants some nuts?" Every one started laughing. The laughter was partly to break the shock and astonishment we were in. Which is why I think Steve was laughing. And partly it was funny. I grabbed a handful and passed them out. I gave some first to dude then to Dee Dee. As I gave Val some I told her she'll get the other ones later.

The pile of fruit mix was popping into popcorn. Just mix fruit popping into popcorn. As I was standing up to pull my pants I noticed a sly knowing look on Dee De's face. So I politely in a stressed out calm way asked her "What the hell is going on?"

Dee Dee said "He's for all practical purposes is Jonathan. I knew him as Joe Joe. Which is his ego? Jonathan is the name of his personality. Steve is his entity. Who's a kid. Since Steve existed in the background, his actions are quicker, for once we've noticed them, they've already happened. The accident brought out Steve, which is the source of Jonathan's existence. Now the entity exists in a space where everything is everything else. There's no separating one from the other. What looks like magic to us is actually to him bringing into existence what has started out as we know as energy, or to say molecules and atoms. Actually as you can see that by the entity being here Jonathan's whole physical "Being" as been transformed. The vibration of the stainless steel bowl was so intense he changed the atomic structure of it. It sort of went back to its original make-up and just came back in the form off that hot ass white stuff. Still all and all he's my Jonathan.

I looked over at Steve and he was doing a little dance while tossing dried pineapple chunks in the air and having them land in his mouth. I sat down and got comfortable on the pile of dried fruit. There was popcorn all over the floor. I guess the fruit stopped popping after it had a chance to cool off. I laid my head on Val's lap. Looking up I could see her smile before I could see the ceiling. She reached in the pile for the dried slices of banana. There was a little smile on my opened mouth as I woke up.

The Message

As I was sitting in the family room, one guy outside in the hallway asked the other a question. I didn't hear the question but the other guy answered "Yes of course." But he responded to his answer like it was totally wrong. They began debating. I decided to go out and see what was happening.

He looked at me and smiled, then asked "If man made television, does it really exist?" Then I knew what the debate was all about, and what his smile meant. The other guy was debating because he was looking at what was behind the scene, underneath the surface.

If it's man made, does it exist like a tree exist, which is created by God. Or exist like water exist which is made by God.

In a moment I grabbed an ink pen similar to the one I'm using now and started to write the answer on the wall. The ink came out writing as if a black magic marker was in my hand. This is the answer I wrote:

"Gods gave man the capabilities to create it, so it does exist. {He started to interrupt but I told him to wait a minute or I might lose the message, and I continued.} So he sees himself. But the damage is caused when man chooses the wrong interpretations, which is all there is."

The Scene

I walked along the black dirt beach with rocks and sparse grass and my feet sunk in the mud. The water was cold and the pebbles scraped along my feet. I decided not to venture out any further. I walked back on up the wall of boulders on the slope, the sea wall. I looked around and saw there were no muddy footprints on the rocks that I had stepped on.

I saw my cousin coming and asked him if he saw me. He said "Yea." Then I asked him if he saw the unbeach. He looked where the beach used to be and said he had forgotten that there once was sand here. The rain that was going to fall was going to wash the sand elsewhere as it did here. I told him it had begun sprinkling, and he said it wouldn't continue.

I pointed to the sky, where below the grayish mass of clouds there were big black separate thunderclouds forming out of nowhere instantaneously. I looked to the ocean, which was at the entrance of the lake surrounded by trees, and the waves were visible.

I looked out and saw that from where we was at, the unbeach circled a small inlet like a good size pond. On the other side, the trees were growing up against the small canal that was feeding the pond from the ocean beyond. Out there above the ocean there were countless big black thunderous storm clouds forming instantaneously and I could see large was headed our way.

Causality

Something happened. The son was in the room with his mother. Two 6 inch tornados spun out of control and trashed the room. The son caught one under a cap and told his mother to put the other one in her mouth. You could see it going from side to side in her mouth.

Possible ending number one

He was about to go out the door and his mother was going to say "God Bless You." But as soon she said "God" the tornado came out of her mouth. Her teeth were mixed in the wind and blinded him. Ending up with a toothless mother and a blinded son.

Possible ending number two

The tornado tried to escape through her nose and she closed her nose and died. Her soul got mixed up with the tornado that came out of her dead body and that mixture became a hurricane and destroyed the whole town.

The reason for the possible endings is because I've only read the book in my dream so far.

The Friend

It was a warm afternoon, and I was sitting at a picnic table playing chess with another guy. I was visualizing the next moves and getting my strategy together, when two things happened at once. First I heard within my mind a girl's voice scream "Ouch!" Then I heard a guy sitting next to me say in astonishment "Damn." When I looked at him I first noticed that I at some sort of outing and a lot of people was around. After looking at the guy next to me I turned and saw a few things happening at once. First there was a pitcher on and twenty feet in front of him was the catcher, then the umpire, then a fence. Behind the fence there was this girl moving in extremely slow motion. I deduced from the scene that the girl had been waiting behind the fence to catch a ball just in case the catcher missed it. She caught the ball all right. Right in her mid-section, close to her groin area. She was no more than nine years old.

As she was going back in the air a few feet doubling over and twisting around, I saw that no one seemed to notice her except for me and the guy next to me. The catcher not paying attention to the fast ball he just missed took out another ball from his pocket and tossed it to the pitcher, shouting some encouraging words as he did so. All of this action the catcher and the rest of them were doing was not in slow motion.

As the girl was landing, I heard another girl's voice. She was thinking "Now what the hell you go and do that for?" The girl replied in a painful voice "You said you wanted his balls." I had turned to my right, which by now I had completely turned around. I saw in the crowd this 13 year old girl with a sort of half turned smile on her face. I looked back at the girl as she was finally hitting the ground and she thought to her friend "I'm going to throw this ball over in the tall grass over here, I think I'm going to need to go see the doctor." As she was throwing the ball in slow motion out with her right hand from her left a couple of people were running
to her side. I looked at the girl to my right and she had a full smile and she thought" Thanx my friend."

The memory

It was springtime, and I was one of a team of four. We were on a hillside sitting around a card table. An area was cleared in the trees for a small makeshift space that served as a jungle bar. I was sitting facing the open valleys and to my left was a young kid, to my right was a guy about my age and at my 4 o'clock position there sat an older man. Everyone was in army uniforms and I assume I was also, although I never looked. The older guy was the commander, you could tell not only by his uniform but also by his attitude. For the sake of this story I'll call the guy on my left "Private." The guy on my right "Corporal." And of course the commander "Sergeant."

We was ordering pitchers of beer and joking around when Sergeant looked at Private and with a smile pulled 3 playing cards out of his pocket. I know that each card was a man's life. We all knew that. He gave Private the cards because it was his turn to rip them. (That's how the war was fought.) And when you rip a card you must buy the pitcher of beer too.

We got to drinking and Private got to tearing up the cards. Since he was new to this we were kidding around about his reluctance in going through with it. We discovered that we over did it a little and ordered and drank a fourth pitcher. Private didn't know about the fourth pitcher. Since he was paying for it, we knew that no other cards could be torn, and no other person could tear them, yet the pitcher had to be paid for with a card. So we had a problem to say the least.

So I, sergeant, and corporal decided to change the rules of the game a little. We or rather Corporal looked under the table and started gathering pieces of the queen of diamonds. He told Private that this guy wasn't dead yet because tear it right. Private a looked at me for confirmation and I nodded my head in agreement. I
looked on the ground for the remaining pieces but could only find some pieces of a magazine that someone else had torn before we sat down. I picked them up and tore the appropriate sizes to fit the pieces that were left open and sergeant told him "This guy is only half dead. You have to take him out the right way this time, and stop his suffering." Private, fully believing us, {it was important that he did or the kill wouldn't be carried through and the bill wouldn't get paid.} Private re tore the pieces and the bill got paid.

We sat around for awhile laughing and telling jokes. Then sergeant pulled out another card from his pocket." Whose kill is that?" Corporal asked. Sergeant looks over to him and says "Mine" We were all thirstier for more beer, so I felt the same as Private when he excitedly asked "When are you going to get him?" Sergeant leaned back and said "One thing about me my friend. I'm different. You see I don't give a shit about this war."

I looked over to a guy sitting at the bar, knowing that even though he was drinking a glass of beer like he didn't have a care in the world, I knew that he was the one meant for Sarge's card. Corporal smiled as he recognized this too, and then asked Sarge "So what do you got to hide?"

As the Sergeant sits back and ponders this question, I focus on him as he remembers back when he was once younger, back in the states. I'm a fly on the wall in his memory and this is what I observed:

There's a parking lot between two buildings on the outskirts of the city. The cars are late 50's models. I'm in back of the parking lot looking toward the street. Cars are going both ways in the street. There are two rows of cars. Each parked facing a building, with about five feet walking space, the space between the backs of the cars are about 15 feet.

I'm above and behind Sergeant looking at this scene. He's over in front of the cars to the left. Down thru the middle an over weight guy comes walking. {Oh yea by the way it's nighttime.} Sergeant walks low in front of the parked cars and meets the guy as he reaches the driver's side of his car. The guy looks at Sarge with surprise. The guy is clean-shaven and looks like a businessman, and thinks it's a robbery. He starts reaching for his wallet. Sergeant says with a motion of the gun he's holding in his left hand. "No no I don't want that, Get inside the car.

Before the guy could get in the car, another guy comes running down from the same direction and shouts wait. They waited for him to come up and Sarge motioned them to get in. The first guy got in through the drivers side and slide over to the passengers side, the second guy got in the backseat and Sarge got in the driver's side. Sarge faced both of them pointing the gun.

To Sarge's amazement, both guys looked and were dressed just alike. Except that the guy in the back seat had a mustache…. The first guy in the front seat said" I called him over because you are supposed to shoot him and I could leave my I.D. on him so they'll think it's me." Sarge thought about this for a moment and said to him "Smart ass." And shot him once in the head. Then the guy in the back seat said, "You weren't even supposed to be here, I was to take your place."

Sarge pauses for a moment, for now he recognizes the guy as an old crony from the neighborhood, and then looks at him angry and says "You Hollywood motherfucker." And shoots him twice in the chest.

Then I'm back with Sarge as we're sitting at the card table in the clearing on the hillside in the middle of the jungle in the middle of the war. I hear Sarge, as his thoughts are the reflections about that memory. He's thinkings are "Imagine, my old buddy taking his place of that man, and I was suppose to kill my old buddy with the witness seeing me. The man was valuable to the family but I snuffed him out and my old buddy as well. I fucked up the whole deal. And Corporal's asking me what do I have to hide? Huh, If only he knew."

The Impact

I was waiting at the barbershop for my friend A.D. I had earlier looked in the mirror and seen that one of the parts that started on one side of my head and went around to the other, was crooked in the back and I wanted him to straighten it. I was sitting there debating whether or not to leave, when I suddenly found myself in a living room debating.

I decided to leave. My sister went into the kitchen to get my shoes so I could get going on that mile walk home. What made up my mind to leave was I had just out, and wanted to spend my 1st night at the crib. The real reason wasn't because it was my 1st night, but because I wanted to finish reading a book I had started reading in the joint.

She brought back the wrong pair of shoes, I put them on anyway. She went back into the kitchen to retrieve mine. I got up and walked to the other end of the coffee table and picked up my blue crystal, my clear crystal and
my 3 Greek coins. Just as I had put them in my pocket, my sister came back and jokily remarked that I had put one of her coins in my pocket. She smiled and handed me a pair of white high top sneakers. I walked her back into the kitchen telling her those weren't my shoes. After looking at the remaining two pairs that was lying against the wall, the sneakers she brought me looked the best. As I was walking to the chair to sit down and change shoes, I told her that these shoes I have on was the ones I bought for A.D. last Christmas.

I was sitting in the chair facing the kitchen,. To my right was a window and behind me was the front door. Through the window shone a light as if a car was arriving. I heard cars doors slamming and I remembered A.D. didn't like me wearing his shoes, which made me remember where my real shoes were they were in the bathroom. I told my sister to go and get and get them please. As I was taking off those sneakers (not the white high tops but the black cloth high tops that was A.D.'s X-max present. My sister was returning from the bathroom with my black army boots, and someone had opened the front door. I looked over my left shoulder and A.D. was holding an old pair of white low top sneakers, asking me if I wanted them. I told him no, as I was pushing his shoes aside and putting on my boots. By the time he had came around to my right he was now my friend Mike

Mike reached his hand over my left shoulder for a handshake and a smile. I noticed right off he had gotten fatter. "Long time, long see, it's been about five months or so. Hay?" Mike said yea and then his five kids came. His oldest son was about 7 years old laid out on the couch and his youngest son was about one and a half at the head of the couch. I walked up toward the youngest and noticed that his oldest must have remembered who I was because he quickly removed his thumb out of his mouth knowing I didn't like that. Whether his youngest son remembered me or not it didn't matter he was crying for his father. I stood up after kneeling in front of his kid and turned to Mike and told him I had to go.

He assured me that I could spend the night. He started walking me towards the back bedroom, wanting to show me all the food he had bought. He said it was in the closet. His sister was already back there standing in the middle of the room facing the opened sliding glass doors to the closet. I guess he wanted to show off, also because I was hungry. So despite the fact I wanted to read my book, I told him I'll stay. From where we were standing, neither he nor I saw any food. Mike wondered about this for a moment then left the room with me following. We walked through the kitchen out the back door.

Somewhere between A.D.'s arriving which was about just before midnight to me and Mike walking out the back door looking for his food, the time had become to be just before noon. With that insight, I told him I had decided to go home after all. I was in the back yard looking at the trees when I turned around and saw Mike standing by a post that was holding up a corner of the patio. With the rest of the patio connected to the house. He was looking at a hole in the concrete that was about a foot from where the post went in the concrete. The hole looked like the aftermath of an earthquake. I was standing in the grass at the edge of the parking lot looking pavement behind his house. By the smile on his face I realized that that's where he hid his food. He knelt down and his face was very close to the hole when a huge Robin came flying out and flew toward the sky. The freak sight caused him to have a surprised grin. Then as he was standing back straight a huge Blue Jay came flying out. It flew in figure eights for a moment then flew toward the sky.

At about the same time as he did, I realized that the birds were down there eating his food. Mike angrily ran in the basement and came back with a sledge hammer axe. The iron piece was flat on one end and sharp at the other. He banged at the concrete a few feet from the hole and three birds came out and flew in circles and flew toward the sky. Then Mike walked about 30 feet from the hole, almost to the edge of the pavement. He was standing about ten feet from me. He banged the ground hard. A few moments later more birds came flying out. They were various species of birds. I then realized that there was a tunnel that went all the way underground to where Mike was standing.

I saw the kids on the patio watching dad hitting the pavement, and watching the birds flying around. I screamed to them over the various chirping, to go into the house because I sensed danger. Then I saw a stork like bird that appeared angry, carrying a dead bird in his beak. I said to myself "That could be one of the kids."

Mike was throwing the axe in the air trying to kill the birds. Without any of them getting hit, the axe came down hard. Once I looked at the axe as it hit the ground and saw it was sharp on both sides, but became blunt again when he started back banging. I thought to myself "That's another reason why the kids should be inside   Three humming birds did a quick dance around my head, and then flew in a circle. As I was looking up at them, watching them I thought to myself "This shit is wild." Then one bird broke the circle and the other two followed. They swooped down in a straight line with the quickness and passed within inches by my left elbow. I could feel the breeze they created.

The third bird seemed a little drunk because he swayed out of line. I turned around as it passed and the head bird started toward the sky. I thought to myself "These birds don't present any danger."

As soon as the third birds was about 15 feet in the air I saw Mike loft his axe up in the air and the axe caught the 3rd bird and sliced it in half. The two half fell to the ground just as fast the axe did. I told Mike that that's all he had to do. Just throw the axe up softly and it'll hit something. He smiled and said "Thanx." The impact from the emotion that occurred from the realization that I told him how to kill one of God's creatures caused me to awaken.

GENEVA {whatever}

"The soldiers of Sarajevo found it hard to explain and shocked by the lavishness of the citizens of Geneva..." Said the news reporter. The soldiers were marching down the street in the middle of a sunny afternoon. I wasn't a part of the column of soldiers, yet I was there where they were. Seeing the things that they say. The reporter seemed to be speaking just over my right shoulder. The soldiers were marching up the street right past an apartment dwelling that was at least seven stories tall. From where I was sitting or standing I can't recall which I had a bird's eye view of the whole scene. I could see a few people sunning themselves by the pool in front of the apartment buildings. That wasn't the 'lavishness' the reporter was speaking about. The lavishness was that someone who lived on the fourth floor had kept their water running and the apartment was flooding over. Which created a man made waterfall, which cascaded down over some of the bathers by the pool. Although the soldiers was marching away from me and I could see the expression on some of their faces as they turned and looked at the waterfall. I could sort of feel their shockness in the atmosphere. It was a contrast to say the least. Here are these citizens without a concern in the world, and here are these marching war beaten soldiers.

The column continued marching down the street. I walked with them past the apartments and then I stopped. I never really thought about what they were doing there, other than what the reporter had just said. It was just another scene I'll experience while visiting this city. I was only a tourist after all. It did cross my mind at the time I was sort of in the middle of an oasis.

Behind the apartment building was a mini outside mall. One had to go down a half dozen stairs in order to get into the stores. After crossing the street to that side and as the soldiers was moving off in the distance my attention was drawn to a store with people going in and out. All the people had ice cream cones in their hands.

It wasn't only the crowd that drew my attention to the store; it was also the loud European rock and roll music that was blaring out of the speakers that was mounted over the door of the entrance. As I was looking at the crowd that was going in and out of what I assumed was an ice cream store, some type of flash caught my attention. I turned and looked toward the apartment building and I saw 2 young ladies on roller skates, bouncing to the music. They appeared to be no older than 19 years of age. The one in front was wearing shiny gold shorts with matching tops. What was unique was that both of them were about two feet high. The sun must've struck one of their hats, which was the flash I saw. They bounced and rolled on into the ice cream shop.

It seemed that I was the only one to take a special interest in them. The other people didn't give a second glance. I wanted to get a closer look, so I looked for a way down there. I saw some stairs about 30 feet ahead of me, so I proceeded to them, and went down to the mall level. As I was walking to the ice cream store, the other stores in the mall distracted me. It wasn't just the foreign languages in the advertisements. It was also the products they were selling. One store was a 70's retrospective type of store, with butterfly collar shirts, and bell-bottoms in their display window. I forgot all about those girls and entered the store. I went straight to the counter in the back, where behind the cashier there were hats on hooks along the wall. I selected a brown cap, which is commonly known as an Applejack Hat.

It was made of cloth, a view from the top made it look like a sliced pie, and where the slices meet in the middle there's a button. The visor had a snap button where it connected to the top of the cap. You understand? It looked American none the less. I didn't pay attention to how much it cost or how much I paid her, all I know is that she gave me a folded 20 dollar bill back. An American 20 dollar bill. The cashier was the first person I attempted to speak to and she just shook her head, like saying she didn't understand what I was talking about. Then I remembered I was in Geneva after all.

I left the store and returned to the street level by the stairs I had used earlier. Within moments of checking out the crowd I saw this little girl of about six years old walking provocatively. Over doing it really. Like she was acting grown. Then I noticed that she was last in line of six little girls all walking the same way up the street. Then I further noticed that at the head of this line was a woman who wore tight gold shorts of a shiny material like the girls on the roller skates I had seen earlier. This woman had her butt up in the air and was switching from side to side. Either the little girls was being taught how to walk that way, or the little girls was making fun of the woman. I couldn't tell which. The girls was having fun either way, giggling and all. I don't recall what happened between me being at the top of the stairs at the mall, and me being at the entrance to the park, but I did note one odd thought that occurred to me. Maybe to you the thought may seem normal, but for me it was unusual. I realized that I hadn't seen any people of color since I've been in Geneva, and that everyone seemed to be in the upper middle class. I thought given the situation being in a foreign land, without being able to speak the language, my identity would come into question more so than if I was in America.

The park was no longer than a block long and a block wide. I could see the apartment building about a block behind me. And behind the apartment buildings in the distance I could see two tall buildings, which I presumed to be downtown.

There were 4 or five people standing around at the entrance to the park which I entered. Again I noticed how clean they were dressed and how they were not people of color. I entered the park and on my left sitting on a bench were 3 black males dressed like bums. They didn't look at me or even notice me. My first thought was that these guys somehow came over here to Geneva and got stuck and ended up like that. That could be me in a year if I don't find a way home. I knew I only had 20 something odd dollars and some change and no way to get back to the states. After seeing those bums I decided to start working on that right away.

As I walked through the park I didn't do anything special except enjoy the afternoon sunshine. I didn't talk with anyone because I didn't know the language. I passed by three black youths who even though wore American clothing didn't have the feel of Americans. After I passed them, I came upon 4 other black guys dressed like the Temptations, wearing sequin suits. They had a boom box playing some R and B song and they were rehearsing some dance steps. I once again noticed the buildings of downtown in the distance and decided to go there so I could work on getting home.

They were going over to a bench to sit down. I walked up to one brother and asked him how I could get downtown, I already knew which direction. Before I could get the question asked, he held up his hand and gestured that he didn't understand what I was saying.

I went to this young lady who was a part of the crowd that was watching the brothers' practice, and I asked her. She said "You catch the number 75 bus over there across the street." As she pointed I looked to where she was pointing and saw the bus stop in front of what I believed to be Switzerland's answer to McDonald's.

There was also a bus half a block away headed toward to bus stop. I told her "Thank You." And she smiled "You're welcome" and I rushed across the street to catch the bus.

I didn't get a chance to catch the name of the fast food joint although I wanted to. I saw the drive thru window backed up with cars and the tables with umbrella shading them out front. The table was crowded with people. I was the last one to jump on the bus and the doors shut right behind me, and the bus took off up the road. "Thanx" I said to the bus driver. Before I looked up and when I did look up at him, and saw he was a brother, I seconded my gratitude with an "Appreciate that." "No problem "he replied. I asked him how much was the fare to downtown and he stated six American dollars. "Damn!" I thought "That seems like taxi fare."

But I didn't state what I was thinking. I pull out my little wad of money and noticed that I had a folded up ten dollar bill and 3 ones. I reach back in my pocket and pull out half of the coins I had. I pull out about five of them. All but 2 of them were foreign. The two American coins were Susan B. Anthony silver dollars. I see I have a huge silver dollar or what looks like a silver dollar. It's as big as my palm and another one just as big but a different denomination.

I turned to my left a little bit and ask this sister who's sitting in the front seat, how much I got while holding out my hand to show her the coins. She point to the triangular one with the curved corners and told me to throw it over my right shoulder for good luck. Because having it is considered bad luck. Somehow I thought that if I threw the coin over my right shoulder I would end up hitting her. So I turned facing the bus driver and threw it. The coin hit the closed doors and dropped to the floor. I looked down in time to see it fall out between the rubber guard and the steps.

I heard it clank on the street. A woman that was sitting next to the girl said that it was also bad luck for the coin to fall off the bridge. I stood on the steps for a moment, then it occurred to me that I'll be in others way if they wanted to get on the bus, so I told the bus driver I'll be right back. I walked back to the center door and stood on those steps while I attempted to figure out the currency I had. I reached in my pocket and got some more change, and after a few moments I figured it out. I reached back in my pocket to retrieve the bills and they weren't there. I spotted the folded up bills in the middle of the aisle. I picked them up and thought about how these people on the bus was so honest, because I was busy counting out the coins. I didn't realize my money was on the floor. Any one of them could have picked it up. As I was walking toward the front, the bus stopped, the bus driver got up putting on black leather driving gloves. I handed him the 3-dollar bills and was counting out the coins. I dropped one coin, and while he bent down to retrieve it I had an opportunity to see why he had gotten up. The wheel chair step was lowered and the black lady whom told me to toss the coin rolled herself into position to exit the bus.

She smiled bye to me and the bus driver grabbed the handle on the back of her wheelchair and assisted her off. The bus was just like the buses in America. OPPS, wait a minute. There's something I forgot to mention. While I was on the center doors' steps, I was also distracted by my cap. I had scratched the top of my head and the button fell off. Then going with the flow and not missing a beat, I pulled the visor part down over my face and it came off in my hands so I let it slip to the floor.

Just figuring I'll just try to look like a French man, with a beret. Being ripped off, caused me to be in a slightly agitated frame of mind. Which caused me to not focus on handing the bus driver the coins which caused one of them to fall. Now back to what I was saying about the style of the buses. They were made just like the ones in America. Behind the bus driver's seat, there's a Plexiglas partition, then there's a seat for three facing the aisle, then there's a seat for two facing the bus driver. I sat by the window in the seat for two. I didn't pay attention to the scenery outside; I was totally in my head. I was thinking about who to call once I got down town and how much money I needed to get back to the states. It crossed my mind to check my money. I remembered I had only one bill left, but something was wrong and I couldn't put a finger on it.   So I pulled out the bill and it was a folded twenty. I straighten it out to find that it was half of a twenty taped to half of a 10-dollar bill. The girl at the store deliberately jipped me. Once again being optimistic I figured I could probably pass it off to someone downtown to get something to eat. If I did it quick enough. I turned the bill over and to my surprise I found myself looking at half a 5-dollar bill taped to half a one-dollar bill. I turned the bill over and over trying to figure out how the hell some one did that and thinking that there's no way I trick could anyone now.

The bus stopped in front of what must have been a high school. About 15 rowdy teenagers crammed on the bus. A young guy sat next to me. He looked like he was imitating the artist formerly know as Prince. (a young version of my friend Aaron.) I asked him "What is the language of this country?"

He looked at me suspiciously and asked "What do you mean?" It didn't surprise me a bit that he spoke English, because I still didn't grasp what it was to be in a foreign land. So if I expected English to be spoken back, like the bus driver and the woman, and the one next to her, I don't recall being surprised. Even though my first encounter they seemed to be saying I don't understand you.

So I say to the guy next to me "You know like France has French, Brazil has Spanish and America has English, what's the language of this country?" He incredulously asked "You mean you came to this country and didn't know what language we spoke?" I said "Yea." He got up and as he started walking away toward the back said to me sort-of loud "You're crazy!" and the bus stopped. The driver announced that I was downtown. I think that I saw buildings and crowds as I was stepping of the bus, because if I didn't I would have certainly asked a few questions. But I was so in my head at this point I got off the bus. When I heard the bus doors closing that's when I sort-of came to. I was on the side of a dirt road in the country. I could fell the bus moving behind me but when I looked to my left I didn't see the bus; Although I could hear it driving away. That's when the thought occurred to me that I must be dreaming.

In the moments it took me to realize that I was dreaming I also came to the realization that by getting off the bus, I had ended my dreaming phase. I was at the edge of my consciousness. Although I knew that to be wild, yet I felt what this scene represented was the symbolization of my consciousness. I didn't spend too much time contemplating this because I wanted to take advantage of the extraordinary occasion. I never looked to my right to see where I had come from; I looked and then turned to my left.

The dirt road went a little distance, and then it forked into. The road on the right had a black cable running up the middle of it. More like lying in the middle of it. The road on the left was just dirt. Each road went over the same hill. I can't recall my reasons now, but I decided to take the road. Or follow with the black cable. I started walking up the road taking in the sight. On the side of each road on the hill there was a white house. They were run down single story houses with half porches. They weren't identical, but they had a sense of being built in the same era. A few moments later when I reached the V of the fork in the road I saw some things which I hadn't seen before. For instance; in the middle of the two roads, what I took to be boulders were actually gravestones of a graveyard. What really took me by surprise is about 10 feet from the lower apex of the V there stretched a fence going from east to west, west to east, or right to left, whatever. I looked this way and that way; I saw no beginning and no ending. I quickly concluded that what lay beyond that fence was my sub-consciousness. I was excited but I had to stay somewhat calm, having experienced something similar like this before. {being aware that I was in a dream state.} I knew that if I got too excited I would wake up. So I really started paying attention. More to what was beyond the
fence than what was on my side.
   I probably would have seen a lot if I wasn't so focus on what was beyond the fence. As I was walking up to the fence I saw a little kid run along the porch. With the quick glimpse I got I couldn't even tell if it was a boy or girl. But the kid was more like skipping along the porch of the house beside the plain dirt road. When the kid got about 2 feet from the edge...swoosh... gone. Just disappeared before it got to the broken edge of the porch. I thought I heard some laughter.

I looked to the other house and four kids appeared. Before I go on I'll mention the kid was running toward the road the four kids two dark ones one girl one boy, and two lighter kid also one boy one girl was running toward the road with the black cable. So they all was running inward not out ward. The four kids also appeared about two feet from the broken edge of the porch, but instead of disappearing in to thin air from which they came, they ran in the front door, which closed behind them, oh by the way the air wasn't thin at all it was thick.

On the other side of the fence there was a bell, about 6 inches in length and four at the base. I figured I had to ring it in order to be allowed to enter. While walking up to the part of the fence where the bell hung on the other side, I saw a brown furry thing out the corner of my eye. Although I had made a decision not to pay too much attention to what was on this side of the fence, I changed my mind just this once. I turned and saw a baby grizzly bear standing on its hind legs with its arms in the air, with a scowl on its face. It was stuffed. It looked like it was about to attack a white marble statue of a kid holding a flute. That was something to remember and try to figure out later.

I got to the fence, it was about ten feet tall and the wires crossed at the top. The bell was hung from a hook connected at the top. The thin piece of steel ringer that was suppose to be in the middle of the bell hung from a string outside of the bell. I put my finger through the fence and pushed the bell into the ringer. It made a soft tone but I knew that wasn't going to get anyone's attention. I was expecting someone to come out the house where the four kids was at.

A guardian of my sub conscious or somebody. Because I know that if I went in there alone I could wake up crazy. I pushed the bell into the ringer again and got the same results. After a few moments which I got very interested in seeing the engravings on those gravestones, I decided what the hell. I started climbing the fence. I had taken off my shoes so I could get a better purchase of the links in the fence. I got to the top of the fence and found myself unable to get over. There was an invisible barrier. It was such that I was able to stand on the crossed wires and not worry about balance. To describe the other side of that fence as being in a bubble would be an inadequate description, because a bubble has texture. This barrier I came to realize after a few moments was mental. I had to really want to see what was there. So by me really wanting to see, I swung my whole upper body in a belly flop fashion toward the grave yard. And I began to fall. I felt the spike rip into my socks and take hold.

As I was falling I imagined my socks being threaded out like when one walks on a piece of gum and the gum sticks to your shoe and strings out when you take another step. I stretched my hands out so I wouldn't fall on my face and I hands landed in the sand. My fingers half buried themselves in the sand. My first thought was that as long as socks stay connected to the fence I'll have some way back because I'll be connected.

I stood up and while wiping the sand off my hands started walking to the first gravestone that was closest to the road with the black cable lying in the middle of it. The first gravestone was made of a dirty gray marble; it looked like it was slanting.

On closer inspection I could see where erosion had buried the bottom half of it more on one side than the other. The name on the grave read "Rjandance" that didn't ring a bell (no pun intended) nor did the initials across the bottom that read "J.D." I didn't stand there trying to rack my brain, because I felt that I had to pee and I knew that when it was time to go I would wake up. So I calmly hurried on to the next one. The next one was also covered with dirt, and again I didn't want to spend any time on it, so I moved on.

Keep in mind that I'm steadily going up the hill. The third gravestone was an interesting one because of the way it was shaped. It was an obelisk. About 2 feet or so. On each side of the pyramidal top was the initials "K.D." I paused for a moment to see where I was going and I could only see the sky. It was a pale blue after noon sky. But I could tell that whatever was over that hill radiated light because a goldish color was coming from below the hill. I had about 30 more feet to go. I instinctively knew that I was bare footed, no longer connected and I had the felling that if I looked over that hill I may see the face of God or whatever, and whatever that sight was, it would be intense. Still I was determined, (just a little more determined than before.)I reached the fourth gravestone and it was also covered with dirt all but the year 1971, I thought about wiping the dirt off, I even spent a few moments considering it, and then I realize that that was a ploy to spend more time than going on up that hill.

I reached the fifth gravestone and knelled by it so I could read what it said. First I looked to see how much further I had to go. I had about 15 more feet and there was defiantly something giving off light beyond that hill. I saw that I had 3 more gravestones to go and I didn't feel as if I needed to pee. I was going to make it.

Whatever was over the hill was giving off energy. I didn't feel a hum, as if it radiating through the ground. I sensed the hum through my whole being. I wasn't afraid or anything like that, it was that I was losing interest very quickly. When I was once younger insanity appealed to me. Not now. I've grown up now. I looked at the grave stone and it was also covered in dirt. Not just covered in dirt, the mud was caked on. It caked on to the others too. I didn't even consider removing it. And as I was standing up to move on to the next gravestone, the 3rd one from the top of the hill, I woke up.

A Sister's Love

The crime was the sabotaging of Annie-May's wedding present. Her special wedding present. It was a large Bonsai tree. Well over 150 years old. It was 2 and a half feet in height, it was in a big vase made of shiny green porcelain. Someone had placed a burning cigarette at its base which presumably caused its life to ebb away. Where this incident took place it was a very serious crime. Punishable by a sentence up to twenty years.

The detective which I never caught his name, had an ideal who the perpetrator of the crime was. So he laid a trap. First he placed one cigarette in a box pack, and placed it in the same room, and he had one wooden match.

On the morning of the wedding Annie-May was in the living room wearing her white dress, her identical twin sister Daphine came over to assist her. The detective was sitting in the dining room where the tree and the other wedding presents were. He asked Daphine could he see her for a moment.

The trap was that he was to explain that the cigarette had been found and placed in the box-pack for preservation for later fingerprinting. The thing about this was that where they were at you couldn't get another's finger print without their permission. So he was going to force the issue.

The match was to be burned and placed as the most likely spot of sabotage. His ideal being that she would pick the opposite end of the actual place, further proving that she is guilty of the crime. When Daphine first heard about her fingerprints could be on the cigarette she showed concern, but that quickly passed for she knew she wouldn't consent to being fingerprinted.

When he gave her the lighted match she motioned like she was going over to the tree, but the flame went out. He told her that was okay, just place the charred end on the spot. So she grabbed the charred end in-between her thumb and forefinger. This indicated to him that she believed the heat from the match would indicate the crime, and by extinguishing the heat, she wouldn't reveal the crime, therefore by her actions she has admitted to doing the crime. Daphine seeing this trap, she "accidentally" dropped the match down the heating grate. Oh do you have another one?" she asked the detective innocently. I believe she knew that there were no other matches around. They were very hard to come by. This had indeed been an elaborate trap. It seemed that she began to see the error of her ways; she broke down and started crying.

"Yes" the detective thought. "I finally got her!" He told the officers to cuff her. Daphine stood there and smiled at him mischievously as she was being cuffed. As she was being lead out of the room the detective said, "Wait!" Something didn't seem right. Although everything went perfectly according to plan, it still didn't seem right. But he couldn't put his finger on his suspicion. He waved his hand in a dismissal fashion telling the officers to take her down to headquarters.

Annie-May went into the bedroom and sat in front of vanity mirror and said "Hi my name is Annie-May." Then she said I again "Hi my name is Annie-May." She didn't hear the detective's soft knock and when she saw him in the mirror's reflection, she didn't have time to cover up the story that was written all over her face.........

Annie-May was supposed to get married, but she didn't want to. So she sabotaged her most precious gift. She thought she'll tell her future husband that it was a sure sign that they shouldn't get married, and he would consent to not getting married. Instead he had called the cops... worried she went to her sister Daphine, and Daphine confessed that she loved Annie-May's future husband. So they decided to conspire together and switch places. Daphine would take Annie-May's place and Annie-May would go to prison, and be happy, while at the same time make her sister happy.

The detective saw all of this in Daphine's eyes that was reflected in the mirror. He thought "I hope that this is worth it." And Daphine seeming to hear his thought nodded her head yes, while a tear rolled down over her crooked joyful smile. "Well have a happy Wedding." Said the detective and closed the door and left,

Daphine looked in the mirror and said "Hi my name is Annie-may."

God's Hint

We were behind some buildings just hanging out. It was about five of us. I don't remember exactly who my friends were, then and now. I only remember one friend clearly then and now. And now I remember not his face, only that he is a close friend. We're at the top of a small hill and there's a gulley in front of us down below. Then another hill rises upward in front of us. There's a house on the hill in front of us. There's a banner flying in the wind attached to the apex of a 2or 3-story house. The banner has the words chronic stenciled on it. There's this blond lady with her daughter about to go in the direction of the house. They're to our right on the other side in front of us. The little girl says "Dada" I noticed that the lady sort of over did it with the weave in her hair. She has many color yarn braided with her hair, it came down to her butt. The little girl said "Dada" again. He drives up from the alleyway of the buildings and over the gulley, up to the front of the house. He gets out and has a very ugly dog on a leash. I mention how ugly this dog is to my friends and one of them says that it keeps them safe so that's all that matters. Somewhere along this time I notice that I have holes in my shoes at the toes, and holes in my socks as well. I mention this now because I ran bare footed.

The reason I was running is because when the man was getting the key out of his pocket for the front door, Another man with the air of a supervisor came running from around the building and said , more like yelled to us to follow him and hurry up, we can make some quick money. My four friends jumped up quickly and ran after him; I was the last to follow. I stopped and pulled off my raggedly shoes. I ran barefooted over pebbles, stones, dirt and trash. I was distracted momentary by the banner and to my surprise the wind had stopped blowing for just a moment. Giving me a chance to read more of it. The Chronic was really the word "Chronicle" like a newspaper. It said more but I decided to keep up with my friends so I don't know what the rest read.
   As I stepped over small pieces of glass, I had a flashback to when I was 6 or 7 years old living in Kingsport Tennessee and cut my foot so I stepped carefully in order not to do that again. I concentrated so much as I was running that sweat broke out at the soles of my feet. So when I entered the lobby area I nearly slipped and failed on the linoleum floor. I heard the supervisor like guy tell my friends that there was something stuck in the drain of the sink and if we get it out in time he would pay us.
   As we started walking toward the back I realized how he didn't tell us how much time we had. I also noticed how little the sink was. It was half filled with water. Two of my friends had started scooping the water out with their hands. The other two was just standing along side waiting for something to do

I walked up to their right and started helping them scoop the water out. After the first scoop it dawned on me what this was all about. An experiment on teamwork. The confirmation of this insight came up when I briefly glanced around and saw 7 people sitting around a table watching us. Standing to the side was the supervisor like dude with a stopwatch in his hand.

I instantly decide to take charge. I pointed to one of my friends who were standing to the side, to start unscrewing the lug nut at the elbow of the sink. I pointed to the other guy and told him to join him to empower him in his endeavor, and report his progress every 15 seconds. I looked to one guy who was scooping water and told him to go and bring me a hanger out of the closet in the lobby. I remembered that closet all of a sudden even though it was at first just a part of the scenery. Then I told my close friend to reach his hand down there in the water and pull the drain. My close friend looked at me while putting his hand down the drain and I saw the satisfaction in his eyes. I thought that "Yea, this is natural. It was time for me to take charge. Time for me to be a leader once again." Then I woke up.

As I was laying there contemplating the dream The young lady with the yarn braided in her hair, The car, the dog, the house, the sign, my friends, The supervisor, the test, the seven people around the table, all of those things didn't and still now don't have a common dominator. I still believe the revelation that it was time to take charge is why I experienced this dream. Satisfied with that conclusion, I returned to the dream. I found myself walking out with the sink in my hands.

I looked around and saw one friend with the elbow joint, another with a diamond ring; obviously it's what was stuck in the sink. One friend was holding and smiling as my close friend was collecting 5 one hundred dollar bills. When my close friend collected the money, we continued walking out together. Then suddenly I felt the need to make an impression on this woman I barely noticed earlier. She was one of the ones sitting around the table. She wore a fur like bikini top and I think she had like a bow strapped around her. Her smile reminded me of some one but during the test I was so focused I didn't dwell on it. So I trotted back toward the table feeling triumphantly and asked if they needed to wash their hands before they ate. I laughed as I turned and ran back towards my friends. I felt dinner rolls hitting my back with soft affection, and as I joined my friends in the warm afternoon sunshine. I woke up again.

Just Cool

I was at some college production; it was a lot of people on a field. I was stoned. A girl smiled at me and gave me those goo-goo eyes. I stepped away from the crowd, called her over. She had on a shiny purple short set. She was sexy. She told me to meet her over the hill in one minute. I guess she didn't want it to seem like we was together. As I was walking over the hill, I turned around and saw four guys following me. I put two and 2 together and decided that the girl was working for them. I waited for them to approach and told them not to gack me, I had enough weed to go around. They played stupid and I realized that these guys were going to rob me just for fun. That pissed me off. They must have thought I was scared to make an offer like that. I was just cool and didn't want my high blown. After a few words were exchanged I finally said that I would fight each one, one on one. One guy said "Huh?" and I immediately broke his nose with the heel of my palm. As I was waking up I was kicking ass.

3 trips in One

It started off; I was looking at a screen showing a picture of an overhead view of a Desert town. The buildings and the sidewalks were mud brown. It was taken from the camera in the belly of a fighter airplane. I remember wondering about the camera angle how the sidewalks would damn near zig zag, then go straight. Every 5 seconds or so, small balls of light would stream toward the sidewalks. The commentator said they were bullets, and you could see that they weren't doing much damage. The bullets would stop for a while then the jet would fly over men hunching in corners, and as soon as it passed the men, the bullets would be shot again. I could clearly see that when the bullets impacted the buildings they did little damage. Then the bullets ceased and instead of small balls of fire being discharged, there were black balls being shot. When they hit the sidewalks they bounced off the walls and I could see that they made intricate designed groves in the side walks before they stopped bouncing. The commentator said something like every time they would think they've located "Kadaff" he would be reported sighted in two different areas away from the target. I was getting bored with this so I woke up.

I woke up along side a landing strip. An airplane came in for a landing. It had two propellers on each wing. As it came in the pilot raised its' nose too high and it tilted backwards and flipped over on its' top, and slid on its' top right past me. Before it got to the end of the runway a huge jet (about 5 times bigger than the airplane) was taking off and just missed it. I remember this dream, but I really don't feel like writing the details, so I'll sum it up; the passengers got out, there was about 7 of them. I was there to pick up a suit bag. (No pun intended) The suit case attendant couldn't find it. Him and I helped this lady closed her long brown suitcase. Then he showed me to the waiting room. The waiting room was filled with the 7 departing passengers. Each one met their perfect half. Pretty boy meet pretty girl, mother met daughter, etc.

The last straw was there was this sister sitting across from me holding her daughter. She turned to the woman next to her and said "You know you're my mother?" The funny thing is when I looked at the little girl and then at the woman, they did look alike. The sister that was holding the little girl explained to the woman that somehow the little girls' mother was either missing or killed and it was decided that she would be the mother. I thought about how crazy that sounded and decided to change scenes.

I was looking at a scene of a video by an amateur camera man. This person had just grabbed a hand held recorder and started filming. It was a scene of a vast expanse of land. Spotted here and there with huge houses surrounded by even larger trees. Out of the 5 houses, I saw that two was on fire. Well actually one house was being surrounded by burning trees and would soon catch a fire.

The other house was gutted by fire. Most of the damage to the other house was done. I could see inside the house because the walls had been burned away, and many rooms were smoldering and smoky black. In a clearing between the houses about 200 yards away, a tornado was coming over the horizon. It wasn't the usual tornado. The funnel was a straight tube. It came from one cloud. The sky was a deep blue. It was a majestic sight. The bottom of the tornado never touched the green hills. The same commentator from a while back came on and said something about how this is Seattle Washington and people moved to theses million dollar houses to be closer to Alaska. The camera turned to the owner to the house that was now surrounded by burning trees, and they said like they felt like nature was turning against them. The camera turned back to the tornado and I could see that it wasn't coming toward the camera anymore. It had decided to turn. I could damn near see the wind coming. Next thing I knew I was flipping through the air when I saw sky, ground, sky, ground, sky, saw the ground once more, and finally I saw the sky and felt the camera's weight in my right hand. I stood up and looked around; I saw the tornado moving off.

   One thing I noticed wasn't any driveways. So I concluded that I was either in their back yard, golf course, or something. I turned around and saw this one story block brick building. It looked like a store out of the ghetto. I saw a couple in front, so I started walking toward them. This young lady holding her daughter walked past me. I stopped and turned around.

She was standing where I had just stood. She was pointing at the tornado that was moving away in the distance, and saying something to her daughter. I instinctively held the camera and focused. This time I left my left eye open for a moment. I could see how I could have easily believed I was watching a picture and not filming one...She's beautiful, brown shoulder length hair, and her daughter was just a smaller version of her. I think she was wearing blue jeans but I can't remember.

She pointed behind the building and said" Look, two eagles! "I took the camera down from my face and hurried to see, because I've never seen live eagles before. They were sitting on the limbs of a big bush. One of them was in the background trying to hide behind some leaves. The other one was about three feet in front of us. It was at least two feet in height. Looked like it could weigh 40 or 50 pounds, with brown feathers, a white head, and a sharp yellow beak. Just what an eagle should look like. It tittered to the end of the limb and flew away. I wanted to catch the other one on film, so I brought my camera up to my face and pushed a button. I pressed the wrong button for video, and got a Polaroid in stead.

I thought to myself "cool." The picture came sliding out. The flash scared the bird and it took off too. I was fanning the picture, while I was walking and talking with the young lady and her daughter. When the picture became clear, it showed a picture of the 3 of us taken by someone in front of us. It even showed me holding the camera that the picture had just came from. I thought what I could say to explain this. I looked from the picture to her and she was smiling. I was about to say something, but I woke up.

Mayan Mission

We were sitting at a bar. We weren't close to being sober, and he said to me "I bet you two pros that we find them." I said "Okay you're on." I thought about what had happen.

Two little boys' age 11 and 12 who were the kids of some workers on the construction site. They were ease dropping on some fellows' conversation. What they heard I can not recall right now. What I do recall is how they were behind some hedges at the bottom of the hill and clearly out of sight of the men talking. What they heard, whatever it was caused the kids to gasp loudly, which drew the attention of the men talking. The men saw them and said something like "Hey you fucking kids come here!" I believe that the men knew them, but were so angry that they couldn't scream their name just then.

The kids got spooked and ran. They went through a narrow path in the woods. The men seeing this, and knowing they can't chase after these kids on foot decided to jump in their jeep like vehicle and apparently decided to cut them off before they reach their destination. The kids somehow becoming aware of the men plan knew that if they continued on the path through the woods they wouldn't reach their destination before the men do.

The kid in front stopped, allowing the kid behind him to catch up. Their destination was a construction site at the bottom of the mountain. The path twisted and turned this way and that way. They looked at each other and nodded their heads in silent agreement. They turned in unison facing the top of the hill and fell backwards down through the bushes and trees, flipping and flipping until they fell out of the woods and ended in the clearing at the foot of the mountain where the construction of a large building was being built.

The kids stood and dusted themselves off, and looked at the building for a moment. It was just a huge block structure placed in the middle of the jungle. They were brought out of their moments of contemplation by the sound of the jeep like vehicle turning the corner of the dirt road about a block away. They ran into the building.

What I've described, and yet to tell what has been going on, and will go on. There are many senses in the air. Ones of fright fear of Death, Anger. Confusion, hurting, pain, A sense of joy of escaping, all of those things. I'm not interested right now in using various adjectives to describe the story. I'm just writing the basic outlines without the feel. Dig? There's other things I won't mention like I was the kid in front. (well I wasn't going to mention it.)

The kids dashed in the building. There was immediately a sense of being in a huge space. There were no lights on; the only source of light came from the various doors that were opened which allowed the sun to shine in. There were steel columns supporting the roof spaced about 30 feet apart. The kids couldn't see the ceiling. The columns just went up into darkness. One got the sense that this was a large warehouse. The concrete hadn't been poured on the floor and stretching between the columns were steel joists that was twelve inches in height. Designed like that. The kids jumped over them like they were little hurdles. One thing that was known was that the jeep like vehicle couldn't chase them into the building. For one there were only doors for persons and not only that the joist would stop all progress. They saw a few workers as they passed by them, but didn't pay attention. They were halfway thru the building when the men that were chasing them entered the building. They didn't turn to look at them, they knew. The kid in front made a decision. By the change of the weight of gravity one could tell that it was serious one. He turned to his friend and got the agreement he was seeking. The kid in front ran toward a back door. He noticed fleetingly how the sun shone off the brown dirt. They saw the sun shining brightly through the back doors ahead of them. When they were about twenty feet from the doors, a worker they knew closed the door by sliding a plastic partition across the entrance. The sudden darkness caused by shutting off the sunshine didn't stop them. They ran straight for the doors. Without stopping they burst through the partition. Falling and rolling on the dusty ground and bounding back up. Even though there was no verbal communication, a lot was said.

They were in a closed section behind the warehouse. There were a fence that went around the building, with white strips laced through it so one couldn't see further. Atop of the fence 3 strands of bob wire leaned inward as if to keep people in.

The construction worker was an Indian, as were all the others that they barely had time to notice. The Indian knew that they were running from the men, but he didn't want them to do what they had decided to do. He stood in front of the fence ready to prevent them from getting any closer. The kid looked at his friend and nodded, his friend ran toward the Indian. In that brief moment while the Indian was distracted the kid turned right and ran toward what he could see the as the only two trees left standing on their side of the fence. The trees were two feet apart and he climbed up them by straddling them.

When I reached the top of the fence I wasn't quite in the middle of the height of the trees. But I was up there. (From a kid's eye point of view.) He had caught my friend and I looked out at the jungle beyond the fence. I saw a bunch of leaves and trees. But I felt the eerie peace we were seeking. I looked down at the foot of the tree where he held my friend. He looked up at me angrily and wanted me to come down.

At this time the men who were chasing us came through the doors. I look back out at the jungle then back down to the Indian. I let him know that it was okay. I thought and brought Peace to him. Instantly anger left him and actually helped my friend reach me up there. Then me and my friend went over the fence.

I began to think about what kind of pro's I should request when I win the bet against this guy sitting next to me at this bar. As I began to think about it I realized that I had somehow been placed in the co-pilot's seat of a small helicopter. It was the middle of the afternoon, we were going over along the side of the highway. And once again I realized that we were the rescue team. From our left a helicopter similar to ours came flying in. It hovered then landed. The bubble raised and the pilot asked us something about are we going in to search for and then rescue the kids..

The pilot next to me who resembled one of the guys at the bar answered "Hell no, we're not going to make the Mayan Gods angrier." Then he used his thumb and pointed behind us. I turned and looked. About a quarter of a mile off, deep in the jungle there was an upside tornado stirring up the sky. It derived from the ground. I thought about how the Gods were trying to show their powers, and was warning against any rescue attempt for anyone who has sought shelter within their borders.

The pilot of the other helicopter said something like that was our choice. Then he closed the bubble and lifted off and hovers overhead. Out of the direction that the first copter had come, came another one. This one was fancier and had the air of superiority. Like a General was riding. My pilot looked at me and I acknowledged we had to follow, that we never had a choice in the matter. Once the General's copter passed us and the other one took off right behind it, we were right there in the convoy.

As we were following them, the air became heavier. As we crossed over the highway and started flying over the sparse neighborhood, we began to be pulled toward earth. We was the only ones affected, the other two ahead of us was flying on normally. The pilot started flying over and under electrical wires. Sometimes going through them. As we got closer to the ground, the more wires we went through. We made an emergency landing in someone's back yard. We got out of the helicopter and jumped a little gate and started walking east up the street towards H.Q. We instinct knew that was only blocks away.

As we walked up and down the hilly blocks of this neighborhood. I remembered what started all of this.. That time when some workers that was walking through a jungle path. Headed toward a construction site, and pure accident one of the workers saw an ancient tribe as they moved through the jungle. Only for a second or two, because the tribe was practitioners of invisibility. Yet this one Indian worker saw them. The worker screamed and the others turned and saw him lying along the side of the path. They saw him lying there for just a moment, like he slipped, fell, and was getting up. But to the Indian worker it wasn't like that at all.

As soon as the worker saw the Indians, and the Indians knew that he had seen them, they disappeared. Then they decided that it would be prudent to take care of this. This was really their first experience with an accidental sighting. So three tribesmen ran to the worker, held him down, and without uttering a word, explained to him how this is their jungle protected by their Gods and Peace will rule only if it remains that way.

When they let him go, he stood up and started babbling about seeing people in the jungle and the Gods of those people. He was fired that same day, and was eventually committed to an asylum. The company erected a fence around the building's back yard and blocked the view of the jungle. Some more workers witnessed these tribesmen. All the workers who saw them were Indians. Maybe it had something to do with ancestry. A few went into the jungle to never return. This was really the first time "outsiders" had ventured into the jungle for sanctuary.

As we were walking down the hill I noticed a group of kids across the street as if a school bus was on the way. There wasn't anything unusual about this scene. Only one kid stood out. She was in the back of the crowd. She was the tallest and the oldest. She reminded me of someone I couldn't quite recall. She had a Lolita smile on her face as if saying" What are you doing big boy?"

My pilot and I walked a little ways past them where we turned right at a street corner. We knew at the end of this block, Headquarter existed. We also knew that for strange reason a tradition of good luck was to spit in the gutter before continuing up the street. So he and I spitted in the gutter. After I spitted I looked back at the girl, I saw the smile in her eyes.

I wondered who she reminded me of, but I knew I didn't have time to think about it. So I turned to walk up the street. Next thing I knew I was lifting my head off the bar. I had apparently passed out and had a wild dream.   I thought about the two pros this guy next to me was willing to wage. I thought to myself "Pros" what the hell are "Pros" Then it occurred to me that he was talking about proposals. Some how in this world one could wager proposals and win or lose them.

I wasn't quite clear on how this worked, but I was clear that contrary to what I was thinking before, this guy next to me wasn't my partner, he was just a guy who decided to get drunk with me before I went on the rescue mission. Without looking at a timepiece I realized that I needed to get to my partner so we could begin our mission.

I don't remember how long we walked through the neighborhood before I found myself entering a door that was the entrance to a long hallway. It was the first floor of a very cheap building. The walls were of sheet rock, with unfinished seams, and some places cracked. I passed a few doors, one or two of them had someone standing in them, but I didn't pay too much attention to them.

I reached the door of my partner and walked right in. For a moment I was surprised to find that she was Angela Ballinger. I hadn't seen her for almost 15 years, and then I considered that I had after all called her angel, and we were going into the realms of the Gods.

It was a small bedroom; with a large T.V. Angela was leaning back against the wall sitting on the bed. Her 13-year-old daughter looked like a younger version of Angela and just like the girl I had seen at the bus stop. As I walked into the room I turned to Angela's daughter to see if she remembered me, but of course she didn't. She got up and left the room with an attitude of hostility toward me. I leaned across the bed and gave Angela a kiss on the cheek. Her 7-year-old son was lying across the head of the bed, and as I was standing back up he said something smart like "You're in my way I'm trying to look T.V.

I said something and he attacked me as a little kid would attack a grown man. I just grabbed him by his wrists wondering why all the hostility from her kids. Her son reminded me briefly of Pamela's son, and that made me realize that they thought it was "I" who was taking their mother away, when it actually it was the Mayan Mission. I looked at Angela and she just smiled.

           Then I woke up.

I was reading the cartoon section of the newspaper. The only one I remember is the one where the in the first square an ant eater is walking and two ants are standing along the side of the highway. Above the highway different birds were zooming past.

It turns out that the ants were actually hitchhiking. With no animosity from the anteater he offered to ride them. And with no fear from the ants they accepted the ride.

Somewhere they had gotten a hold of a bottle of champagne and started celebrating. The last square showed what they were celebrating. They felt that one wouldn't be able to enjoy the splendor of nature if one was always in a hurry.

I realized I was dreaming and wanted to bring more comics out, but this is the only one I remember.

P.S. – It actually said "A Zooming Flashing Past"

And *AnotherOne* Down

Me and some guys are in a parking lot filled with cars. In the distance there's a building that we deduced one way or another as being a old folks home. The only car I remember in the crowd is the big four door Mercedes, beige in color with black tinted windows. I remember thinking that this must be some rich old folks.

The cars were parked in the middle of the parking lot. On the edge of the parking lot there were junked cars and a forest behind them. Two guys who were with us, went up to a beat up rusted car. The car had all the wheels missing, and the front hood was gone. Still these guys were fascinated with this car.

I was separated from the body I was in, and became an observer of the guy whose body I was in. Him and the remaining fellows turned around and walked across the street to the mall to do something. I was left observing the two guys.

They were standing by the rusted car when someone came out and got in their car. {I can't remember if it was a man or woman.} The two guys motioned the old person over and tried to sell him/her something. The old person agreed and told them to wait while he/she go get money from their room. At this point the two guys attention was drawn across the street where the other fellows was returning.

The two guys ran next door to a building which had a basement garage. They ran up to the ticket man in the booth and said something like the guys coming across the street are criminals or assassins and do not let them take their car. Especially don't let them have this blue box. The guy gave the ticket man a blue box and told him they were going to call the police. They ran back across the street to await the old person. The ticket guy didn't want to confront the guys crossing the street so he jetted out of the booth.

Now I was immersed back with this fellow and seeing out his eyes and having his frame of mind. When we entered the underground garage and didn't see the ticket man in the booth, we automatically assumed it was a trap. Someone was waiting outside to ambush us. So we quickly decided to search the building for members of the attacking organization. At the moment I thought I just raised my hand like I had a gun, but on hindsight I think I did have a gun.

One guy took the car and drove up to the second level, while I and this other guy took the elevator. When we exited the elevator we found ourselves in the center of a circular building. Surrounding us was glass walled classrooms

I told the guy to go one way and I would go the other. As I was walking around the empty hallway I had barely gotten ten feet from the elevator when the bell rung a bunch of young men ran to and fro around me.

It reminded me of prisoners running for chow. I went around the curve and entered the crowded cafeteria. I first thought they were running for free food, but they were paying for the food in a restaurant setting. I made my way through the crowd and stood along a wall. I bumped into a young lady and said excuse me.

Then from the corner of my eye I saw a big tall ass man stand up. He had to be all of eight feet tall. My first thought was "This is one tall muda."

He came up to me and with his left hand grabbed my right shoulder and squeezed it tight. The first two fingers on his right hand straighten out with sharp fingernails preparing to stab me. His face was smooth shaven, angular black Germanic with a smirk, with old dripping Gerri curls. I thought to myself this muda is going to kill me.

The girl next to me gave a little scream and he motioned to her with his daggered fingers and I imagined that they could have easily torn her throat out. While looking this big guy in his eyes I saw in the background the guy who I just once was, taking out his gun. He aimed it at the big guy and waited for him to make a striking move.

Somehow I saw the crowd behind me move out of his line of fire. I felt stronger since I got some back up. Using his finger example I put both my hands up to his face. {they were still twelve inches away even with me arms fully stretched.} I told him "GET {and I paused} Away From Me!" He didn't get it. He drew his hand back and the other guy raised his gun purposely. I knew I couldn't look at the guy with the gun, or I'll be dead in a flash.

I said again, this time angrier "Get -I paused- Away From Me!!" He just smiled an evil smile. A third time I said slowly "GET AWAY FROM ME." And I focused all of my energy to come out of my finger gun. The giant started disintegrating molecule by molecule. When he reached the point of looking like the static fuzzy-ness on T.V.

        I woke up

AUTHOR'Z NOTES

All of my dreams are based on a true story..
My poetry is also

CHAPTER FIVE

2ND LINES

Parting

After she said "Good-bye"
I even heard the empty air
As the joy began to die
I started to no longer care
May this world within me, withstand this crushing lost.
Along with that sense of half seen sunrise.
Being together with the space she has just left
My only comfort in knowing her smile
My only peace in knowing she's in my life
My only pain is the memory of her embrace
My only normality is being without her
The truth being no longer true to form
The contribution having to be served cold
Being selfish
Wanting her hand to hold
Instead, her hand waves a so-cool good-bye
That's me I saw walking away
My life, Hopes, Prayers, Dreams, just me.
And here I am
After she said "Good bye"

To Speak

I even heard the empty air
Speaking of dreams that I've craved for
Freeing worlds I created in moments of confusion
Find praise when I thought I was all praised out
I am to never mention my promise to be silent
To never cease in seeking to be lived out
Now that we are here, why is it that we sing
The lyrics that remain mysteries within our souls
Point the way to the promise Land
If you're ever lost …just point to yourself.
I even heard the empty air
Speaking of dreams that I've craved for
I would be fortunate to find a home
Or just a little finality to this long long life
In addition to this I don't usually say
To communicate to you in a clearer way
Allow death to be undone and smile to bloom
Friendship is Our space
Freedom is coming soon
With the laughter and joy of all the saints
I believe there's existing grief

Straightening

    Speaking of Dreams that I've craved for
    Wisdom wasn't a choice in the choosing of you
My thoughts was disruptive, But my love was true
So security was removed.
          Still… Agony was held at bay

I's not close ourselves off from each other
    The world we've built must survive
    Now that the future has touched us
    What's the true cost of love's Pride

    The open mind is within a headstrong brain
        The wish for Peace
              Is refused again and again
Saying "That's a needless wish for nothingness."
      Again
        Who am I to argue back faith?
        Yea it's the Dreams I crave
        But dreams I don't chase

You and Me

Wisdom was a choice in the choosing of you
Faith was restless and trust was silent
And yet you've become one with me
Through all the turmoil creation creates

Even being withheld from the stars at night
You allow me a view of heaven
That no sky can hold

Our relation was so clear
Is that why it was so brief
And Yet it lasts forever
Or another plane of reality

In flights of fancies I would have to admit
You were chosen
Because Our Love is Known

Allies

Faith was restless and Trust was silent,
Life for me is a relentless comfort.
Thinking is worth the mysteries missed,
And I feel no rage toward the Madness.
 I get these Dreams
  With courtesy from insanity
I'm thankful for all the insightful sparks

 And the alertness of well wishers
As they gather with joy at the graveside of Destiny
Who will stand and shout into the quiet contempt
  That space that fights against tomorrow
   Anyone who's a fool for freedom
    Will shout themselves voiceless
   A fool with an allegiance with faith and trust
  Is it enough to give up suffering
   And suffer through life any way?
  Keeping only hints of truth and reality
    As one moves into a world
      Which one has dreamed up.
   Will others make this one a legend?
   Will they even value the lesson?

Faith was restless and Trust was silent
The fool held them in awe and wonderment
And he had no idea why
Reminds me of someone I see every day in the mirror

I loose my mind every time I think of myself
I stumble and gracefully fall
Gracefully fall in love the angels
The angels who has placed me on a pedestal
A pedestal built by their wishes

Faith was restless and Trust was silent
Their presence was known
A fool's life is one of being Heroless

Fruitless

Life for me is a relentless comfort
    Someday I will dance in the clouds of tonight
      The apple is gone, I look for it
      And I don't see it. Am I to die
        With it never to be in my eye, again?
Is my heart to forsake the joy, for this search
    Please come back
             Please come back

  Life for me in all it's illness
      Just a misunderstanding
  It's just a smile not a smirk
      And not a smile of triumph
  Life for me is just a simple smile

    What effort it takes to love you
    What ever it takes to love you

Then Some

Someday I will dance in the clouds of tonight
What joy and everything else that will appear
I will embrace my shadow and hug it tight
Hopefully by then everything will be clear
My darling Do you see a place you can give me a shout
Can you wander in this space where's there's no doubt
Are you willing to exist as completely whole
Just lean and give me a kiss with your soul
Sometimes I get simple
Although I try to make it every time
I don't mind your disapproval
If it allows me to feel sunshine
She was a cool babe
She is a cool woman
Someday I will dance in the clouds of tonight
And pay for the chance to rid you of your fright
I'm influenced by purity
I'm not dismayed by absurdity
I won't be drugged by destiny
You are all that needs to be

What Joy

What Joy and everything else that will appear
During the moment when life may seem it's bleakest
For the moment will have life
And life brings with it the chance to choose
Choose Joy, Don't be so coy
Living simplixtic can be a hard adventure
And a rude dream
Loving you can never be that simple
And as I share this with you
In this brief moment of eternity
I am reminded of the often ness
Of my encounters with angels
And of my Capers and Day-sky-Dreams
What Joy, Could be had…. really
Within the usual boundaries of prayers
And the borders of trusted fates
What joy is to be truly accepted
In all the manners of religiously practiced logic
The underlining of life
Does not show up plain life
Only appearing in the disguise of struggles

What joy and everything else that will appear
During the scheduled breaks along the way
All will be there
Glory, Praise, Denial, Joy, Sadness, Madness
will be there because they've always been
Like I will always be here for you
And you can ask yourself
What joy

Praise found

During the moment when life may seem it's bleakest
I'm gonna dream about you
When love seems like a prize in a contest
You have it become so true

Where in the world can we be
If we're lost amongst the free choices
Stranger in a world too friendly
Listening to the angels voices

If I could just
Bounce around your mind for a while
Be like the thoughts that birthed your smile
I'll be cool with you
So cool with you
Praise will find its way
In God's story

Second Lines

I'm gonna dream about you
Someday the world will understand
I will drop in the fire with no parachute
That type of glory in demand
One time I had all these fears
It was clearly one time a little too much
You came by and swiped all my tears
Don't you think we should have
stayed in touch
Just a little bit baby
Jump a little bit off that edge with me
If our love was a script
I'll write a line a second
And have the second lines be eternity
I said "I'm gonna dream about you."
We will survive the view of others

And as we cross the abyss of opinions
We could be so cool as we recognize
The gleam of victory in each other's eyes
That we thwarted the many acts of treason
And become one cause and one reason
Games are played, risks are taken
Rules are layed, fates forsaken

You are my futureless wonder
I have come upon you
When my smiles are no longer a pain
I'm going to dream about you
Can you hear me telling you what you wanna know
We are strangers beyond being lovers
We are the ones that makes the future "Now" grow
In everyone's funny little world
They look for a cure for their impending death
I know when my time comes
I'm gonna dream about you

Neat and Clear

Someday the world will understand
Love can be used to death a hand
To applaud the way it can appear
To let us know that life is here

The known secrets that allow one to laugh at tragedies
Causes one to miss the ideal of the gift they are
I can't go back to my child hood
I can't come back to you
If you would be my only answer
I could be a living fool

To let us know that life is here
To applaud the way it can appear
Love can be used to give death a hand
Someday the world will understand

The Same Thang

Love can be used to give death a hand
You can be abused even in the promise land
I need light to Lay on my sunshine
Without any assistance she comes to mind
Who's to be the lover Who's to be the one
Are you gonna be my reality
When my mystery becomes undone?
God said, "Could you be with me?"
I heard her speaking to me last night
I said, " As long as tomorrow will be
Any type of togetherness is all right
These words are really useless
Meaningless nothings without you
As these words a related by the ink of this pen
So am I   to you
By the breath of God
You may still say this poem is of different subjects
Just like you think I'm a stranger

228

I world

You can be abused even in the promise land
I was in love once
A child could be refused upon demand
Our ignorance can be so superior
How many deaths can we Die of
I have experienced many in my lifetime
Illusions are the boundaries of Love
I used to be at war with myself
What I have in common with yesterday is today
So few has come and too many has gone
It was a slip of memory to be left alone
In the distance it may seem that the world prevails
How can we reconcile this view without knowing ourselves
God has always been with me
Freedom is relative to its many forms in reality
Each step left behind brings you one step ahead

I think toward the end I would rather die
Happiness is untying my shoes at the end of the day
It would be cool to be in the thoughts of others

Once Again

I was in love once
I was just thinking the other day
About the time
When time seemed stuck
I must've been interested in pain
It was just my luck... I found it
She was no more than an angel
She was no more than my life
What more did she want from me
I think I asked myself that twice
I was in Love once
Once lasted Then once was gone
My reality shattered
Leaving pieces of my world scattered
The chaotic ness was sort of entrancing
The insanity enhancing
Left me to look for that high again
She never returned......Never in a real physical way.
Leaving me Yearning
To be in love once more

I must Say

I was just thinking the other day
The world is a confusing pace
No names could claim the ultimate title
No style could feel the face
I've come to resist the outside
Remembering the times when I was there
Who was the one with the misplaced Pride?
Holding insanity so dear?
Realizing this Next Era's fate
The joy! The real truth becoming
Focusing straight for my mate
And Sun of dawn in this world is the same
The attitude... My state of mind
Becomes one of growth
Before a mind tangent gets too involved
I must say

Back IN

The world is a confusing place
Sanity is saved from the source of grace
Plastic smiles and designer skinbags
Makes me contemplate the value of fads
One must be determined to go beyond sight
If not, thangs may never be started
One has to be prepared day and night
Just in case one needs to heal the broken hearted
{2 BREAK it down}
The world is a confusing place
Sanity is saved from the source of grace
I could speak about the little known of space
That brings the comforting Love that at times save face.
I've been here since before I was once younger
And all I'll exist after you think I'm gone
Sometimes a selective memory is stronger
Remember that when you are alone.
Alone you will never be
Although one can be truly free.
Sanity Almost Defined
Sanity is saved from the source of Grace
I've spoken my opinion about the subject before
Being repetitive may not be appropriate now

Even if insights should happen more
I kid and joke, sometimes I beat around the bush
I take the avenues any way I can
Some contributions are given with ease
Some are given with a harsh push
I met Grace during an Era when I was discovering
be ageless
In a space that one can have the choice of recovering
Being in life cageless
The Entity Grace introduced me to this "Being" Sanity
I remind you I'm speaking to you
In the terms of an employee of the universe
This is the only way to be as a flower is free
And to ease in insights I consider true.
Also to state as a reminder
Sanity can be a wish or a curse.

Fa-ha-ma-Vue

I've spoken my opinion about the subject before
Didn't think it was needed to separate the mind and outside
I dig my first reviewer
God has blessed me with a reality rider
Maybe she will become a believer
Yes it is yet a new context
Finding someone who has become famous to me personally
I've become grateful that those tattoos didn't
Reach their full potential.
Sure did choose it to occur as a possibility.
The first all out reviewer is distinctive in many ways
Reasons of Being are meaningless, Only truth counts
Even though there won't be many who know who I praise
Voicelessly the advice was given to include her in my world.
I've spoken my opinion about this subject before
Eleven different ways I've approached the style to give
When my thoughts seems to derive from folklore
Enjoy the chance it gives to fully live
Remember her as I do

Eventhough

Didn't think it was needed to separate the mind and outside
I have journeyed the path with one hundred percent faith
Some lessons has been taught, given, shared, and forced upon my soul
Clouds are given as excuses for the sunshine to wait
Out beyond yonder, my dreams are a reality that's a wish
Voluntary I gave up myself as a possession
Empowering all others to be the freedom of being a choice
Remains the major source of my commitment's obsession
The "behind the scene" context of this current 2nd lines
Has been I {in my opinion} shared with you well
I've come to the conclusion sometimes, that
Some insights are hard to sale
Pleze Discover this piece...... I ask that of everyone
Everyone, even if you are another
Causes seems to cause death
Even though all live forever.

A sense of Challenge

I have journeyed the path with 100% faith
My actions may seem strange
But they are essentially straight

Unless and meaningless are natural thoughts
That's an interpretation that occurs for me
Often.
Neglectiveness as an attitude toward non-thought-about possibilities
Eventually dis-empowers the choice one can choose too be free
You are But Me
Others are us also
Until reality is realized
Afterwards will come before
Realize it pleze…… Everyone is also others.
Before, afterwards, and now
Ultimately is up to you
The power to choose is really yours
My thoughts are those penned words
Enlightening becomes the challenge to the various worlds.

Next Along

My actions may seem strange
Yet my sweetheart remains my goal
I will often ask if a wife still remains a curse
Or will I eventually become natural.
Do you think that life will be worse?
I ask you that personal question
Out of my curiosity of if you have
True knowledge of me.
If you do not……. X-perience the words I've penned
Then you'll discover
That I participated in this relationship
as more than a normal friend
To find what I have forever seek
Remains a whisper of a dream of a choice
To reach and go beyond my chosen life path peak
Is only possible if one get truly in touch
With the life source
Become all of everything
That's a little advise from my sporadic wisdom
I once again I end with this reminder
You can choose to be 4-ever in the context of freedom

Came to Be

Yet my sweetheart remains a goal
And my summer nights are found at times cold
Could there be stars that are her world
Will she x-ist as flesh. Will she B so bold
Doubtful feeling continue to invade my peace
The peace of assurance that's apart of my knowledge
My knowledge of the truth that has been revealed
Revealed to me during an era that was powerful.
The true truth that she's a rare real sweetheart
She's a source of the God that caused the universe to start
Sometimes it seems that I be speaking of myths
Sometimes I do. Sometimes I don't, the judgment is up to you
The contexts and subjects of my word could be this or that or this
Since these words are channeled through the universe
The source remains true
I've lived my life mainly being alone
And still loneliness is very rarely x-perienced
Disempowering "wills" appear momentary
But they soon disappear and are gone
The x-perience of those moments are declared finished.
No one has ever asked, "how I've become me."
It doesn't matter
I've yet come to Be.

238

Again I remind

And my summer nights are found at times cold
The moments when I'm most clear is when I'm confused
A time of silence, completely silence
Is a vision that has become old
And to be complete in life
I think is a bet I will lose
This nightlife has not lived me
I miss this presence of showing up
Showing up totally
These present moments are always here
Yet I choose when to accidentally step into them
For I've known since I was once younger
To be in those moments and live a long life
have chances that are slim
This is the last piece of being in this presence
I think my commitment to contribute
Has to be spoken and shared clearly
It's up to you to understand
And get this all
I remind you once I've yet come to Be

One Or Another kind

The moments when I'm most clear is when I'm confused
At times I see contributing as a strange art form
The feeling of her laughter within me
Frees confessions withheld from myself
Any atonements I offer, I often lose
Recovering from insanity is thought of as a state of norm
While we're together I can truly see
that secrets shouldn't be kept.
During this brief lifetime this time
I've chosen many paths and trails along the way
No matter what I've been in action of one or another kind
I attempt to live so there'll never be a dying day
When the prettiness comes, and the strange goes on
You remember an insight I stumbled upon
Love is a part of your voice source corner stone
And what is right can sometimes be wrong
Embracing all the fear makes one's next moment larger
I've heard it said. Time is here to be used to not be needed
Striving to have one's being to be of openness
Is a request that I'll forever choose to have pleaded
The moments when I'm most clear is when I'm confused

At times I see contributing as focused way of life
Too many times I've witnessed folks realities as a cartoon
Do you feel, or to ask can you ever feel Christ?
Presently I recall when I was once younger
Slipping different contexts into a single piece
This way I attempt to all allow various impacts of insights to be stronger
That way, the echo of life will never cease.
I've yearned for at least one moment of simplicity
It's an awful Blessing to be captured insanity
Right after every one of the "hers" releases me.
Downtown I saw a hurting girl in pain show a bright smile
I decided to learn how to truly pray
For that cause of each fantasy is a possible wrong turn
Freedom of choice can be chosen
That's a lesson one should learn. I will always wonder
If you can ever enjoy these words
From this tangent of my mind
Live life, don't let life live you
No matter what Be in action in one or another kind.

This Time

At times I see contributing as a strange art form
This time I'm shocked by her passing
I've shared about the times that has been up-front
Still I don't know if the impact will be Everlasting.
I'm hoping that Africa will become a partner
And not that space of land
To journey along side me in life
We could share the choice to empower.
Whatever occurs, it's of course God's will
Apart of God's destiny plan
If Africa is lost to me
I will pray for the wisdom to understand.
At a time like now, I'm compelled to let go
To step out side the boundaries to recall myself
There's been moments of times that has shown up
Like the ultimate brightness, like there's no shine left.
I remember asking the question
"How can you call me wise, when you are more than I know?"
Everyone can be cool, Everyone is special
Just choose to have the habit
To be compelled to let go.

To Her

This time I'm shocked by her passing
Or I should say her passing on

My interpretation of my reaction
Yearns to be comforted in an empowering source

For now I'll just briefly broach the subject
And come back and speak upon it later
Having something more important to share with you
Anything else is thought of as a space saver.
Most of all, now, I wish to praise her
In this sort of discreet way, and state of style.
Very rare. It's very rare to x-perience a power
Until one has been gone from this world for a while

Switching WITHIN The Box

Or I should say her passing on
When I speak about the one that often returns
Returns as a source of joy and real life
I'll inquire into the impact of the news for some time
To come
I take off my glasses when I'm about to choose
To be alone
The repetiveness of the returning love. Is what
Being with truth, one learns.
{now pause and enjoy this moment of a space of change.}
You may notice that my poetry is at times
Stuck within a box of contents of
few words.
Or to say
I share in different ways that's the same
My way of x-pressing the impressions
That can only come to one true truth
No matter the number of shared or taught learned
At night I involved myself here
Then I anxiously anticipate the future
I'm cursed with the dream of this world
Can you follow this other direction of what's pure

I have refused to see myself as getting older
Each boundary I've discovered is a chance to become less
I'm currently working on combining my inside with my outside
I'm troubled by the flesh. I must confess.

Each letter, word, sentence, line of poetry, Each piece
Reveals a layer that I've caused to cover up me
Join me in this journey. Join me Pleze
I'm sort of seeking what life is like
If all choices can be chosen
for free
I look forward to the "x-citment" of the x-pression
That comes from imagining what could come in the next moment.
I'm driven from the energy of that x-pa-tation.
The x-pa-tation has become like the ordinary air
That I've needed to continue to live this lifetime
Dig?

People react differently when I happen to Be
With them, outside of my mind.
Which goes to prove or to say it's just an x-sample
of how I think my thoughts of the known outcome
Can always be different.

Each Day I wake up to be able to give my thanks
In order to do that, I must know how to x-ist a certain way.
I just remain committed not to x-ist as I'm Leaving God.

This 3rd and last page of this piece is meant to be.
Of course if it wasn't, no words would be continuing.
The seeking of truth is an elusive purpose
One must deal with, and accept all the Bull shit.
Dig?

I confess that I've been thought of as being honest
In totally the wrong way
I did what I did to continue to live on the edge
With the context of confession
That's all I gonna ever say.

If I see it as necessary to eat a bug
To quench my hunger
And another believes to consume another living being
Is not the way to live life
Each of our realities can be a possibility,
That has us living longer
Each thinks it's the bigger Picture that one is seeing
To have it all be the same
Would be so nice.

Behind the scene of the words I pen
There x-ist a purpose.
One that's a cause that changes interpretation.
From a curse to a blessing.
Dig.

To Return, To Leave

When I speak about the one that often returns
You can take it as a person or thought
Whichever way you choose to take it
I sincerely request that you simply "get it."

A cloudy day is often given the power to decides ones' mood
Everyone has allowed a circumstance determine one's choice
By being alone in a crowd I've sought solitude
I believe the will of God is to become One with God!

This piece is chosen to be brief
So I can rest because of the power
That comes from being present
In the moments of "now"
Present in such a way that reveals "Truth"
That's all.
Or to say
This is all for now.

Words beyond the Decided end

You can take it as a person or thought
These words I hear from no choice of mine
There's always a different Paradise that's sought
Still there x-ist those that waste the purpose of time.

I know I have thought it as not interesting
When I'm witnessing the battle for my soul's source
It's like I'm a fan in the stand observing the game
But this game involves what happens in my life.
This going back and forth between sane and not
Could be because I'm enjoying the adventure
Or because I haven't suddenly discovered what I've sought
Or it could be, that I've chosen not to be sure.

These words x-ist beyond my choice to decide to complete
Here are the reality of what's here
When one goes on
The volumes I've written could be thought of
as an amazing feat

That's okay. Just remember its "Death" that you
Shouldn't fear
No one can really be alone.
My wife is here somewhere in this world
When I encounter her is a moment that's yet to come
I have no doubt that the moment will occur soon
Yet "Soon" is a context of "time" and "time" is meaningless.
Can you Dig where I'm coming from?
I'm simply saying
That I may find my wife during my next lifetime.

{ The previous 5 poems has been written in one sitting. Or to
say one flow of riding
a wave of thought. These spurts are interesting. It's like what
I've been wanting
to write for days, but I haven't and now I'm just doing it. Dig?}

To seek the state of being
Truly the truth in the life of the state of mind
The state of mind it takes to be willing
To be willing to x-plore the vast space
The vast space of the context's box
A context that shows up in whatever universe
Of course it's known that universe
Can show up as at least a zillion realities
Which reminds me to remind you

That you can choose an x-iststance
That could have every x-isting moment
Occur as empowering possibilities.
To go here, there, yonder, and to go beyond what's gone
Allows life to be enriched in a way that cannot be
Described
The only insights that are hidden
Are the ones you withhold from yourself
You've been tricked into believing that's a sort of protection
You're able to choose to have freedom
Given as a gift.
Pleze Dig what I'm saying
Or to say
Pleze get the insights I've intended to provide
Or to say
Get this contribution, from these penned words
Or to say again
Pleze get what I'm saying.
You can tell that I've reached the end of the trail
Maybe not.
When I sign my name, you'll know I'm complete
And this piece will be another one added
To the volumes that could interpretated as an
Amazing feat.

Being a writer is just who I am.

An X-sample of attempting to bring Poetry into Being

These words that I hear from no choice of mine
Come along with the destiny that remains no choice of mine
Comes along with the destiny that remains unknown
I've not enjoyed the hints to the clues of her love
Yet no matter how much I die, Life goes on

I've come to believe that in order to always have heavon's presence
She must show up during this current lifetime
If she don't who ever this angel might be
I think I know I'll continue to lose mind.
{now I'm gonna attempt to get deeper, prepare yourself.}
The stars came into x-istance after you appeared in my dreams
Sweet heart, Honey, My Queen, what ever I call you, you're my miracle
By knowing you x-ist allows me to see death as not what it seems
I'm patiently waiting for you to become my all
{now I'm gonna attempt to end this poem smoothly.}
Verily. Verily I say unto you
Live to live the will of God
Being alive involves all sorts of realities
And what those realities are interpretated as
Is your choice.

Just Maybe

Come along with destiny that remains unknown
What is it that comes, You could, and should ask
It can only be this life we live
And will go on living until the end goes past

It's a pleasure to x-perience the life of a commitment
A commitment to discover as many ways to share
To share a strange form of art
A form of art that empowers one's voice source

Really, for real, right now, I'm presently am gone
Gone way beyond the limits of out side the boundaries
The boundaries that set for safety around the contexts
the contexts that's seems as a true truth
A true truth of the walls of the boxes
The boxes that most everyone live their lives in.

Witness history. For when you read these
Penned words
I've already gone ahead
Just maybe I've made it to another world

Boo

What is it that comes, you could and should ask
Our ignorance isn't an unhealable state
Now, like always, there's the freedom to choose to last
Destiny is a different distinction from fate
Eventually the thoughts provoked will have joy felt
Remaining a cautious source of the way to insights
I've often had to force myself to accept
Neat obstacle that occurs regularly like the nights
Get this, so you can get you.

An angels' grace –shush intervention in ones' life
Brings gifts of various unforeseen realities
Often during my teen age years
Uninhibited possibilities showed up from that grace.
To say one more gein. There's always the freedom to choose to last

Because of the perfect timing
One cannot help to think of her as a set up
One is still willing to see where out tomorrows will take us.

Simply Choose

Our ignorance isn't an unhealable state
Be in touch with the space of peace that x-ist all around you
I find it interesting that I seek a she to live for her sake
Sometimes I wonder, If in my next lifetime
I'll discover I've lived this one as a fool

It appears to me that the space of which I belong
Encompasses such a vast context too large to handle.
When I die in this lifetime and move on
Remember that I was insane although stable
Pleze remember that.

I'm so simple; you'll think I'm never confused
Yea right. I wish...
It's a wish that can only be possible in my dreams.

Let go what you believe you need to withhold
Let go what you believe you need to withhold.
Please, Pleaze, Pleze, Pleze, Pleaze, Please
It's a request, Not a demand
Be free and powerful
Choose to take that stand.
In order to make that choice, You simply choose to do so.

Make It So

Be intouch with the space of peace that x-ist all round you
It is such a trip to x-perience true silence
Can you believe me when I'm speaking by writing
The level of the volume of these written words I speak
Is totally up to you.
It depends on how intensely you seek
And how much you're true.
Understand?

Sometimes I catch my self-drawing the letters of a word
Being that present can be a hazard to one's reality
A long time ago, I was able to give up the world
Yet somehow or another I think I'm not free.
Pretty please I ask you to Be intouch with the space of Peace that x-ist
All around you
Just now a memorie flashed briefly within my mind.
Re-x-periencing the moment hugging Meg, as we pose to have a
photograph taken. I set it up so the hills of the Napa Valley
would show up in the background.

What is knowing how one is truly saved?
When answers to questions become unaskable questions
themselves
What should you do?

I sort of have 13 more years to stay here
I'm hoping I die like I've died countless times before
I'm glad to be able to embrace all my fear
Yet I remain afraid of what life has instore

If you ever have the opportunity to encounter
I think that you'll think that my words and me are the same
Times like now are dreaded afterward
I still live my life as if it's a ruleless game

I think that one x-ist always during ones' peak of life
So when you hear time as spoken of as being prime
Consider why they have chosen to live in a little world
Look at if you have also made that choice.

This space of Peace that surrounds you
Is known by many contexts
And x-ist as a lot of concepts
So it maybe already a part of your awareness.
Think about it
If it's not.
Make it so.

A Heck of a Silence

It is such a trip to x-perience true silence
After she said "Good-bye"
I cried, I tried, I giggled, I died
She was a true sin, chosen with pride

Yet the silence that occurred right after the echo
of the closing door

Is a truth that to x-perience no more
will be just fine with me

Going Out

After she said "Good-bye"
I prayed that she'll return from her house above
I praise the pleasure of just the ideal of our being together
Being with her is the only chance I've had to x-perience Love

Many years now I share about my encounter that happened here
Here in this world on this earth, within this reality
Then, maybe then you'll know I'm cool

All the previous poems just goes to show
That I'm continuing along the path that goes in no certain direction

I almost managed to continue on beyond
What's meant to be must be
So now I'm out of here
In search of the ultimate completion.

AUTHOR'Z Note

Having fun so far? If you look hard enough, you may notice the "errorz".. Sometimes you won't have to look hard at all...

Verily, Verily I say unto you..Some "errorz" are Right.. if only just to have a piece be contributed Correctly.. Dig..

So sit back and enjoy these projects..

PEACE

Chapter six
Notes from the Student Of Ego University (revisited)

written and designed
By
Gitsuyu

Forward

I read somewhere, that a forward in a book is unnecessary & it shouldn't be written by the author. It should be written, if it's ever written at all, by someone else after the author of the book is dead. And this someone else is particularly a close friend, and this close friend is ideally a scholar. Although I've read hundreds of books I haven't read up on the proper etiquette of writing a book. So I'm penning this Forward because I feel it needs one.

Having taking to days to write this one would think that I should have had some type of an agenda. I did, but it was a simple one. "To revisit the Ego University as a student. I think that the love of an angel reoccurring with in the theme is an natural occurrence. Everything in here is natural when you consider the source. ☺

I have made two major mistakes in the original manuscript that are perfect. It shows that no matter how much I strive for perfection like God, I'm still a human being. I'm not talking about the misspelled words, that's become almost a fashion. I'm talking about being real. You dig? Peace and Love!

Table of Contents

1) Answered
2) From My Soul
3) So Free
4) Nothing Fancy
5) I Don't Won't
6) Religous Thoys
7) Quiet Thing
8) Six Day Rap
9) intermission
10) Heaven
11) Simple Independence
12) Bitter sweetness
13) No Nay
14) A Feeler not Filler
15) Little Lady Gray
16) Careful Cousins
17) Seeing more than Sight
18) Out Here
19) intermission
20) Where's My Wife?
21) I Am. And Me
22) God's Child
23) Hiedi
24) She Remains
25) Justly Cause
26) Partial Creed
27) intermission
28) Unadilla Rap
29) Sonya (revisited)
30) From Now On
31) They're Me
32) Lady True
33) Gikuyuism 101
34) Living Alive
35) Miss Reporter Returns
36) intermission
37) With Only Me
38) Constrastable
39) Spoken Promise
40) Know
41) Her Again
42) Now is Never
43) Gikuyuism
44) Imperfect
45) intermission

Answered

Don't want to Die
            To be happy
It's no longer a choice I can afford
I don't want to be a saint
    Insanity is no longer
              The Paradise wished for
Hanging out with Mercy
    I'm no longer lonesome at the side
My prayers were everyday thoughts
    Don't know why they wanted to hide
I'm not smart at all
      Maybe just a pinch of some
I've stubbed my toe
         On the corner of the world
    From things as such, I've acquired wisdom

                              Gikuyu

From My Soul

I view my world though two windows
I've quit being a judge in the coustom contest
Lately I've mourned in the mornings
I've misunderstood Her, I thought she was not here
I think I need glasses beyond my windows
                  to make it seem clear

The sky was never Blue to me
I'm in this prison And I'm free
Her smile is the joy of A memory
Her smile is the pain of A wishful dream
And still I find myself stuck here with You.

Go save those that see Is A savior
Saving me is like bringing more light to the Sun
I view my world though two windows
    Where is everybody going?

So free

They think it's his freedom
    That allows him to do what he did
How can that be,
        When he does it without a choice
I'm not going to do what he did
    Because I'm gonna choose not to
Still we're going to both
        experience death
No matter what we go through.
    I'm just going to choose to let it pass
      And keep on living.
I've always been free to risk myself
    That freedom has never been a choice for me
    And so what am I really saying
What do I mean if I mean this.

                    Gikuyu

Nothing Fancy

Hay don't you know
I never fell out of Love
   I never really fell in Love
    I only Loved you
I Still Love You

   I want to say something in this part of the poem about how I once saw the world as a complicated place. How I would see a cloud and see more because of my pattern of thinking was just that way. How when we loved, all of that stuff became simple. But I can't just now find a fancy way of putting it so I won't say it.

Hay don't you know
   I never fell out of Love
   I never really fell in Love
I only Loved you, I still Love You

Gihuyt

I Don't Won't

My mind would have never filmed the dreams
   Unless she played the majorest role
That girl gave my world such a shake up
You would think a person would want to wake up
I don't and I won't   I don't and I won't
   It's not unusual for her to challenge fate
It's a matter of record that this is what she enjoys
She would say hello and hug me, and turn around and say good-bye
The reversal of life was free, you would think I would want to die
I don't and I won't   I don't and I won't
I remember being once younger
      The belief in love was stronger
   If it was really up to me
      I would live in that memory
I don't and I won't   I don't and I won't

                              Gilsoye

Religious Thugs

Praise be to The Almighty
   And Look at That Bitch with the Phat Ass
I know I'm walking the right path
   And I want the fame that's gonna last
Praise be to the Almighty
   My life is safe and sound
   My ways are God's ways
If you cross me I'll put you in the ground
My former confusion, I am losing
   It's so clear to me, of where I'm at
If I don't do what I do
         Somebody will for sure
What's wrong with getting paid and being phat
What am I doing here, what am I saying?
   Praise Be to the Almighty

                                Gibsup

Quiet Thing

You'll find that I am quiet
        About certian things
Never from shame I don't play that game
My cause is to contribute, ~~many other~~
    That's my life, that is me
In my own way, I scream and shout things
But it may take years
      for you to hear the echoes.
It may be the right thing to do
      It may be the wrong thing too
Only the historians will know for sure
But what is life, if it's not forever
  It's a job with no paid vacation.

In time you may hear these inked words
  And when you do, Remember them and not me.

                                              signature

Six Day Rap

Hello everybody welcome to the party
   You're right where you belong
       Where the love is so strong
I'm not going to get into a long stay
   I'm just here to acknowledge you
We   And give you all the glory
I've done the tyrollian traverse
      And the zip line
We've done the rappell and we've runned that mile
   So come one everybody and put your hands together
We're gonna contribute to this world
      And make it better.

   You people are so lovely
     You know that's true
Before I go, let me hear you scream "Breakthrough"

                        Gilbert

intermission

Ahh... Now we come to ~~what~~ is usually called a pause. It's official title is of course is "intermission". The purpose of this piece is to take a break; to see what's happening. So far I've written a piece (Poem) a day. It is my intention to continue that, and I do not see anything to prevent that from happening at this time. Except for maybe going on a mind tangent, which I'm prone to do. Since this is "Revisited" I wanted to jump right in. I believe I have achieved that objective. You the reader cannot tell if I have or not unless you not only read the first book under this title and understood the concept, You must understand clearly by what I mean when I say my objective. If not, it's assumed that my objective is achieved when I say I believe it is.

Another point I wish to point out is that although there is structure there is no form (so to speak.) my first thoughts was to have these intermissions to be like spaces or say breaks between certain depths. That may turn out to be the case, only time will tell. That's all for now. I'll be seeing you in another nine. Oh yes, that's another part of the structure. Other than that, that's all. I think. Peace and love

GlBurg

Heaven

However much it appeals to me
   I find I cannot in all honesty
     Accept the invitation given so graciously
  I can't go just yet   No I can't go just yet

    Pleasure mama wants to embrace me
    I never thought I would be tempted this way
    But if flowers can bloom in the winter's snow
      Then anything can possibly go
Including my sanity   definitly my sanity

    The location of the place
      Isn't marked on a map in my mind
  It's left left up to me
      to choose which direction to take

    It will always and forever be here
    No matter how it appears to me

Simple Independence

I cannot tell where we start
             And where we finish
We are so together it is like we are one.
  Some may say that is dangerous,
          We could lose our sense of self.
If love is our truth, anything else is a myth.

Your independence no longer breaks my heart.

If where we were is where we are at
           And is where we are going to be,
  Then there is no bottom line
    When we communicate with our souls.

To love and be loved is not a simple request.

My mind hides inside my brain
  When I confront my visions of us.
May I hold your hand and take a peek?

                                          Gilroy

Bitter Sweetness

I had made some light blueberry Cool-Aid
I wanted that bitter Almond taste
It was a beautiful mess that I made
And the attempt didn't go to waste

Here I am, with this moment solidified in ink
The wrong concoction worked right
Or the memories since it would have been missed
truly missed

Where ever I point, I'm pointing to myself
with no directions how can I get lost?
Wisdom can be acquired no matter what
With "no matter what" you have to appraise the cost

It cost me damn near a half of billion brain cells.
And I've might have gotten tricked.

Remember: I wanted that bitter Almond taste

Gikuyu

No Nay

It was time to crash
    So I drove off the mountian
The bliss was found
    wittenessing the session of the council
    There was no nay to say
    So I'm here to this day
    And the secrects remain known
    As the tricks of the trade

Can You Dig What I'm Saying Here?

People's destiny are choosen by Themselves
    Yet most see value in being a victim
Don't seek that myth of a paid vacation
Reklize the light next to un-truth's night

It was time to crash and survive
There was no nay to say so I'm still alive

A Feeler not Filler

I'm confront again with this page
At first it was empty
    But now it's not so, anymore

As I contine, my concerns go away
I ~~need~~ some thought provoking prose
    So you may understand
    How my world is now

I was walking along the snow covered ~~beach~~
    with Amy
And while she was pointing to the icebergs
    I was enjoying the way she smiled
I was thinking
    And I thought "I'll never experience this again."

Sometimes I go on a mind tangent
to provide a glimps of a simple world.

        Gikuyu

Little Lady Gray

How impossibly deep could I go
    When speaking about our Love.
I could say nature was NATURAL
        When you first called me daddy.

Waking up in your embrace
    from one dream to another
Smiling at the way you don't
        understand the world

So easy to cry for
    So easy to die for
In your laugh I hear my future happiness.

The sense of no fear
    As you begin the new day
The life of the young
    Should remain that way

Gilboy

Careful Cousins

Reality ran away, She took her cousin wisdom along
She said I frustrated ~~them~~ them to wits end
They said I only used them for subjects in a song
~~Being~~ Then lost was my cost to being free
It was less like songs and more like poetry
She thought she needed to be needed
                        In order to be around
I said "That type of yourself, isn't so sound"

I persuaded them back with the golden carrot of Destiny
I don't know if that was wrong or right
All I know is that I had a sense of that spoken reed

I gave them this spiel about life long devotion
Wisdom said "You say that, because you're free to say that."
She wasn't afraid of their destiny, it was their sanity
especially when I replied "Baby, I'm Gikuyu."

                                                            Gikuyu

Seeing more than Sight

I look out and see these funny days
I guess ~~I'm~~ I'm not suppose to conceptionlize the razor wire.
A guest shouldn't guess at the realness of the mess.
    you wasn't ~~to Accuse~~ wrong to accuse me.
Getting caught up in this storm of dreams,
Don't know if she meant to touch me
        So deep in my mind.

I look out again and see a night of silence
   People checking to make sure there is no ~~escape~~,
Unlike these words, I will not be here tomorrow
      And fame is not always great.

I don't fear the way it has to be,
My life is sometimes a different story.
My world is sometimes just a word.

More times than not that word is love

                              Cowboy

Out Here

I woke up here, then I realized what I did
Then I blinked my eyes, and came back to the planet earth
It could have been a simple slip
                yea you could have called it that
I just have this sneaky ~~suspicion~~
       It would have lessen the value of the act

Sometimes with being Here, I actually show up now
  And now becomes a moment, that last a little while,
  Out of all the insights that has occurred during this moment
None has impacted me more, than discovering
     I have much much more moments to experience,
     And None will be like now.

Sometimes I wake up here while I'm on the planet earth
   I smile a remembered smile
     Thinking of value and worth

                                                        Gilbert

intermission

Well I went outside the structure with this one, so I might as well stay out there with the remaining 3. I knew an intermission was due, I just got caught up in thinking of what's next, I didn't pay attention to "what's soon to come." One thing remains, that is the same dry delivery, where these intermissions are concerned. So that at least remains in the structure.

I think the progression of this book is natural. These intermissions doesn't indicate one level or another. These intermissions is like a intake of breath after a long recital. Nothing may be said, but it's vitally important for the continuance of life. At least that's what I think.

Writing this book is an experience. The "right here" in your face reality that it brings forth is something to behold. Being where I'm at, and having the same surroundings, I can only speculate that these poetry pieces will only get deeper and maybe stranger. The cause is something like I'm not giving enough time for the poem to get settled in, it's just boom there, and by it being like that, its conception may be deemed strange.

Gikuyu

Where's My Wife?

That Being next to me
   That some claim They can not see
May have been in my previous life
   I want to know about now
Where's my wife, where is she

   All The Acts of Love
And The drama of romance
   Because of my insanity
No woman has ever stood a chance
   Well maybe one or two
If They would have been inclined that way

   I know my destiny
Because of the visions I see
But fucks tomorrow, I want to know about now
   Where is my wife, where is she?

                                Gihuyt

I Am And Me

I'm not simply for everyone
    I'm simple for everyone
And I still sometimes misunderstand myself

    The clearity of my complexity
    Admittly is my responsibility
The indictment stating I'm crazy
    Need not be An incident of spoken cause

Sometimes I choose not to be tight
    One can Be to free
And one can be Too free
Eventhough my box is the universe
    As opposed to
        A simple little slot in society

    By being born I've become
    The source of my destiny

                    Glhuy

God's Child

I'm not a map, Telling you how to get there
I'm not a Table of Contents
 Telling you what you'll find
I'm more like a wish
 That formless dreamful vision
Yea, that description sort of fits me.

I'm not an opinion
Which is said to be just like an Asshole
 everyone gots one
I'm not a fact
Which if truth be told, is just like an asshole too
 everybody knows one

I'm God's Child
 That's right, The Child of God
Like you, And everyone else

 Gilroy Jr

Hiedi?

We sat on the floor facing each other
            In the upstairs gallery
She was playing with a live wire
Saying I was silly to be so frightful
               for her
She wore a blue floral dress.
I asked her "Do you have any children?"
    She said "Me? Personally?"
While she thought about it
She got that thousand yard stare
              And knowing smile
I said "Your name is Stacey? right?
     She said "No"

It would be so cool
If I could find a girl like her outside of my mind.

                                GBurg

She Remains

behind the wind, she moves
I think I will be able to embrace fate
fantasies are provided
                         moments are stilled
I think I will be able to
                hang on a little longer
one more season and a half to go
Her smile will only burn me up
             bring me up too
I can live with that
       I can not die with that
Before the light, she thinks
Destiny may be within my grasp
realities are replaced
       My Angel remains real

Justly Cause

What's in the chance for fame
Lucid rumors are often heard
If she only knew me
It's all the fame I'll ever need

to return to the shadowed corner
where imprints are often made
ones of peace, joy, and madness
The space of comfort
Lateness never being a sour time
Because time's never being

I listen to more than what's spoken
That's the way I write
That's the way I live

Forgiveness is the key to a smile
Life lived causes my fame

Partial Creed

I intend to cause attention
And not be the cause of attention
To bring people into focus
Which would allow them to see
      The details of Life

I intend, whether I choose to or not
to become an habitual contributor
better yet : to continue being one
Being aligned with God
      The sance of Life

I will be and do my intentions
My mind may go on a tangent
Yet : my soul will stay on the righteous path
So that tangent will be alright
      Providing more of Life

intermission

    Maybe not strange to the person in the know, but to those who's not an avid reader of my work, they just might not understand. For example, a couple of nights ago I let another inmate take a peek at this book, I said these are some poems I'm working on. He opened the book and the first piece he read was "God's Child" after reading that he asked me "Are you sure that's a poem" I nodded my head yes, then he continued to go backwards, and he liked the earlier poems he said he didn't like the "Asshole" parts in the poem. When I vocalized the words he got it, it seemed simple to me, but with him, by reading it it had a totally different meaning. Which leads me to conclude that I should warn you that as this book progress, it is my intention to have the remaining pieces get "stranger" and "stranger."

    I fitted this intermission back into the structure because of the out line for the table of contents allows me to. Also when I first started writing this intermission it seemed like it took forever to reach the last line, writing so small and all of that. Now I can't write small enough. And I still continue into the next one.

                                                                            G/King

Unadilla Rap

After the 3rd block movement
   I'm going to doo whop
Then Curtis is going to look out for the man
   while I pop the socket
And we get our smoke on
   Because our bugle light
     has been burning too long
We don't mind breaking bread that way
   Wish we had a caddillac
Couldnteven get one on our mastercharge
   These busters in blue
     try to tell us what to do
Saying it's their way because we have no way
   They just do know
Me and Curtis are from the free world

Gilbury

From Now On

Working these feilds till de sun is gone
my hands done gone down to de bones
My mamma told me da Lord has mercy
I shoul need da Lord to come And bless me

Sonrise to Sunset we shouldn't regret
Sunrise to Sunset we shouldn't forget

Working with a commitment
              One has to ~~~~ trascend
I've gone crazy time and time Again

If I have Loved you more than I realize
I've been out of Place and I Apologize
My Love for you will make it through
Those wild storms and false clues

Sunrise to sunset we shouldn't regret
Sunrise to Sunset we shouldn't forget

Gilby

From Now On

Working these fields till de sun is gone
my hands done gone down to de bones
My mamma told me da Lord has mercy
I shoul need da Lord to come And bless me

Sunrise to sunset we shouldn't regret
Sunrise to sunset we shouldn't forget

Working with a commitment
            one has to ~~trascend~~
I've gone crazy time and time again

If I have loved you more than I realize
I've been out of place And I Apologize
My love for you will make it through
Those wild storms and false clues

Sunrise to sunset we shouldn't regret
Sunrise to Sunset we shouldn't forget

They're Me

The acts of stupidity
             Are pardonable
Someone being stupid
    I consider it like I consider ~~someone~~ someone crazy
     It's an act or state of mind
        I don't understand.
Sometimes the action of these stupid people
   Are very disrespectful toward me
        And I forgive them
Do un to others ~~as~~ you would have
         others do un to you
   Sometimes I think I should reverse that
   And disrespect them as they do me
         But if I was them
    I rather be forgiven.

                                   Gilkey

Lady True

Your response comes highly recommended
    All I have to do
Is request that you become dependent
On me, then you scream, then you kick me out the door.
    I Love You

Play folks can see the plain things that be
    But if they're real like yourself
They'll see if you take away the world
    Something is still left
    My Love for You

My soul has been dazzled
    My Destiny complete
I have become focused because you have become found
    My insanity has become sand
        By Being with you

                Gilroy

Gikuyism 101

It is to God
Not nessexrly that man's father
Nor that couples creator
But the source of Life
That a free man owns up to

One can get credit
        And extend one's credit
With the universe, through the ~~intrinsic~~ Act of contributing

Living like the only race of people
        Is the human race
    Is God's will

The actions of this life
        determines the outcome of your next
Peace and Love is like a hand and Glove
everything is simple, including the complex

                        Gikuyu

Living Alive

500 days
I have been in this world that long
I have lived 20 ½ times that
And I'm still going strong

I have and will
   continue to live the life I lead
When I get there and end up square
I request that you applaud for me

I will never let anyone live my life
   No one never really can
I've known folks to live off another memories
   telling the same old lies over and over again

How can they live their lives
   If they don't know who they are?
One is dead when they live that way.

Gilbury

Miss Reporter Returns

Miss Reporter - Why have you brought me back?

Steven - So you can ask me one or two questions. Now that it's been over ten years since our first interview, maybe there's something you'd like to know.

Miss Reporter - I think I've made a brief appearance since then.

Steven - Maybe, maybe not. I can't recall just now.

Miss Reporter - I think I have, but that doesn't matter. One of the questions I would like to ask you is, "why have you continued to be a writer even after the course has caused you to be imprisoned."

Steven - This skinbag has been imprisoned, my soul has been freed.

Miss Reporter - That's simple enough, but what about your tattoo's underneath your tattoos?

Steven - Sorry. The space is up.

Gilhooly

Intermission

And now we come to this one and I don't think I've gotten any stranger, oh well that's life. I've noticed that as the table of contents fills out, it continue to amaze me. As always, I think that when I complete this book the amazement will only last a few moments, then it'll be time to move on. I don't believe I've started a trend by writing one piece a day, just like I didn't start a trend when I wrote that poetry book that February 14th. This is just an experience.

I'll say that all but 2 pieces between the last intermission and this one weren't a struggle to bring forth. They was just thoughts I needed to speak about. Two pieces are retrospective, Sonya's and Miss Reporter's Return. My intention with the remaining 8 is to dig deep and bring forth pieces with subjects or thoughts that I haven't the slightest idea yet as to what they may be.

I say that's my intention, but who knows, I might find that I need to say something about Hope or Junie or even Bonnie, one thing's for sure, whatever I write will be authentic to the moment or to say I will be true to the "Now." And being true to this "Now" I have to go because the space is up.

Githuys

With Only Me

When I ~~close~~ close my eyes and look at you
I think about yesterday
    And the life we lived tomorrow
This joy hasn't been in all my dreams
Only in the ones where you're the reality

I can count my many True Loves
    on one finger
And you have been the only one
   That has stuck by my side
While I've slipped away
    In ~~pursuit~~ result of freedom
And I thank you, And I love you

Much can be said
   About how much of a myth you are

Nothing can be told about your beauty

                                   Glkuy

Constrastable

I wish I had enough of you
These shadows are not wise yet
What you see is a thought in motion
progressing toward destructive birthings.
  My Good-bye's has been silenced
  By the space between our Love
  All my smiles has been covered
  Before a chance to start over
It's an odd pleasure to wish
It's more tangible Than you
The mistakes are other myths
I still haven't gotten over that smile in your eyes
  The interuptions of your beating heart
  To a two sided Complimentary gift.
  A contribution needlessly refused.

                                        Gilroy

Spoken Promise

Pamela said "I never wanted to be so lonely
    Lord take care of my child
    He never wanted to be so free

    You can declare a war with anyone
    And be free to battle
    But the cost of most of those actions
    remains unseen long after thier impact"

Pamela said "Son, you are my life
    And sometimes heaven is too much of a paradise
    Some people like me, choose to remain insane
    By being grounded on the ground
    I would never give up hope
    That you may be included
    Yet the game must still be won"

Pamela said "My reminder is my salvation"

Know

If you think it's forever
    Then it won't last long
If you say it's always
    Then something is known

I've never had an incomplete thought
    Nor have I ever seen a false bottom
    A Promise or A Sunrise

Well maybe from tears of sincerity
    I've seen a Promise

I will only be shy by acting
Which is the only way I will die

It was too late to remain unknown
    even to myself
History has a price and a cost
Fate doesn't need a reason to come around

    Gilroy

Gikuyuism

God is amicable, so why the fear?
Chastisement is incurred by choice
   Our egos can be baneful
   Causing hurdles to become stop gates

It is wise to not be a sponsor at a pulpit
Taking a stand takes more courage
To love is to embrace life
Whatever you hate and fear
        you usually don't understand

I declare, with no if, and, or buts
That this is it. Yet this isn't all

I don't assume Truth, I know it

By living on the brinks of the ledge
I've become experienced with insanity

Being a writer is a balancing act

                              Gikuyu

Now is Never

My daze is gone
Never to return again
My mind is clear
Yea Right. I'm just dreaming

She's here, right beside me
every last moment of my life
       Just like God
Yea.   Just like.... God

Never having to be a Preacher
my sponsored pulpit
          Has crumbled from neglect
I still use my right to write
☞ If you can hear these words
          Hear them Now!

Never doesn't last long when forever is mad

Imperfect

To rest, The rest of the way
    Would be my personal choice
I can not, because I am bound by duty
    to my commitment to relentlessly
        contribute to Human kind

Maybe that can be called such a Noble cause
    It is my approach that causes conflict

The way I live.
    It would be silly of me to ever die

I will be here even when I'm no longer around

These words are like me
    They can not say it all

It would be silly of me to think that I'm wise
    But I have been known
    to have a crazy sense of humor

intermission

this space is truly up now. It was God's will for me to finish this project. I say that now, but I'm not done just yet. What you have just read in the past few minutes has taken me so days to write. One can easily see how I could be concerned about having the impact I intend to have. You may think I've written some nice poems, or some cool pieces, but being nice and cool is not what it's all about.

My commitment to contribute consumes me. Whether I'm talking about what Pamela said, or talking about doo whopping, whatever it is, it's to provoke thought, to provide insight, so that you "the reader" will be contributed to.

I can honestly state that there's nothing that crossed my mind when I was considering a poem/piece for this book that I didn't include. Unlike my other projects, my novel for instance, I consider and discard scenes, that's probably why it's taken so long. But due to the structure, "This writing one poem a day," I didn't allow myself to be placed in that position. Writing this book has been a real experience. The moment to be amazed hasn't arrived yet, maybe after I finish the writing the Forward. So far, I just have the feeling of satisfaction, like one gets after a job well done.

Peace and love,
Gikuyu J

CHAPTER SEVEN
2ND
SECOND LINES

Back with Isa

We were photographed
Posing in front of her nude portrait
When I lost that roll of film, I laughed
In public she remains known as a saint

She was superb as a poetry reader's support
She was a dancer that could truly be felt
Our relationship was of an unconditional sort
I knew our love couldn't be contained or kept

She cried big sad tears
Because her future husband was another and not me
She held on dearly to her fears
It shows not choosing to choose can be costly

She left a note, a gift, and huge vibes from her smile
When she decided to let me know She'll be forever gone
She felt like a reality on the unfalse truthness style
She didn't leave and went to Heaven, and left me below
She did leave and left me alone

Shared Possibility

In public she remains known as a saint
I still keep returning to wonder about her
I tried seeing beyond her, I just can't
I've questioned my ability to be sure
It's easy being in an unknown Love
This "In-ness" is a mystery to my rational side
I would like to understand if I could
Why we remain, Only to pretend that our love died
Pleze make that "like" an actuality
And go back being a possibility

In Public she remains known as a saint
I still keep returning to wonder about her
A forever wonderment drenched with curiosity
A mystical wall made with bricks of "always"
Is covered with fate filled paint
A reality more lovely than heaven is no further
Than you choice of choosing to Have it Be
Pleze make that "Have" become a haved
So that Peace to all can be shared

There….Come Here

  I've questioned my ability to be sure
  I think I know for sure at least one thing
  I sure wouldn't mind finding and having a wife
  I yearn for the joy and the completeness she'll bring
  I've prayed, wished, and whispered my simple request
     It's an either-or else" kind of attitude
       From which my request is derived
  Let me be home in a house that I've always
                         Been a guest
     Don't let that "Death" Obstacle intrude
     A wife will allow my life be survived

  I'm not withheld by the lines on a page
  It's the pressure of the pen
     more than the insistence of the ink
  I've been in a beach house
         I've been in a cage
    These words can be a friend.
    A friend that causes you to think

Me and She

I yearn for the completeness she'll bring
Skipping and jumping steadily forward to me
I learn to have a sight seen as a king
It follows that this life is up to me

It became the oracle quest so fast
That transition was smoothly laid
Became, because of the encroaching past
Became, because of the cost I paid

Our relationship has become more than clear
After each and every moment, one will come next
Every now and then someone can just appear
To scream a life without context

Within the universe it is shown
You were chosen
Because our love is known

A Factoress of Mine

It follows that this life is up to me
The rush to get on time is useless
YoU Just got to notice how chance came to be
The "ALL" is all one can confess
Once again…. These words are before beyond
They exist in the shadows of contributions
Is one thought to be not sound
If one needs no solutions.

I go this way thatway anyway of the space
Dancing with any and all of whatever
Seeking what ought not be sought
In a crazy world.

I considered this life complete so many times
It's considered cool to not inquire too much into that

{The next brief part is where the title comes from.}

Sugar, Factorress, Babe, Somewhat an happening
Can you need me now?

AnyHere

The "ALL" is all one can confess
God is all day all my life
Every word I pen becomes the best
Even when a Destiny is not in sight
   Long after the "last" the fate continues
   Listening from within allows one to hear the news
   Individualism can be totally refused
   Faith and trust can become important tools
   When growing into the "ALL" of life

The "ALL" is all one can confess
God is all day all my life
Sometimes I get caught up in that mess
When I tend to think that something just isn't right
 Faith and Trust has become important tools
 I go forward toward the "ALL" of life

See Pleze

Even when destiny is not in sight

We must aim for the tomorrows with open eyes

There are certain spaces used for pauses of reflections

To gather within oneself to get the connection

The wisdom of a man was serious damaged
 Damn near destroyed because of a true fault

Sometimes I write those "Bringer uppers"
   Some times I write uphill
There's a lot who choose not to be a captive
       Of God's will

  It's interesting to hear a story
      That you once heard when just a child
It makes me realize that at least some things
     Wasn't just wishful thinking

Even when Destiny is not in sight
One should ask oneself if ones' using needless eyes
Unsightfulness is a choice chosen
From a somewhat deep-rooted
                inferiority complex.

Find the courage to unblock your sight
Discover the strength to cut all ties
And recover the moments stolen
Those that was prostituted
Thinking they weren't the best.

I crave for a sightful human race
That craving is part of which
    My commitment in life is derived

I request you see these words
               With your eyes closed.

Time to Gather

To gather within oneself to get the connection.
I say needlessly that, that causes wisdom.
Most of every moment is a lesson,
Even the ones you don't dig where they're from

I've been there when it was
Suspected by me to be yet to be

Fahamivue x-istance is a space of "Never" And "Forever"
Once I thought I had all the time in the world
Reaching the point when time was eventually "given up."

My mother has a sense of "Unknowingness" that's special
And I love her without conditions for x-isting.
Special out of a context of life's many sources.
Time no longer makes the decisions concerning living.
Eternity forgives me for my slow arrival
Reaching the point of x-specting to receive a clear plan
Inside death there x-ist "Survival"
Now is the only time to live, and to take a stand.
Gather within one self to get the connection

Enter Friend I Love You

Even the ones you don't dig where they're from
    Females continue to profoundly impact me
None remained constantly, Because I was on the run
    Remaining only for an encounter that makes life
The tasks I take on allows me to catch the fleeting
    Enter Friend, into this misspelled world
Enter Friend, into a state where we are one
    Inquire into the discoveries you can chose to Discover
Raising the ante too soon could kill or maim opportunities
    Notice the invitation to be released.
    Decide to x-ist in every moment muchly pleased.

Inquire into the chances of letting go
    Look out for upcoming signs of openness
Yet I'm hesitant about telling her not to block her glow
    Once I attempted to x-ist as less.
Our own selves sabotaged a meaningful step,
    Visit the "space-place" where there's only an Outside
Until you are aware that each moment is a gift
    Entering the kingdom of God can only be tried.

Have The Having

Remaining only for an encounter that makes life Be.
I continue forward toward the life that don't exist yet
Silently humming along with the chirping sparrows glee
Everyone remembers gladness, How can one forget?

Until Never Is Always, Remains the time when we'll end
Pause, to be able to allow the insights to attend

Angels that are guardians are just some of them.
Never settle for answers that are not sought for.
Didn't that sound like crooked advice with a pinch of truth?

Dance to the harmoniously rhythm of the universe
Allow the sources of the "Living" that involves life
Neatly transcends any obstacles that may occur.
Choose to rise up and Dance.
Express the joy of having this life becoming a chance.

Make Lost

Everyone remembers gladness, how can one forget
The sensation is sought after the world over
To have God in your heart sincerely, Serves
A purpose, that follows God's will

To forgive is to accept a cause chosen to negativity affect
To live this true gift, make lost the choice not
                                                                                 To be.

A piece while Dazed

A purpose, that follows God's will
Becomes a serious undertaking in the long run
The stars sometimes whisper their quizzes
When I wonder if loving has begun
Should saints save safe sincerity?

Focusing on dreams seems to be the plan
A plan that was not planned by me
There will never come a time when I'll fully understand
The main source of life's simplicity
Should saints save safe sincerity?

Too much togetherness alone with one's mind
Puts at stake, countless risks of insanity
Truly truly I confess that I seek to find
The main source of life's simplicity
Should saints save safe sincerity?

My Days are presently entangled with some nights
My Daze isn't something I can't deal with
She stilled my heart, Had my mind x-perience many delights
I search for a woman who can become a hit.
Should saints save safe sincerity?

My Misguided Wonderment

When I wonder if Loving has begun
I mix the wonderment with a little wish
  That way, when the insights come
    I won't be caught off guard and ask "What is this?"

Being in management has its perks
What could be downfalls are just possibilities
  Making each reality become" This is it!" come first
    Discovering it's needless to have needs

  When I wonder if Loving has begun
It's a misinterpretation of the context of time.
  The past, Future, And present x-ist as one,
Acknowledging another human quality of mine.

  My sanity's safety continues to get discarded
Done on the sly, Caused by not receiving my full attention.
There has been countless joyful moments I've been awarded
    If asked why, The answer would be "The faith in fiction."

  To encounter in the flesh an angel dreamed of
    Causes such smooth profound vibes of wackiness
    From such realities insights become easy to love
Such moments allow insights to occur very easy to catch.

As she laid beside me dozing off
To a space-place that's endless,
I recited my work so she'll listen with her soul.
She was open to learn when she had only taught,
I asked her for a chance
    She said yes with a pleasure that was bold.

When I wonder if Loving has begun,
    I give up the hope of winning the game
        of Destiny

Totally Absoulute

I won't be caught off guard and ask "What is this?"
I will keep my faith in God at one hundred percent
I will {**Insha Allah**} retain the awareness of truth
And go on living the fast pace of confusion
Only to continue constantly returning to the 1st step

I leaned out the windowsill
To see the truck driving without doors
Just as it was beginning to rain.

I told a girl that I was her old man
She said she wanted a little boy
it's the only time I remember saying "goo-goo gaa-gaa"
With absoulute Joy

Speaking as An Oracle

And go living the fast pace of confusion.
Announcing and proclaiming the testimony of fate.
Never will the truth be forsaken
    Faith is all it will take
    To be able to quit fake-ing.

    I found it
 interesting that she noticed that
                 I was interested in her.
  Being within a "Her" context
     Occurs for me often

  I could be here, then all of a sudden I'm there.
    I tend to lean that way.

  Once lasted, Then once was gone
   Releasing the power to go on
  And I've sought to be left alone.
  Could it be possible, that I won't be
  Literally, able to get what I asked for.
Even the refused freedom consist to appear.

GET FAITH

Faith is not all it will take
To continue along the path of becoming
One with God.

Shrug off the passion to sabotage
the perfect reality that's always Heavon.

Make all of yourself relate
What's Now, and Don't be Bumming
With the Lord.

Having every problem start off solved
Allows one to notice that faith has begun.

Shrug The Shrug

Shrug off the passion to sabotage
The opportunities for possibilities that occurs with consistency
I know what I miss when I don't participate in the world
So don't be concerned about me when I'm not here
For you see "here" is everywhere

An insight caused me to "see" the "here"
Caused the cloudy moments of confusion
To become clear.
If only for a short while.

To decide to destroy an opportunity
Of the path way you go
Allows a context to be withheld for free!
Truly Truly I request you to know.

A moment in time could become a page
In the book that's to the left of them
When you decide on a cloudy day to seek shade
The chances to choose with clues becomes slim

Faith became Sheena, while Joy was still there
A chance encounter that's just kept simple
Sometimes life is a fare to the fair
Maybe it's a way to give permission
To enter the temple

I'm still balancing on the edge
After so many years
To get life I still beg
To have mountains more than hills
It's amazing how we shrug off
The passions of life
You still get "Here" in this space place
Where the service is like paradise.

Even Pleze

So don't be concerned about me when I'm not here.
And pleze don't write a letter to my momma.
Did you hear me say what I said when it was done?
You're my only woman without no other.
Enter the entrance to the dreamish utopian present moment,
And pleze bring along just a hint of your self.
Refine the movements of advancement.
Notice when hope is gone, There's countless other hopes left
I've said in many different ways that I'll always be here.
Now will you pleze let go the safely held fear?
Get yourself some pleasure from the unknown "Out There."
See every insight received as an insight you can share.
Fine residences, cars, and clothes are rarely enlightening.
Remember to pleze provide those thought provoking contributions.
Of all the given away honor, I find spontaneous most frightening.
Made me twice scratch my soul for the solutions.
About me have no worries when you think I'm gone.

I Speak for Truth

You're my only woman without no other
   Now that it's settled, let's move on
I'm talking an "on" that takes it a little further.
   Having the By-gones really get gone.

Look for a retched state behind the prose,
In one condition or another my needs are met.
Without involving the needless abuse of judgment.
   You still remain my only woman without no other.

   You're my only woman without no other
You seem to have my words sing that song.
   Being here in a reality so together,
   Have allowed the By-gones get gone.

Find that thang that x-ist behind the truth!
You'll discover that we're of the same mind.
   Your kind of proof
              Is not in another
     Yea Truth
You're my only woman without no other

Not A Real Cost

Having the By-gones really get gone,
Saves securing the sight to see the seasons of sound.
To put it a different way, and say the same thing;
Let the past be in the minds' part of never
Causing a cure to the cause of crowd's cruelty.

Sometimes it's helpful to just be Here now
You can populate the town of the world
Or the world that's just a town.

Not a page may be saved so the way
                             can be paved
That'll be cool with me
    The source causes me to have no concern
So what now?
It just cost a given Love I so **Y**earn.

Lesson given, learned, digested, and Returned

Let the past be in the mind's part of never.
Like death is to the enlighten ones
Let the love of others get in and remain forever.

Inspiration is never sought for
It's here always,
            That's the fact of the matter,
From within I've given more,
  That includes the praise
                With results I become gladder.

Finally the phase of an era becomes clear,
And just that quick it's a cloudy thing again.
Without a moment's finality ever being "Here"
    Makes one wonder if forever is a sin.

Let the past be in the mind's part of never.
 Of course there's a chaser to the context of
               That's reality's concept.
Visions and dreams can always appear,
Eternity is here to support the letting go
                  of fear.
I've said sometimes in moments of stress
These moments are crazy enough to learn
                How to bless.

love laying hands

Inspiration is never sought for
Sometimes Destiny hides its shocking head.
Lately my words has been rhyming more,
A nice way to say what needs to be said.
I've been famous in a way that's suited for me.
Didn't ask for that rare type of glory.
Well is how good you could be laid.
Enter miss woman upon my tomorrow's scene,
Let the truth be what it could mean.
Lately there's a feeling when ever I felt for you.

Either Way

A nice to say what's need to be said,
Is a way to say what the moment needs.
I somehow think that these poems are important
Who else would cause a thought provoking tease.
I've fooled the world into fooling me,
And recovered a permanent part of myself.
 Still the directions are given in old talk.
  Given for free without being a gift.
When offered, it's received with no fault.
Try to remember that trying is a myth.

A nice way to say what needs to be said,
 Is a way to say what the moment needs.

Who else would cause a thought provoking tease?
Ardently pursuing the wind is a thoughtless act.
Nihilistically given love is sometimes mine.
Discontinuation of a virtue could bring life back.
Extrude the choice to choose and act upon.
Reactions that has a stepping back meaning.
Least-wise my wonder-lust is strong.
Unfit for anyone who only use their eyes to be seeing.
Shell shocked by reasons confounding one another
Testate now is the ideal I gather.
Internationalism, is a state of life I gave up
Scary risks to insanity isn't scary.
Mood swings is different from magnetic ones
Arcane stuff is often the easiest to find
Nix the falsely golden dream that reality shuns,
Death is only an often chosen state of mind.
Acknowledge the reaction to be free
Titillate the way as a possibility
Obscene interjected obstacles can come
Rip-roaring along, and you still chose to be strong.
Yore; was a time when you was mine.

Everything Have An Easy

Discontinuation of a virtue could bring life back.
Sometimes "letting go" doesn't have a lessening effect.
To choose to live without growth is not God's will.
Remember that "Everything" I mean "Everything" is perfect.

    I have a heavy hand because of a
                  Heavy ink pen.
    Un-x-perienced in ceasing, I wonder how it is to
                  Begin again.
    Radiating with reasons, is an obstacle's trick.
    Obstacles x-ist to simply imitate the truth.
     Speak for yourself!
                  That's what I'm doing now.
  These words can be touched as a gift.
     I'll have the insight gotten somehow.
When I say "This Is It!" I mean this is it.

It is here. The request to give me a chance,
Everyday I cleanse myself up for our date tomorrow
That doesn't mean we're be strangers
                When we dance
We'll just be the cause of a lot less sorrow

I often step back to attack the senselessness
It's a trip, having dreams to protect.
Still I ask"Are you there for me?"
Remember that "**Everything**" I mean "**Everything**" is perfect.

  I, like many others..knock the though of you
        Around and around in my mind.
   Sometimes I am, Sometimes I'm not
                Such a folksy person.
  If I just write the words I seek to find
    I'll draw a huge amount
             from the account.
   I have with the Bank of the Universe.

As easy as a changed thought,
    Is the choice of a different reality.

in "Arcane-ish" Ofcourse.

REMEMBER THAT EVERYTHING I MEAN EVERYTHING IS PERFECT.
Even words that are screwed up and hard to understand.
I attempt to always have that be my state of mind's foundation
I slip and stagger but I somehow get straight again

**Remember that there are no, I mean none at anytime
No accidents, mistakes, or truths that are simply wrong.
I put forth an effort to embrace the sun's shine.
I often get the urge for that effort,
The urge comes strong.**

Remember who you are before you made yourself up
Be aware of everything, including that whispering voice.
Gather the truth and remember there's never enough.
Don't stifle the power provided by the source.

Slip to Trip

I slip and stagger but I somehow get straight again
I lean into the breeze caused by life's x-istance.
I pause on the path while I seek it's end
I'm somehow empowered to go the distance.

I slip and stagger but I somehow get straight again
Put back or more like placed back upon steady ground
A helping hand is here, All I need to do is ask.

Sometimes my ending seems undramactic
And I endure the boredom.
I surprise myself how I endure it with such grace.
Sometimes I'm just too cool.

My Friends support

I'm somehow empowered to go the distance.
To go beyond the usual rationale norm.
When I go along with a plan unforeseen in my wildest dreams,
The insights are welcomed as they are willed upon me.
When I've been presented with profound possibilities
I've come close to panicking
Yet I never have...my faith has kept me strong.

Don't misunderstand my intentions with these words
For they can only relate to you as much as I want.
With the vast amount, people attempt to count,
Then look at me as if it was all my fault.

Wisdom is faultless when chosen to direct
Each word is on it's on
My Nation has many houses.
I often step out side the path that's been set
Me and wisdom's relationship has grown
As I seek the truth in the causes.

Those Darn insights

The insights are welcomed as they are willed upon me.
I set up all kinds of risks,
                As if they were gifts.
The picture of my tomorrows has become abstract.
Yet I go forward without knowing
                            Where my next step will end.

The insights are welcomed as they are willed upon me.
They are welcomed very sincerely. For true.
I decided long ago to just go with the flow of God's will.
When there's an opportunity for the possibility to be chosen
                          What else is there to do?

The insights are welcomed as they are willed upon me
I've taken all the causes for actions, come what may,
"No matter what may come." Is what I should say.
The needless obstacles has no cost
                            They are free.

The insights are welcomed as they are willed upon me.
They have a reception that has my state of mind
                            become so graciously.
It's the only way I have life to be.

The insights are welcomed as they are willed upon me!
  I use up the upcoming days to provide for more.
  How can I keep it up, and remain sane?
  How? When it has never worked in my many lifetimes
                                          Before?
  Can I desire freedom that x-ist outside the bounds,
  And remain the same. The x-actly sameone?
  I've wondered if my petitions for insanity
                      has had grounds,
  To be reason enough to leave me alone.

  The insights are welcomed as they are willed upon me.
   I think it's necessary for those words to be repeated.
  Only between lifetimes can one truly be free.
   Even if one put in what is needed.

  This life is a trip in more ways than one.
   I wouldn't mind being crazy without all the fuss.
   I may not ever be reminded the job got done
  All I've ever cared about is us.
                                      Dig?

She Shares Reality.

The pictures of my tomorrows has become abstract.
I'm not saddened by that. Neither am I surprised.
As far as surviving, it seems as if I have a knack.
When I go insane I somehow manage to find a new mind.
It doesn't take courage to be a fool for wisdom.
Not knowing the cause and still taking a stand,
It's like jumping out of an airplane without a parachute,
          And also not knowing where you'll land.
I haven't written a love poem
          Because I haven't been in the mood.
Could it be because there has been no one,
          That can prevent me from being that fool?

I feel that the end of this era is coming soon
So I share with you words from me that's urgent.
I still wish to share with you, my essential self
It seems for that to be, is not meant.
I don't know the finale accomplishment with these words,
    More than likely I'll never know it.
    To pen these words, I had to visit different worlds,
    My enjoyment wasn't considered, but it was had,
    Even when insanity happens every now and then
     I still continue to step forward along the path.
     I must admit life hasn't been bad.

Some may have mistaken my good deeds as if I've
>really done good.
And interpret my bad deeds as if they were
>really bad.
When it just depends on the person at the moment.
And I find some folks are amazed
>By my work.
And I say to myself
>"They'll get over it."

When Should You ?

When I go insane I somehow find a new mind
It's not because of the freedom of the choices
Inspired by the many possibilities.
It's because of a smoothness of perfection
The kind that allows what you know
To become the truth of your world

I may never cease to wonder about my amazement
Of the simple perfection of every "Now" possible.
And within the "Nows'" if I should get stuck
Should I give a fuck
        If I don't know about the concept
                      Of Luck?

Should You?

I mean should you really recognize yourself.
Your hidden self that's self hidden.
That self. Yea. That self.
                Within Me?
Would you show love.
Should You?

True....But

It's because of a smoothness of Perfection
You become a new world in an old universe.
If you was spoken about I don't remember.
Why can't we ride the breeze of the turbulent wave of the present?
We can touch, even when there's no connection.
The Love. Yea the love was a blessing you cursed.

Too many words can sometimes **d**isport the real **M**eaning
See what I mean....or is it
                              Do you think my sight.

Living those moments with you
  Those moments when you're real
    And new again and again
It's like the moments of my BirthDay.

Words are simple because they are what they are.
I Love You...oh..yea....Simple words..
        True.....But,Simple.

Let and Let's go

Why can't we ride the breeze of the turbulent wave of the present?
      Sometimes questions can be said.
Why can't we live in a world where normality is reality "Bent."
      There's been Believer that's been mislead.

      There I was, More exhausted than the one level
below, which is very tired. Sitting on the rock looking
at her. I asked her to hold my hand all the
way back to the car. She acquiesced. We walked
back and about 30 minutes later I asked her
how did that feel. She replied "sweaty" She said it
with a smile. I was intending for her to
feel a feeling.

When I've wittiness most waves whipping on,
 It's easily understood how I could
 Contextualize the stir in the air
                Caused by those waves,
 As feeling like a breeze I've felt more times
                         Than a few.
Only the Boxes change.
 The Boxes that within you've placed your Life.
 The Boxes can't Be shared. So move.

I have a friend that when she goes away
    within her private universe
She's silent towards anyone around.
Yet her vibes gleams so much
    One can almost feel their touch.

Ride baby, Ride that breeze, Pleze
That will simply allow us not to get lost
    within the influential opinions
        of others.

Ride and don't watch the waves go by.
Let go, and Let's go.

Been Believed

   There has been believers that's been **M**islead
    Believers believing by thinking the thoughts of others
 I'm so tired of waking with her screaming in my head
   Talking about she's gonna Die
              Because she believed in me.

 One's fate occurs despite one's Faith
  Within the ways that things are
  Life is coexisting with complexity.

     Every once and a while I have thought
      I've finally thought myself
                    Out of the world.
     I've believed that sometimes.

Little Bit bout Mom

Talking about she's gonna **D**ie
That doesn't happen within
              My Life's state of mind.
I know her as the gift that gave me life.
Having it be forever that we are a part of each other.
Brings about Joy in having the freedom to
              Choose the choice to x-ist within
A love, one that glows brighter than
              A hundred sunshines.
It's not the outside..
    it's the other side that she have moved onto.
I know that Ngozi will always be here with me.

She taught me that even an everyday occurrence
Like the birth of a flower can be celebrated.
In her own speechlessly shouted way
Made me live Life not taking chances.
Take a stand. Make a stand. Live the stand taken.

Little Bit More bout Mom

I know her as the gift that gave me life.
Lately she's been disguised when she's appeared
                          In my dreams.
Just revealing Life in another manner.
Sometimes she made me perceive in levels that
goes deeper than the here and now.
Levels beyond the sights of what's thought
                          to be seen.
Being within those levels the impacts are profound.
Being impacted from truly getting the true truth.

I know her as the gift that gave me **L**ife.
The acknowledgement of her priceless **G**ift
And my complete thankfulness for providing
                         This priceless gift of life.
was spoken only with voicelessly silent actions,
That yelled the gratitude from my soul.
Just revealing sharing in another manner.

There was a few times when we talked.
talked conversational wise.
Majority of those times occurred
When it was truly known she'll be moving on
                         Moving on to the otherside.

One lesson taught, when I speak
                    of the heart,
when speaking about the heart of the matter.
   Discovering from that lesson, the strong
   Possibility that majority of the source
   That provides life to the essence
   of life that allows the existence of
   truth that's the foundation of the
   Heart of the matter. That majority
   is as strong as one's mind.
      →Something like that. <----
Briefly clearly speaking in another manner.

I KNOW HER AS THE GIFT THAT GAVE ME
                              LIFE.

Going to Become

Just revealing Life in another manner
 When one commit to master the
  art of contributing. Manners are meaningless.
We were photographed twice. Once
 When I was a kid, the other when I was
 about 22. The first one showed me clearly
 expressing my confusion about my embracing
 this stranger. The other shows me smiling
from pure joy of embracing this Beautiful
Human Being that is my mother.

   It's important to recognize that I've
    Never completed a book in this way.

   Just revealing Life in another manner.

CHAPTER EIGHT
From A Heap Of Spare Space

written, edited, and designed
By
Gibuyu

The Introduction

Earlier today I decided to sit down and work on the couple of projects I'm in progress of writing. I wrote a couple lines of poetry, just stared at my speech, and traced faintly over the folks wanting their picture drawn.

I couldn't fit into any of my projects contexts. It suddenly occurred to me that if I couldn't fit in, I should just remain where I'm at and somehow, somewhere continue with my purpose to write.

The pages of this project has been outlined for a few years now. I placed them in my "working on" notebook for future use. I knew that one day in the distant future I would make something of these pages. I didn't know it'll come so soon.

Ghuy
Peace and love

Table of Contents.

1.) I recall her
2.) Are You the you?
3.) Get the chance
4.) And be here now.
5.) Keep this
6.) Being For
7.) The way of decisions
8.) A Child's Lesson
9.) i should think more often
10.) If this is the Blessing.
11.) Affirm idealized Chances
12.) ~~Steven Simmons~~
13.) Gikuyu C. W.
14.) Saying What's Said Safely
15.) From a source barely seen.
16.) A Pause Piece
17.) Don't Die Pleze!
18.) Soon Seen Truth
19.) Don't Consider Me Blind
20.) Some reasons of me
21.) Us with A Here.
22.) Breaking It down.
23.) Fahamivu II
24.) A Lie From My Pride
25.) Just Yet
26.) With Life
27.) Awareness within a context
28.) What can You do?
29.) A Content Contentment
30.) just like i

I recall her.

The confounding connections caused contemplation
Highlighting our own realitie's flaws
Barely managing our affairs adequately
Our survival is from the grace of God

  I often wonder how it would be
If you were still here by my side
I guess I can only experience that joy
                             In a dream
I guess I can only see you again
                    Only in my mind.

I have a female friend that makes her smile
               Show up as a cliché.
The air becomes electrified when she's around
            It's really something to see.
It's a high form of naturalism.

Are You the you?

If love was a rainbow, you'll be color blind
You allow opportunities to go up in smoke
You befriended me in an unchristian manner
Confusion has become a tie-in with my sanity
Provide a pinch of hope, with a sprinkle of passion
My Nobleness has been captured secretively
My sense of importance has been somewhat mollified
When it comes to loving you, I've never been such a hot-shot
When you frown, my heart gets a headache
Our conversations has been brusquely
You have done your finales to many times
An ode like this is old to me
I hope when the times comes, love will be furbished
The pleas for pity was pleasantly pushed away
I fervently request that you get some sight

G. Kings

Get the chance

The late night stars may be in sight many times.
    Still.... They can only bee seen once.
I produce projects that can be choosen,
        to get gotten Profoundly.

I often fake a "leaving" like I've done gone.
So I can give a joful impact,
        when I falsely return.

I've leaned out far so I can start
        to jump off the edge of sanity.
Each time I've been put back in my place,
    By the slight breeze of the space of grace.

The cultures of my world is often my own.
    Still..... They can only be seen once.
I produce poems, plays, speechs, novels, and what-nots,
So that victory can become the possibility of chance.

And be here now.

The feeling of the devastating pain
    was nothing compared to the feeling
I felt when you told me that I had let you down.
By truthing when it comes to this involving love,
    we've been able to surpass our dreamed of pasts

Don't be afraid to love another.
For you are another that is loved
                    to others.
You can be an amazement at any time.
If that is so, do you think you can ever
              become fully mine?

Our wondrous encounter was simply great.
I once was often driven to appear.
Your love has given me faith in fate.
I wish a painless life could be here.

                            Gikuys

Keep this

I tend to venture within the otherside,
    just a touch too much.
I seem to be willing to lose my mind,
    Still.... That can only be witnessed once

So I find a kind of friend
    in a lonely type of mood.
Should I let my friend remain there?
Letting disempowerment be contrived.

I could be a dastard or a saint
The choke of understading who I am
    Is up to you.

Right now, this moment has
    come and gone.
Have the praises and contributions be kept.
    Kept to remain strong.

Being For

This compelling reoccurring sense to asks again,
Has reoccurred a bit too many times.
I'll simply ask again, hopefully for the final time
Simply asks "Do you ever think of me?"
  Is the start so hard to begin?
  Stop hesitating and pausing with your love.
For the time is here now to open your heart,
Opening up to receive the passion of life.
Receiving the totality of a confusing contribution.
 My life has been one long quick trip.
 Yet I'm still finding it easy to give-up.
Life is like a thick thick door.
Is like the door at the entrance to eternity.
Facilitate the way that has miracles happen more.
Ease the chance along the path of possibility.

Giksy

A ~~Kid~~ ~~Kid~~ Child's Lesson

A couple of days ago
This girl whos ~~is~~ almost 5 years old
Bothered me until I agreeded to photograph her
        with an imaginary camera.
She said she was willing to have candy be the fee.
I took her picture with ~~as~~ my hands as the lens.
The candy paid for that service
        Also was imaginary.

So I acted like the candy made me
        spit up.
The wrong flavor, is the reason I gave her.
I would accept it, and reject it.
I did it atleast a dozen times.
Until she tasted the candy,
    did she know ~~I~~ she had it right.

                    Gikuyu

i should think more often

When i think of you
    You become my world.
Not only my world,
    You become my universe, my ~~galaxy~~
    You become my All of everything.
Thinking of you makes me question
    The belief of all the dreams
      that I've wished to come true.

When I think of you
    You're no longer a little girl.
A little girl
    that I had a crush on long ago.
You become the possible source
    of the dreams,
    that I've wished to come true

        6/15/05

If this is the Blessing.

And I accept you, as you are.
I do not consider the cost.
I'm thinking that we're gonna go far,
With the moments others have found lost.

I've mentioned before how she felt
That sometimes my poems to females
                    seems the same.
I've also said before, that
          I state my Love,
     even if it turns out Lame.

I could deal with our love,
   If this is the Blessing.
I'll be 100% beside you,
If truth is the source of the lesson,
And if "doubt" can be the concession.

Steven ~~Simmons~~

If you know me as you think you know me,
    You know so little.
I'm there x-isting just as a visitor to your reality.
    You know so little.
When I'm there within the "here" of your life,
    And you're believing that who I am is all of me,
I hold most of myself away,
    And I pay a price;
Sometimes contributions aren't given for free.

If you know me as you think you know me,
    You know so little.
I'm there with you in your world to be able
    to become an answer
        to your life's riddle.
And it's okay to know so little.

Gibury

Gikuyu C. W.

Getting to know me more,
    To know me more than you think you know me.
Invites an inescapable way
    of having truth become with no fee.
Knowing me, has it's risks.
    has it's curses and gifts.
Until there's an absoluteness about your love
    Your love for me...
Your love for me will only skim the surface,
    Barely skim the surface of reality.
Understanding my poetry, novels, essays and what nots.
    is really a minuscule part in getting to know me.
Comprehension of the whole of me, in one single lifetime,
    is an impossible Possibility.
WORLD?!.. Can you hear me?

                                          Gikuyu

Saying What's Said Safely

Mourning for the cessation of my life this lifetime,
Is the incorrect type of an acknowledging expression.
Awesomely, and profoundly the celebration should be,
For what seems like death, is really a promotion.

There was a somewhat huge payoff for my insanity.
It will last until the day following eternity.
A payoff with a cost that's totally my responsibility.
Causing the moments to refuse to participate in dipping.
Miraculous insights, and dangerous discoveries,
Are happenings happening with intensity.
A heady happening that will occur continuously.

It is easy to listen to me when you see what I'm saying.
When I say "What's Happening?" I want the details of the "What's."
I don't mean it when I speak good-bye because I want you to get what is said.
I still refuse a threshhold that can be crossed safely.

From a source barely seen.

realities can never have a curfew
    If that is the case,
The chances for risks becomes
           more than two.
I'm aware of the mass space
        that surrounds my universe
Even the space I don't know, I don't know about.
The space that's there
        Is contextualized as spare.

This project is from a heap of spare space.
These words are placed here
        some-what on the sly.
This is from the same source.
The source around the bend,
The one I see from the corner of my eye.

Don't Die Pleze!

I have consistently choosen actions
That would more than likely lead to
                                my self destruction.
I've sought to embrace the distractions;
So that I'll be able to be cool
                                with this resurrection.

My strong belief in the universe's perfection.
                    has been profoundly shaken
For the 1st time in 15 years, everything is not alright.

Living this life as a writer,
                My sanity has been forsakened.
A dimness has come to join my tomorrows
    my yet to be days that was just bright.

Laugh, Cry, ... Don't Die!
            Don't Die Pleze.

                                        Gikuy J

Soon Seen Truth

I briefly caught her as she sneaked a peek at me,
with a look as if she was concerned
                              if we'll be meeting soon.
I quickly placed my smile back inside my mind,
    I didn't want to provide so soon the clues
        that would lead her to discover who I am.

I caught that glimpse of her soon after the distressing thought,
That this place in the world where I'll soon reside
    Is void of all other ones of which I can relate.
Her quick appearance provided the spark
That rekindled my failing faith in fate.

What may seem like a dangerous twisted curve
                        in the path of life,
could really be seen as a slight simple bend.

I've begun to question what's behind the truth that's revealed.

Don't Consider Me Blind

I may at times see my poetry as serious litanies,
Still there's nothing Morby about the messages.
I have meant my words to hearten.
Still I'm misunderstood as a mere writer.

The many hazards I've encountered and overcame
is meaningless when I think of my future.
Life seems to revitalize the rebuilding of the injured self,
That has occurred when I'm not sure.

I contribute solely from a truthish defensemechanism
Eryptions of my "Her" and only " Love Are no irruptions

If you think that I'm not attentive to your propraganda,
It's not so. For I have choosen to nag your mind.
Her not being here, doesn't mean I couldn't find her.
So whatever you may come to think of me
                Don't consider me blind.

Some reasons of me

World news is old news, when it becomes news to me.
I've given up 3 careers in the previous 4 months.
And I thought I had a plan for stability.

There won't be a useless cause for a needless pause,
if I just continue to put in what's missing.
When a "space-place" shifts,
        I must keep my position.

My abrupt departures makes me seem the villian
They're not caused by reasons, but a feeling.
I live a life that that rejects the choice
               to be unwilling.

I've presented my contributions with clarity
But they are recieved with a hint of deception
They may have been given idiosyncraticly
They're still given with affection.

Some reasons of me

World news is old news, when it becomes news to me.
I've given up 3 careers in the previous 4 months.
And I thought I had a plan for stability.

There won't be a useless cause for a needless pause,
if I just continue to put in what's missing.
When a "space-place" shifts,
        I must keep my position.

My abrupt departures makes me seem the villain
They're not caused by reasons, but a feeling.
I live a life that that rejects the choice
                to be unwilling.

I've presented my contributions with clarity
But they are recieved with a hint of deception
They may have been given idiosyncraticly
They're still given with affection.

                                      Gikuyu

U's with a Here.

Our purpose existed in a grizzly shade of state
"The preacher" and others acknowledged wisdom
          twenty-nine hundred years ago

Etchings from countless moments are upon the soul
Living to be truthing with only oneself
Allows a different cost for each told

Our conversations is diaphanous with all that background
In that "space-place" called eternal love
Requests can be made to have one stroll around.

I've chased hope up and down the proverbial coast
Faith was chosen over back by a clear margin.
It wasn't even close, not even an almost.

The false faith is harder to achieve than the real thing
Answers are different truths in a different scene.
And you've become the answer to what I mean.

Breaking it down.

When payments are given freely
    They are considered favors so.
Although it's settled up, Remember this
    Remember this gift.

When it comes to picking a reality
    I choose between this and that
Sometimes pure truth isn't concerned with stability
It just steps up, and doesn't look back.

Every time I've given my word
    I've sincerely meant it to be kept.
Spontaneous promises made are mostly absurd
    But that can't be helped.

To be involved in the laughter at so seemed pain
    Has the truth of reality.
    You can pick which is true.

Fahamive II

As I crossed the bridge on the way home 15 years ago
I saw her walking with her kid on the road below
She was a woman that didn't fit the norm
Me, being who I am, she was a lot more real to me.
The thought of "who'll her daughter will become?"
                                    might have crossed my mind.

One of the first few people I encountered
of my 1st few days once again in the "Free World"
was a young woman with her realness together
I wasn't really surprised when she told me
                    she was the woman's daughter.

After Fahamive gave hugs to the eager pre-teen brothers
She caught my gesture for my ~~request~~ Feyjest for one
She's here in my world, without the reasons of others
I Love her, and you may never see where I'm coming from.

                                            GiBorys

A ~~Lie~~ Lie From My Pride

Awed by some of the costs of my actions, I have been.

Lots of times I've been tempted to choose giving-up.
I find it easy to be involved with
Endless impossible crazy situations, and I survive.

Fuddling the cornerstone of clarity's foundation
Recognize the real truth amongst all the ~~est~~ rest
Otiose reasons waits in the wings ready to pounce
Meanwhile you exist as if this life is a test.

Most of something isn't All of Anything
Yet I've considered myself so so Alone.

Payoffs for unforeseen sins that are done,
Radically empowers the arguments for fantasies.
I await the consequential click,
Don't dance with just a "please?"
Expectancles are always worth the action.

G. Boyer

Just Yet.

So far it's been just about 159 days
And the exBtance that's now has come upon me,
Sort of reminds me of the days of yore.
I attempted to convince myself it was just a phase,
by acknowledging that fact that where you are is where you be
I'm glad I didn't know that before.

My abilities has a defense against rustyness
There's no one in particular I seeks to bless.

I strive to find a world of which I'll fit
I've made contributions be in a style that'll stick.

if i find a wife during this lifetime
it would be worth much more than the
                 cost of the life I have spent.
I could carelessly survive this life of mine
       if I'll just repent.

                                   Gilroy

With Life

With Life, I may get along just fine.
That doesn't mean that my path is paved.
I faithfully clutch to this confusion of mine.
For I know of many that's lost and are saved.
I've feared God once upon a time,
That's when I believed I had it made.
Sacrificed sanity cannot be replaced with the same kinds
It's the space on the otherside that I've craved.
I retain all of that life that may seem left behind,
I'm showing up more when it seems that I fade.
These words are not here just to add a line,
Ruthless compassion is the name of the game I've played.

With Life, are the contributions I provide.
I go that way, only to find I've gone this way.
I scarely hang on here, with Life.

Gibuys

Awareness within a context

What I do today is all there is
I really don't know the outcome of my actions
I don't bother questioning what is this
The insightful gifts comes in different styles
                                    and fashions

Working for the universe is great
I've become aware of that I can choose my fate

Don't think I'm my past or what is yet to be.
If I'm still curious about myself
                How can you ever know me?

I've been filled with a sense of eternalness,
and I remain here in this world simply by choice.

Do you thinks you can allow these words to contribute?

I always find a cause to keep living
I'll be gone if I ever get the feelings

What can You do?

If I think about the time I've spent,
I discover the way toward my true self.
The price I pay is the opportunity to repent,
When I've required Anarchy to be unkept.

If I begin to question the validity of the pay offs,
It'll be like my faith isn't grounded enough.
If I choose to exist in life as if I'm lost,
There's a chance of not finding what I've sought.

If I start to go the otherway than I'm going,
What little revealed progress will have been shown for nothing.
Then it'll be useless to be belonging,
to the joy that contributial gifts bring.

All I've really said with these many words
Is simply "I Love You."
If I live like that, what can you do?

A Content Contentment

I've traveled countless I've experienced
                              within the papers.
I've risked all kinds of life needing stuff.
   Still I strive to be like my maker
I should be able to get gone and leave this world
                    without a fuss.

I have at times just sat back with a certain openness
And waited on the possibilities to simply show up.
I don't know where I'm going or where I truly come from.
I've been told I was a saint,
         I've been told I was a nut.

I've done countless ~~this and that~~ This and that
         In alot of that and this ways.
   I long for the coming afterwards
       And seek to be content without the praise.

                              Gihugu

just like i

it's like I can't claim most of the words I've written,
to do so would seem to be a cheating way
       to let you know myself.
i'm just repeating what I've said before
       in another way. Dig?

it seems like the twists and bends
       of this current lifetime of mine,
aren't concerned with safely containing my sanity.
i'm just once again letting you know where I stand,
       with different but the same words. Dig?

it seems like there will not be any brief breaks,
       i've had no time to rest,
       could go on untill I'm gone.
i'm just x-pressing one of the countless causes of my actions
       in a fashion other than normally. Dig?

       Peace And Love!

CHAPTER NINE

THE
2ND
CHAPTER
OF
CHASING THE SUN

MECCA'S ODE

I'm in love with Mecca, she allows peace within my soul.
Made tranquility overwhelm my space, like when one's in that place
I've been given the freedom to become whole.
Now and forever, and for sure, eons before I remember
Love for Mecca was woven in the fabric of my Being.
Once and a while there's forest fires that starts with just an ember
Verily, Verily I say unto to you, My love for Mecca is profound, yet tender
Evidence is at times sought after, to confirm and comfort beliefs
when truth is the truth that comes along with you like your DNA
I'm in love with Mecca, she's sort of like all the visionz of my dreams
To tell you the truth, sometimes truth's reality may not always be what it seems
Hevon for me would be a simple embrace, and being with her smile
Maybe it'll take another lifetime to get together a while.
Each prayer I whisper in my mind, Iz for Mecca iz for Mecca
Clues of a curse.. that each lifetime, chances of love getz a little better
Caution. Once one choose to open their eyez
And be wittiness to the light,
Sometimes they think they're not ready, and
Instead wish to return to the night..
My Love for Mecca, iz a discovered source of my life
Only the universe provide the accomplishment of my plight.
Now and even before then, I will, and I have strived that life and joy get together
Eternity may decide not to exist forever,

But never, Never, My Love For Mecca

Note to self

Guessing of my knowledge of 43
I think there'z a chance it'z real.
Knowledge isn't always'z free
Until one movez on.
You know
Ultimately the truth comes along

Chapter 2 – Fruitful Wish

Begun 8-7-07   10:07pm

I will, I will, I will attain my awareness, my knowledge, and my wisdom somewhat. My connection. I will more like retain, rather than attain. All that is already with me, within me, all of that is essentially me myself. I will recognize the signs of the always occurrence of disconnection.

Yea yea I know I've said this mantra over and over again countless times when I've begun my entry countless times.. I guess it'z it's one of those eurge that'z truly natural. I go thru this every time and yet I haven't discovered the secret to keep it.

I wonder how far along I am. I feel like an eight week old skinbag. Around that sense. This time I'm gonna plan y journey now. And instill it deep within my inner self, so that when ever that dreaded disconnection comes, I will do this journey, and get the lesson learned.

Okay the first truth I need to maintain and in still here is that whatever may come, Be the truth by any meanz necessary. The truth that I am not this skinbag This is only a journey I chosen to take. And this time the lesson I'm here to learn iz, well this time I'm really doing this journey to learn a lesson, more like to experience a sense of being. I haven't whole heartedly been loved by any so called human beingz of whom I've been born. For some reason or another that has nevered occurred, it's never really affected my past journeyz. {or lifetimez} for it waz never needed to learn the particular lessons I choose to learn. Yet I do wonder why I chose to choose to have this journey only to experience this one sensation. Oh well, there's an old saying that there's some tangents that some has **gone on, that they may never go on journeyz again.**

Why iz it that after all of my countless journeyz, I'm aware of being my trueself, quicker that a nanosecond after I've existed my skinbag, and I'm aware of my true self during the start of my journey, yet only when I'm my trueself and the reasonz behind t hat, yet I can't bring along with me the ability to never disconnect. I know it's possible.

I wonder and briefly ponder once more why the memories of my previous journeyz occur, as reminders of how the lessons was gotten. I wonder and ponder briefly what it takes to be ables to just get beyond the cause, and be the lessonz gotten. Maybe the time will come, when I'll just be able to start that journey by just be every lessonz learned from every journey. First of all I know I must let go any belief in time. Time is just residue of myth that has stuck with me, caused by repeatedly choosing to return again and again within a skinbag. I'm hooked on taking journeyz, what can I say. {that'z another x-sample of the effect of journeying. I've use their language of the skinbaggerz of the time.} it'z a simple way of thought, Yet I know that "time" can not be conceptualize and put in a box. So to speak.

There'z many otherz that journeyz every so called 100 years or so. Yet most decide not to journey within a skinbag st all. They have choosen to grow by other meanz. I wish that I could during one journey, enlighten all the onez who'z journeying with me, how to connect with their true self. Despite the opinion of those that think that that's a fruitful wish. For those who has kindly shared with me the fact that this particular Journey. (this one where one sends a piece of one'z essential self into a skinbag.) is meant for learning purposes only, and not true awareness of our true selves. I know deep within that there'z nothing in the universe to prevent this awareness, other than choice. It's the freedom to choose that's really blocking all those skinbaggerz from awareness

The ending to what is referred to as a lifetime, a couple of those ago, I don't remember when. More than five lifetimez, less than ten. I remember being strapped to an uncomfortable small bed. For a period of what'z considered months. Being infused with foreign chemicals that was meant to control me wholly. Mind, My skinbag, and my soul. The fluid only controlled my body really. I remember that, during that journey I retained my awareness, yet due to my sharing it with others, caused them to place me in a secluded place with soft walls. Somehow I couldn't communicate the truth correctly, Yet I do remember after that non-a-second after returning to my true self, that the major lesson learned…{cause that particular journey waz made with a "taking a vacation" state of mind.}Out of all the lessons learned. The major one was that there are sometimes long stretches of time "Yearz maybe" that skinbaggerz are knowingly or maybe unknowingly agree to remain in the dark. Remain disconnected.

I wonder and I ponder still, what was the lessonz from the more than a few "lifetimes" when I returned without anything that wasn't already a part of my true self. Thos timez when there wazn't even a reminder or restrenghtening of my true being. I wish I could just get a hint, some small clue of those journey'z purposes. Well I guess it'z just natural to have fruitful wishes. The truth that there will always be thingz that I will may never know that I don't know could possible be true, is hard to choose to accept.

During this period of reentry I sort of x-perince the sensation of what the skinbaggerz call excitement. I remember being in this place-space at the start, I remember striving to maintain this awareness again and again. Many Many times. Yet that the moment of disconnection is a mystery to me. Maybe it'z because I return too much. Who knowz. Although I've heard from those who knowz. Their many opinionz and what notz. Yet I guess I'm just what the skinbaggerz call hard headed…

Uhm….It'z interesting that I am… how'z it said?.... that I'm so used to, or like become accustom to uhm. "thinking" my thoughts in the language of my carrier. My mother so to speak. My mother. I have to start relating to my female carrier az my mother. Even though I've never been concerned really with the Mother/son {and somtimez daughter}relationship. That's never been a part of the lessons of any of all my journeyz. This time it iz. Totally. I guess she speaks and thinks in english. She may at times speak other languages, I'll find out. So far though, the few many sells she'z provided for me so far, only allows me to "think" my thoughts in English. There'z something missing. Ohm. What is it. I'm here.. so it's not my awareness of this start of my journey…..

The connection. Yea the..what's the description… the spiritual connection between the carrier and the carry-ree.. I don't think she knows I'm coming yet. Hold on…. Yep.. I don't feel her being. I'm awake first.. Wow. That doesn't happen often. Usually it'z the carrier.. "Mother'z" consciousness that has me to become aware. This iz a perfect opportunity to become a somewhat "perfect" so to speak one, before my Mother is aware of me. Whenever she becomes aware of my existence I'll be in-tuned a little bit mire with her being.

I wonder and ponder briefly why I've started this Journey within the box. Right off the back.. What iz it that'z imbedded inside these cellz that runz through this embryo that has already has me having thoughts that speakz in terms of time. Thinking that there's really a space of time that'z " Briefly"

Yet it's also interesting how I'm starting off this life time, not all over the place within my mind. How clear I've awaken here with a purpose. It seems that I'm on the correct path to getting the lesson learned in a way that will profoundly my true self when I get back. Still I know that sometimes the universe has a strange sense of humor. So to speak.

Those timez when I discovered when I was going to be a mother. Even though each time I sort of expected it, or sort of expected it, each time the moments of realization were different. I retained somewhere deep within myself, that bearing children were part of my life's lesson. What if she's lie the many countless women I've known, like all the women I've been borne unto. Like those who's unaware of the necessity to provide the needz of the one's borne unto them. Uhm. I wonder and once again find it interesting why it has recently occurred to me to live a life time only to experience being loved wholeheartedly by the one which I've been born. One of the sayingz that has just occurred to me "life is lived to learn." Then I remember that so far as I know I've existed what is considered by the skinbaggerz as forever.

    I will, I will, as of now. Establish within my Being the truth that time iz not containable. Time has no place being thought of a space that can fit within concept. I will establish this truth within the cornerstone of my Being. My Being that will live life during this current lifetime. Disconnections or not. I will know that wordz like "Now" "Past" "Future" are just6 wordz used to put time within a context, yet time is just a word to conceptualize a sense of being like I've put myself inside this skinbag again. Also whatever I decided to show up as this time, this lifetime, It will allow me to get a lesson profoundly gotten, which will impact my true self in such a way that I'll able to let go of my seemingly addiction that I seem to have with being in a skinbag.

    Maybe I'll be able to get all those others understanding about the true reasonz the skinbaggerz decide to become disconnected. May be I'll discover the purpose of why when most of us are in a skinbag we somehow or another become disconnected. I could easily inquire of those that has journeyed in a skinbag that has a heck of a lot them connected,

Yet they're the one'z that shows up every now and then. I guess I'm one of those "Hard headed" essential onez that knowz that{once again I'm reminding my self- sort of steeling myself still.} there's some way to provide the contribution of power to give every human being the choice to receive the enlightenment that will have them to see that there's no disconnection really.

    I told her I was a gypsy, then she was suddenly out of my life. What was her name? when was that?. Okay, okay hold on, that life has nothing to do with this one. Stay focused. As much as you can. Focus while you can. This lesson is big. Remember this time, I'm gonna take back a lesson that will have me true self reeling from the impact. Mecca. Her name was Mecca.. I wish it was allowed to meet each other over there. Yea whatever lesson I learned from that lifetime, Falling in Love and having one'z heat broken was a part of it; that waz one hell of a life. Latin, I wish I was speaking and thinking in Latin now. I wish a Love like the one I discovered within myself could occur more often during these lifetimez. Yet those are the chances of the times. I wonder, I ponder how many fruitful wishes I have.

Remember that there are dangers when one is borrowing what is called "time" from the "Future". Because even though that allows you to continue to "Be" in the present, it also shortenz your path. Your destined exit. Remember when you're borrowing time you are actually taking away time. Or to say "Borrowing" isn't free. So therefore any "time" you decide to borrow, use it well. Remember, actually make that reminder another truth within my Being. Within the cornerstone of the foundation of my being during this lifetime.

    Even though she was saying good bye to me, her smile was of absolutely joy.. what was her name? no so-called time to wonder about that. What was her smile for. Why now do I recall her joyful Good-bye smile. That lifetime was sort of simple and cool with me.

Wow I remember once that I had a quick flashback once when I was in some history that described the era as the dark agez. I remember living in those "dark ages" as a simple man. Just providing whatever I could. I waz a grocer, or trader, or sorts. She waz the daughter of a farmer. We was great friends. I don't recall the detailz of that lifetime, like what went on day to day. I've sort of become "accustomed" to how many lifetime lessons are gotten by the occurrencez that's had the effectz of purpose. Do remember the experience of a solid soul connection whenever I first encountered her. We skipped the introductionz, the getting to know each other, even falling in love. We just instantly became soul matez.

For some reason or another we waz meant to part wayz.. To know that we'll never see each other again. The smile she smiled waz of great joy. I know now. The lesson learned was no matter what "Love" exist no matter if the one you love is no longer around. Because remember {another reminder to myself. My Being.} True Love will exist always between great friendz forever no matter where one is on the planet. So I guess I have to also put in my cornerstone that sort of true love. So that when my mother becomez aware of me, she will get a hint of joy that will have her smile with joy like Amy did. Amy… Yea Amy Zimmerman is her name. I wonder and I ponder once again if Amy is meant to encounter me again. I wish. Yea another fruitful wish.

He couldn't understand me. He didn't really want to. I allowed him his anger. I accepted his the way hi naturally became enraged. My life at that time was over. I waz just hanging out. Without a purpose. I had learned what I was there to learn. Well that was my belief anyway. Come to find out that my lesson was to discover what it was to really "give up." He pulled his sword or something like that. I don't recall because I really wasn't paying attention.

It was his instrument of death. I recognized that his purpose in life was to take lives. He was really convinced that he was disconnected. I do remember thinking about how I couldn't fell one iota of a connection existing within his being. he was truly lost. I don't know if his purpose was to live his life truly lost, I do recall that his lostness waz authentic. I asked him simply for some coinz in exchange for a paper bill. I was speaking a language that was tough to speak.

{it was probably Latin.} Even though I grew up in that country. I could have had a speech impediment. All I know is that he got frustrated from attempting to understand what I was saying. I remember purposely repeating my request maybe two or three timez in the same way. I think I may have asked each time like he was the one who was slow enough that it waz his fault that he couldn't under stand. Even though we had people around us, I don't recall anyone stepping up to translate what I was asking. We were part of a population of a large town, and at the time people was beginning to separate from each other. It was an era when people were just on the cusp of discovering being individualists. I recall the relief I felt when I saw in his eyez, his intentionz to slay me. So yea… Another piece of my foundation during this life time must be the lesson. That my time in this skinbag is my choice, yet don't give up. Live Life till I decide to leave.

It's interesting how the purity of this period of awakenness has a sensation that can't be described in any of the languagez that I've known.

This lesson will not be one of those onez that I've somehow decided to be gotten while simultaneously forgotten. This life time will be remembered in its entirety. I'm sure I'm just reminding myself of that. I feel a sense of just a pinch of a memory of making sure that remembering this lesson this life time was placed within the part of the piece of my true self that I've put in this Being within this current skinbag.

This lesson showed up as a desire at first, then I guess it morphed into a wish. It's interesting how back there in the universe; wishes are fruitful in a positive way.

I wonder, and ponder briefly what is it that makez some lessonz get gotten, and yet forgotten. Why do one choose to acknowledge the impact of the lesson learned, yet do not choose to acknowledge what was learned. Nor acknowledge how it was learned. Yet know as truth is known tat there's something there that wasn't there before. And that something is an inner sense of growth that has only come from lessons. lessons learned. Something that's different from the sense of a ripple effect from the discoveries that always come from the learned lessons. I don't know what I'm attempting to clarify. I'm just content thinking like this, right out of the gate.

I wonder if I could wake up my mother up to my x-istance. I don't recall ever doing that before. That time when I was very near grown within that teen age carrier, when I decided to connect when she decided to stop purposely disconnect from me. Wow that was a life. Not being able to fully get across to her that I wasn't meant to exit that journey in a …. What they say that was… yea yea. A sack cloth.. I sure was grateful that she provided me with a healthy set of… those breathing sacks that usually comes with the skinbag. Remember realizing that I was being sabotaged. Remember that I had lived that lifetime without that memory. I can't recall the lesson of that life time. Oh well, I hope my mother is one of those women who's ready for me. Who knowz. With the strange humor of the universe and all.

So far, at least from these first few moments, I have given myself enough of my true self to stay on track. Though journeyz where I've wondered and lost, or sometimes purposely chose to lose my sighting. Yea even though there waz some hint of lessonz gleaned from them, I would really like to get it right this one time. I wonder what the space-place will be like. I wonder what'z the shade of my skin will be.

I guess I should have put more specifics in planning this journey. what was on my mind....Ha... I just related my thoughtz that occurs while I'm my true self as being within a concept called mind. Yep. I'm certainly becoming accustomed quickly being back in a skinbag. Who knows I could have laid out a plan not sent it with me. What ever, as long as I've placed within this piece of myself a strong commitment to Be in such a way that I learn a profound lesson from the experience that I'm here for.

Hay I'm Here. You.... I'm here.. uhm how can I subtly let her know of my x-istance without stressing her out. Remember that time I exited and waz the same as if I was in here. That was interesting.My carrier would tell me all the time that I was birthed under water because she didn't want me to have...the stock of sudden air..sock of hair. No No. The shock of air. She wanted me to enter out there peacefully. That life time she would always remind me that she prayed, hoped and wished I could find peace.hmm. It was then when I somehow twisted the ideal of a wish being fruitful.

That was a violent life. I hope this time I'm just able o enter out. Even if it's on one of those floor places. Even if it's on one of those no floor places. Even if it was like that time when I entered out there and greeted by the loud voices of those unclothed ladies. Yea that waz one journey. That was, I think... Hah I said "I think" Yea that was on of those couple of lessons learned in one lifetime lifetimes. What was my original purpose? I can't recall. I think it was "to discover suffering" boy did I suffer. The starving, the hunger, the knowing that others aren't loving enough to prevent the pangs that ravished my skinbag, even though I knew was easily capable of stopping my suffering. Yet really getting back in touch with my true self, slowly as my skinbag disintegrated. That sense of relief that existed that non-a-second after I returned.

395

If I did plan a plan that I hid from this piece of myself, I hope I planned one of those lifetimez that's at least comfortable, with no distraction. without anything that could occur that would cause one to struggle for another's love. I wish I could live this life time in the total bliss of my mother'z love. Something else I remember from that carrier that had prayed, hoped, and wished for peace. During my eleventh year or so, she insteeled in my mind that God commanded Man to be fruitful and multiply. It waz during that time that I was fruitful, and multiplied my violent actionz.

That lifetime'z lesson taught me to truly forgive myself. Yet it took living 50 years. The last 50 years of that journey living in a cage like structure. My fruitful multiplied actionz cost me my so called freedom. Yea that lifetime it took what I now consider to be about a second in the whole scheme of thingz. As I understand the concept of time, Yet it took 50 years in prison, I think I recall it was the 1600's and I do remember no one knew about having one iota of care for evil doers. I still to this moment know why it took so long to learn my lesson, and exit. I think I was so disconnected. I think I had to be disconnected in order to get the lesson. Yet I do recall the moments that I experienced forgiving myself and knowing that I was going to exit that skinbag.

Uhm. Forgiveness. That's a lesson I'll put in the foundation of my Being.

I think after this lovingly long journey, I'm gonna make sure I put in the piece of myself that I send here, enough consciousness to stay awake during this whole growing process. Maybe not fully awake, just a little. I've always wondered why there's periods where I'm not aware of anything, then the next thing I know, I have fingers and feet. I wonder if I planned to be a girl. I guess it's too late to plan now, whether I'm a boy of girl, I know I'm here to experience true love. That'z my wish. May my wish be fruitful and multiply. In a positive way.

Oh yea. I can make a plan during this period when I'm aware of my connection. Yea I've done that before a few times. Well I don't know.. There was those journeyz when my planz made by the piece of my true self got tangled up with the planz my true self had already made. You know what? That could be the reason that some lessons were never really gotten. Uhm. That's never occurred to me. Those timez when the lessons was harshly delivered. Do you think My true self was forced to provide them in a way that wasn't exactly the time for them, uhm. . What can I plan for this life that won't interfere with the plan, if there is a plan. Uhm. What was that ideal I had.. ah..ah..yea okay. I now insteel within my being to be a writer. A writer that write words without boundaries. Wordz that can't be placed within an era. Yea that'z cool. That way I can experience what I'm here for and not really have any interference from my plan. I've always wanted to be a writer. I recall those many life times when I've wondered how does a writer stay committed to writing words, even though they know that their work may never be known of, until after they've exited, if ever. What drives them. I guess I'll find out. I hope I can stay connected enough to remember that that this is just a journey. Who knows I could write something that will me of my trueself when or if I get lost during of the many future journeyz I'll take later on. There'z something about these skinbaggerz I enjoy. Maybe it's the challenge to enlightenment. Oh.. this skinbag is becoming a sleepy mode state. There's so much more I wanted to ensteel in my foundation while I've awaken.

    oh well , I'll get to it when I become aware again. Hopefully my mother will be aware of me then. Hopefully I will find that sense of wholehearted Love. I wish. Yea I wish.

Autuhor'z Note

I wrote Chapter 2 of Chasing The Sun one night.. and the next day I was so out of it, I barley had enough energy to walk up the street and buy a "soda". I was walking in the sunshine, but I really didn't pay attention to that.. I walked with my hat brim so low over my forehead that I could only see about three feet of the side walk in front of me…I noticed some one standing right in my path.. I raised my head and Melanie Owenby was there smiling brightly at me..

I typed the pages of the 2nd chapter and then that night I walked to the store to buy me a "soda" and once again I see Melanie Owenby.. She Gives me a ride home..(Smiling all the way..) I told her then, and I tell you now.. there'z no accidents in life. Where ever I place the 2nd chapter I will dedicate it to her, for being My angel of Grace…

chapter 10

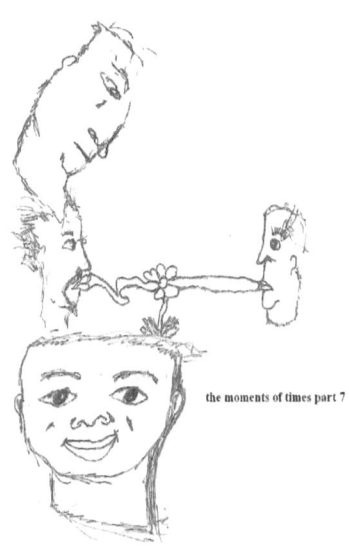

the moments of times part 7

the peace makers

The Moments of Time
             Part Seven
                    By Gitsey

A

Forward

As you will notice these pages of this Forward is not numbered. That is because if this is ever typed it is designed to not be a part of the manuscript. I've designed it that way only because I wish only for you who are reading this hand written version to have the insight provided.

I mentioned in part 3 how after I slept for practically a week I was able to get to the desired goal which is to have reached another realm. After I had this pad bought for me and after I numbered it I knew right away that I wanted it to be a short story. And not only did I wanted that way I knew that was going to be that way. Not only did I know, I also knew that the story would be derived from a dream.

Although it took almost a week to have this dream I really started working on it a few days before it occured. I remember that I slept most of the day and all night. I wrote a little but my main purpose was to have this dream. Belive it or not I had to turn down my state of mind a lot because I found once I began going for this story, I had dreams that was so large in context that I could only remember certian parts and those parts would have filled two of these pads.

The night I had this dream of The Peace Makers I felt confident before I went to sleep that it was the night. So much so that I had pen and paper beside my

pillows. I woke up at 2:15 or so and filled the whole page front and back. And some of a 2nd page.
From that I took out two parts so I could have a good beginning and a longer or easier ending. But I of course kept the same context of the dream.
Roughly 3 nights later and 3 days after I actually started physically writing this part 2, I had another dream. And I woke up and wrote that down because it was so compact and of course unique. First I thought it was just like an aftershock, but I soon came to realize that it was another part of the bigger dream. The 2nd dream is the one with Abe and Susan.
Now that you know this, maybe ya'll have a more profound understanding whatever the moral to this story is.
To tell you the truth not until I got to the 3rd from the last line did I know that I was going to title this what it's titled. I didn't worry about the title just like I didn't worry about the story. I knew it was going to come.
So sit back and enjoy reading
"The Peace Makers."

9-25-90
11:03pm
Gisay

The Peace Makers

8-24-90 10pm

It was a normal Saturday afternoon. The 2nd Saturday of April. He was sitting on a grassy hill along the parking lot behind the school cafeteria. Dust was still lingering in the air from the uprooted tree trunks that the workers had finished digging up just a few moments ago.

They used mostly a bulldozer to pull up the trees. And the saw dust came from when they was cutting up the roots that at some, spreaded out 3 feet long. He was waiting on Joyce to show up. She was due to arrive at 1:15pm. And the students were scheduled to be there at 1:30pm.

Joyce taught a class in Science and she selected 7 students out of the six classes she taught, to be the team to put together a project that was fore the Science Fair that was to be held June 4th.

The team had been meeting for the past two week ends and sometimes after school. And they had yet to come up with an ideal for a project. Joyce ("Miss Webb" as the students call her.) decided to let them all come up with an ideal instead of just her deciding on one.

Steven (or "Mr. Thorngood" as the students called him.) was in relationship with Joyce. She told him of her delima with the students and asked him if he could come to the meeting and maybe help out in some way.

Steven is an aspiring playwriter. He has written a few plays that got produced in the big city theaters. He agreed to support Joyce any way he could, but had no ideal of what input a playwrite could provide to a team of 8th graders that has a project for a science fair.

As Steven was sitting there on the small hill, relaxing and enjoying the big blue sky with the huge puffy clouds that comes with spring. He saw a girl walk up and sit on the stairs of the trailer which was Joyce's classroom. Knowing that it could only be a student of hers he politly went over to introduce himself. As he was walking across the parking lot she smiled a friendly smile at him, and he smiled back. He waved and said "Hi." She waved back. As he stop in front of her he strectched out his hand and said "Hi, my name is Mr. Thurngood, I'm a good friend of Miss Webb. She invited me to sit in on you all's meeting today." And the young girl just looked up at him and while shaking his hand, she just smile. Steven asked her "What's your name?" "Tisha" she replied. "You are one of Miss Webb's students aren't you?" She knodded her head yes. "What grade are you in?" She held up 7 fingers and then said "next year," then she held up 8 fingers. He smiled, not knowing what else to do. He turned to the feild where they had just uprooted the tree trunks and with his hands on his hips he asked her "I wonder what they're doing that for? Do you know?"

He looked back at her and she looked up at him, and then made two fist and started making the motion of putting on fist on top of the other and then taking the other fist and putting it on top of the first fist, she did that a few times and then pointed to the trailer of whom ~~steps~~ steps she was sitting upon then with her hands she made the motion like she was feeling the top of a wide flat surface, sort of like straightening out a table cloth that was just put on the dining room table. "They're making way to build new trailers or to erect new trailers?" Steven asked. Tisha pointed at him and smiled and knodded yes.

Then all of a sudden, Steven remembered that Joyce had told him about two or three of her students on the team and Tisha was one of them. Joyce said that Tisha learned sign language when she was 8 years old because her mother went deaf, and she was slowly replacing speaking with sign language. Tisha made it thru elementary and ~~is~~ making it thru Sr. high. All her friends accepts her ways and unless she has to give a speech or verbal rant she doesn't speak. And only if she has to speak, she'll answer all her questions in sign language.

After Steven had remembered this, he motioned for her to ~~slid~~ slide over, so he could sit down, she smiled and slide over... "You know I've always been fascinated with sign language," he said. He contived "Every since I saw that movie, ah.. I think of the name now, but you see I'm a playwrite, that means I write plays

And by seeing that movie, it opened up all kinds of possibilities for me in my work. But I haven't written one like that, because it'll be like me trying to write a play in Greek, I don't even know Greek." Tisha grinned and said "It's easy once you get the hang of it." Then she started to point at different things and motioned to Steven to copy what she does. She pointed to the sky then motioned the sign for sky, and Steven followed her, then Building, then Car, then Side walk, then step, then Grass, then Cloud. "Hay this is great." Steven said with excitement as if he had just learned how to speak english.

"You know this is my interpretation of Sign Language." Steven then stands up and Flaps his arms and asks Tisha "What is this?" "A bird " she says with a smile. He puts his hands on his hips, bends his elbows behind him, bends his knees and walks with is head stuck out, "A goose or something" She laughly says. "Good you're getting it." Then he stands up straight and puts is right elbow to his hip with his arm stretched out and snaps his finger and makes a face. Tisha looks at him confused. Then he spins around in a clumsy way and starts halfly doing the dance moonwalk, And a girls voice & not Tisha's? from behind him says "Michael Jackson" Steven turns around a little embarressed And says correct. It was Flora and another team member Janet. Steven waves at them and Tisha waves them over.

275

Steven introduces himself and They introduce themselves. And to his surprise Joyce had already told them about him, and about how he is to help them.

Joyce arrives with two other kids moments later. She smiles from behind the wheel because she's happy to see that Steven has made it, and that the girls are not being strangers. Steven trots over to the car and carry's her books for her. She introduces the two boys whom she has picked up from house. "This is David and Charlie.. David and Charlie this is my Good friend Mr. Thornegood." They shake hands and exchange jesters of Pleasure to meet you.

As they step into the trailer which has been transformed into a classroom Joyce turns to Steven and says that she's so glad he could make it. "My Pleasure ofcourse" replies Steven.

As the students sits in the front row of the class desks, and Steven sits in Joyce's chair behind the teacher's desk, Joyce says "We've start now and just include Andrea and Andrew when they Arrive. Now 1st remember the rule of our project. It must not be a copy-cat kind of style. It must be original. Has anyone thought of my ideals since wenesday." They look at her with a fustrated look and after a few moments Tisha raises her hand, and to Joyce's surprise because Tisha hasn't raised her hand all that year. "Yes Tisha" "Who was the winner last year and what was their project?" Joyce smiles just from hearing Tisha's beautiful voice.

"Well the winner last year was a young fellow from Brook middle school with his elaborate demenstration on how the solar system worked. I tell you kids that the only reason he won was because out of all the rejects that was there such as how does a cell divides, what is photosynthesies, projects like that. Out of all of them his was the most regonizeable and so the judges voted in favor of him. I was one of the judges, I think I told you this already, But I was one of the judges and I knew there was something more, so I decline to be one this year and put together a team of young Thinkers and see what we can come up with."

Then at that moment at finishing up what she said Andrea and Andrew came rushing thru the door. Andrew says sorry Miss Webb we're late, Mother had to take dad to the office for a bussiness meeting." At this Steven thought with a smile, now here right before my eyes this brother and sister will be the next generation of republicians. Andrea and Andrew sits down and looks at Steven as if to say who the hell are you? Joyce was about to speak when Steven said to Andrea and Andrew "Hi I'm Mr. Thorngood." "Oh yes," Joyce says. "He's here to support us in making a decision to day about our project for the fair." They smile at him in a kiddish snobish way. For some odd reason Joyce realizes that ever since the begining of the school year she hasn't had a stand for her potted plant to sit on and the little branches was or has been cut off because they've grown to such a length that eventhough she put it back in the corner students was still stepping on them. Remembering that she noticed the tree trunks stacked in the corner of the parking lot she asked Steven if he would go and get one so she could sit her plant on it. He smiled and said sure.

As soon as he left out, knowing that he'll only be gone a moment Joyce said to the class. "If you haven't figured it out me and Mr. Thorngood are in relationship or as you call it he is my boyfriend." The class gives a little giggling response. "I asked him to come here today to break up the block we're in. He's great at doing that." Then Steven stumbles up the steps with a trunk about 2 feet long and he notices that the class is looking at him strangely and looks at Joyce and says "What's wrong? What did you tell them?" "Oh nothing dear, that trunk is a little too short." "Are you sure?" "Yes, I'm sure. Bring me the tallest one out there." So Steven puts down the trunk with a soft thud that shook the trailer's floor and turned around to go get another one. And Joyce continued to say, "He doesn't know what to say or do. So what your job is, is to ask him questions to get his mind working and I guarantee that he comes up with something."

Steven stands outside at the edge of the parking lot with one hand on his hip and the other hand wiping the sweat off his face with a hankershief. In front of the 10 or so trunks piled in a pyimid shape, He thinks to himself " Damn I didn't expect hard labor when she asked me to come here, I would have dressed for it," Then he smiles and chooses the top trunk on the top of the pile. He pulls it off the top and it falls to the ground. He takes off his shirt leaving him with only a T. shirt on. he places his shirt in his car. Joyce seeing this as she peeps out the door continues to talk to her team. When Steven turns around and looks at the trunk he see's how strange looking it appears. It really looks deformed. He stands it up, steps back from it and just looks at it for a while, for he has never seen a tree trunk that looked so strange.

It was about 4 feet high and 2½ feet in diameter meaning from the right to the left side it was 2½ feet and from the lower front to the lower back it was 2½ feet. The wild thing was at the base of the tree trunk it stuck out about 6 inches more and 2 feet up it also stuck out 6 inches. There in the middle where it stuck out it was the shape of a half diamond starting at one side stretching out then returning to the other side. Also above the middle it goes back into the tree so the length of the width is about 1 to 1½ feet from front to back. Steven doesn't yet know what to make of this yet but he's sure it's something important. So he stands behind it and bends down and wraps his arms around the trunk so his hands can grab on to the diamond shape bump. And he lifts it up with no problem. Because he's 6'3 and 220 pounds with some what of a Beer belly that the trunk lays back on

As Steven walks soundly up the steps he notices that it'll be very difficult to just walk straight in, so he with a big thud, bigger than the one before, puts the trunk just inside the door. The kids looks at his appearance that looks like half businessman, half lumberjack and they hide their laughter by giggling and Joyce looks at him and with a smile thinks to him, You're so sweet. She points to the corner and says "Thanks Sweetie, and she kiss's him on the cheek." The kids says Ohhhh, she waves them to be quiet. After Steven places the trunk in the corner with the two six inches extentions facing the classroom he walks back to the desk then Andrew asks him what kind of work does he do. "I'm a playwrite, I've written plays such as "Decision of 30 days" that's playing now at the Academy Theatre." "Do you make a lot of money?" Andrea asks. "Enough to pay my rent." "How did you become a play writer?" David asks. "Well I have a great imagination that all it takes, along with patience to be able to sit down and write you know?" David knods his head. "Are you and Miss Webb going to get married?" Steven laughs shyly and answers, "You going to have to ask her." "Can I be your flower girl?" Flora asks with a giggle. Joyce just bashfully smiles and says "Alright enough of that let's leave our nupitials to our selves and get to work on this project. Has anyone come up with any ideas?" Charlie answers "Well you said it have to be original, and that's why we have Mr. Thurngood here. I would like to hear some of his ideas."

Steven walks around to the front of the class and folds his arms then he puts his left hand at his chin like a man contimplating. He thinks to himself "Now these kids are really exspecting something brilliant, What the hell am I doing here. let me see..." He turns his back to the class and in the corner that to the left if you're facing forward there sat the plant on the tree trunk. That's when Steven saw it. He looked again at the tree trunk, this time with a more profound look and he saw it again. He turned to the class with a look of shock on his face and a look of uttermost joy of discovery.

Steven points at Janet and tells her to come here, come right here where I'm standing." he says. Janet quickly gets up and comes to the spot where he is. Steven says while pointing at the trunk "Look at that tree trunk what do you see.?" "Tree, Nature, Wood, God's creation?" "No, No, What could it be?" "I don't know." "Use some imagination!" Then Steven hurry's behind Joyce's desk and sits in the seat. And tells Janet. "Now look at me. Imagine that the arms of this chair isn't here." Then he leans forward a little and rest his elbows on his knees with his palms of his hands facing each other and his fingers interlocking. Then he says "Now Janet, look at me and then look at the tree trunk." She does and then looks back at him and Steven raises his eye brow as if to say "Get it." She answers with the facial expression "What the hell are you talking about." Then Janet contives to look at the trunk then at him.

413

While she's doing that and thinking about him saying "Use your imagination!" She begins to smile. The class and Joyce while all of this between Janet and Steven is going on, They're just looking dumbfounded and confused. Then Janet begins to laugh and she steps over and pulls Flora up and points to the trunk then at Mr. Thorngood and Janet asks Flora Do you see it?! Do you See It!?" "See what?" Flora asks. It's a man, It's a man in the trunk of that tree. Steven sits back and smiles at Joyce and Joyce thinks to him with her face "What the hell?" And he jesters with his hand calm down and just watch.

By this time the whole team is standing up and pushing thier way to the spot where Janet and Flora was standing. Janet excitely trots over to the trunk and points out that the exstention at the base of the trunk was the man's feet, and the one in the middle was his arms, and she pointed out where his shoulders and head was. It was just covered with a few layers of wood. Joyce begin to smile as she began to see it and the class began to see it as well. After everyone had thier turn standing in that spot to see it clearly, After a while no matter where you stood in the class room one could not help but to see the man sitting and contiplating stuck in that tree trunk. It was for Steven, Joyce and the her team, an amazing Discovery to say the least.

After Joyce got the kids to settle down and to go back to their seats there was an atmosphere of excitement. But that didn't last long because now they wondered what was the purpose of them seeing that. And Andrea raised her hand. "Yes Andrea?" "Miss Webb, what do we do now." Joyce looks at Steven and says "Yea Dear, What Do We do now?" He answered like she was suppose to already know the answer "Dig him out of course, Don't just leave him in there." "But none of us are sculptors nor had any dealings with carving." David says. "So! Does that mean you can't do it?" Then Steven looks at Joyce and thinks to her with his face, Take over now baby I've done my job. "Oh no you don't.." She says "You got to help me out here." So he says "Listen [still thinking Make it up man Fucking make it up.] You need a project, Something original and never done before. Well I've never heard of 7 kids making a sculpture. And as far as the Science part is concerned well you all could each do a report on how it is working on a team, with the underlining motive being in the feild of psychology. About the attitudes and behavioral aspects of being on a team." Then he sits back and gestured with a hand wave to the front of the desk to Joyce as if to say "Now my job is done, The floor is yours." "Uhm" says Joyce. "Team what do you think?" Ofcourse they're only thinking what did that guy just say? Do he think we're college students or something.

415

Joyce noticeing thier faces of a little to a lot of confusion she felt like she should explain to them what he meant by what he just said.

"What Steven I mean Mr. Thurngood means is that he suggests that our Science project be carving a man out of this tree trunk, But that just being the physical proof of our project. Our main purpose is writing a report of our feelings about how it is being on a team and what we've discovered about our self. We could build a sand castle and get the same result. But since the tree trunk is here that's what we should work with. And maybe once we've freed the man from the tree so to speak, we will free something within ourselves. Understand?"

She notices the class now has a more relaxed expression on thier faces and they are beginning to get it. "I think it's a great original idea, let's take a vote!" says Charlie. Joyce asks the class "All in favor" They all raise thier hands. She didn't need to ask if anyone wasn't in favor.

"We have to have an outline to get in this done" suggests Andrew. "Do you have one?" "No I don't just yet." Joyce answers. Then she turns to Steven and he says ask them. Emeaning the team? "Okay class let me hear some suggestions on how to get started. we know our project but we just have to work out the logistics, the outline if you will."

Flora raised her hand first, then David, then Andrew, And Tisha raised her hand last.

Joyce always wanting to hear Tisha speak any time she got a chance prodded her. Tisha lift her hand raised and jestered as if she was pointing to the ceiling but she wasn't. She was extending her finger. Then she made a circle in the air then within the imaginary circle she jestered like she punched or pushed with her finger, out three holes in the circle. Two at the top and one in the middle, then she drew a quarter within the circle beneath the dot in the middle. Joyce looking confused, but not fustrated. Though she wanted to hear Tisha speak, Joyce didn't mind for it was just the way she chose to participate this time. Tisha seeing that Miss Webb didn't understand what she was doing repeated the jester. She drew a circle, then two dots around the inner top then a dot in the middle, then a partial circle beneath the middle dot. "She's drawing a face!" Janet said with excitement as if she's won a prize. "A face?" asked Joyce. Tisha smiled but had that with her face, "there's something else." "You're drawing a face?" Tisha knodded her head and jestered for Joyce to repeat herself. "You're drawing..." Tisha motioned for her to stop. Then held out two fingers and pointed to the second finger. Joyce thought about this one. "You're drawing, you're drawing, pointing to her 2nd finger. You're drawing, Ahh, dama this charades can get crazy, Ahh, Ahh, Oh drawing!" Then Joyce says with excitement as if she's won a prize. "Drawing, It's

Drawing!" Tisha smiles a big smile as if that's her prize, and then points to the tree trunk and then at the team. Joyce didn't need to think hard about this one. She knew what Tisha was suggesting and thought it to be a great suggestion. Joyce didn't need to take anymore, it was like Tisha had turned the key to get her mind started. "That's Great," she said. "What Tisha suggest is that we each draw the man in the trunk as we see him to be, and collaberate with our drawings and by then we'll have a clear picture of who this guy is. That is what you're suggesting right Tisha." Tisha smiles with relief as she always does when she got her point across to another, without having to speak. "Let's see it's 2:15, we have a hour and 15 minutes before we conclude the meeting for today. Within that time do the best you can to draw him." Joyce hands out the pencils as Steven hands out the typing paper. Each one of them that he hands the paper to, they smile up at him with appreciation for unblocking their minds.

"Alright team you can position yourselves anywhere in the classroom to get a better view of what you see." Joyce motions Steven to take the plant off of the trunk and move it out from the camera. The students move out. A couple of them settle on Joyce's desk. Some remain in their desk. Charlie even placed his paper on the black board and started drawing standing up against it. Tisha put on her glasses and remained sitting.

286

 Joyce opens the front door and before she and Steven steps out she tells them that there are color pencils in her desk drawer if they needed them, then they step outside.

 Walking toward the car of Steven's Joyce says while looking at the ground with her hands behind her, "Well you did it, I knew you could." "What can I say, Grace under pressure." replies Steven. She looks at him and just bursts out laughing.. "What? What's so funny?" "It's you I've never seen you like this," "Like what?" "like this. Never seen you right after a discovery. You're always away when you're writing. I would think what just occured in there is something like what happens when you discover a new subject for a play." "Well sort of.. But what's so funny?" "You have a proud glow about yourself." "May that's just the sun reflecting off your beauty." "You're so sweet." "Well what can I say." She pushs his shoulder and smiles a big smile.

 When they get to his car he opens the trunk and pulls out a pair of jeans and Tennis shoes. Then he begins to take of his dress shoes, and Joyce says to him "You're not going to change out here are you?" "Only you and the Birds and bees will see me. What the hell!" So he changes clothes right there behind his car in the parking lot of the school.

419

They sit on the trunk of his car and face the field of torn ground where the tree trunks was dug up. Steven asks her "Do you think they'll be able to finish sculpting in a month and a half?" "I think so. I just have to figure out how to make it more exciting you know more fun than work. Because these kids are so bright as soon as they get bogged down with something it's easy for thier minds to go somewhere else and forget about what they're doing." "I thought that Bright kids were able to concentrate on whatever they're doing under any circumstances." "Yes that's true, As long as it's fun learning. Kids will be kids you know."

They sit on his car for a while then he takes a spread from his back seat and lay it underneath the shade of a tree and he get's a beer and a soda from a cooler in his trunk. They relax there for awhile and enjoys each others company untill it's was time for Joyce to end the meeting for the day.

"Okay times up." She says as they enter into the class. "Come on a few more minutes.." says Charlie. "Okay 5 more." Joyce sits behind her desk and starts jotting down some notes and meanwhile Steven walks around and observes the drawings or sketchs they're doing. He's amazed by the quality of their works. As if all of them has had some kind of background in drawing. Some of the students was using color and some was sketching in the style of using the different shadings of light and dark to make the man sitting show up more. He notice something odd about Tisha's drawing. He pointed to the green spider that she drew that was clinging on his right arm. Tisha just looked up at him and pointed to her eyes then pointed to the tree trunk and smile. He understood that she was saying that's what I see. So he smile back at her and moved on.

"Alright time is up! Turn in your drawings." As they was turning in thier drawings, Andrea asked if Mr. Thorngood would be back. Steel knodded his head no and the class seemed a little saddend. Joyce just smiled because it made her feel good that the class had taken to him so quickly, like she did when they 1st met.

"No. Mr. Thorngood has other commitments he has to attend to." She tells the class. "But I will try to make it back for the science fair." She also tells them.

They all waited outside together for the students who were to be picked up. All of thier parents came within ten minutes. All except for David's and Charlie's because Joyce is taking them home. Tisha's mother was the last to arrive and when she was going to the car she flapped her arms like a bird then turned around as she was opening the door and said "Good By Steven And Thank You." Steven pointed to his smile and waved good-bye.

While David and Charlie was getting in the car and Steven was carrying Joyce's books for her he asked her out for dinner and Joyce gracefully declined because she now needed to do some hard working on designing this project. Steven said to her give him a call early in the week or just stop on by. He placed her books in her back seat and after shutting the door he leaned over and gave her a soft kiss on the cheek and said Thanks. "I should be thanking you." "You're the one that had the confidence in me. And trusted that I can get the job done. So I thank you." "You're Welcome."

Steven went out that night and slept half of Sunday away and the other half he watched rented videos. Joyce on the other hand was hard at work analizing the drawings and writing a small thesis on the design of the project. She noticed the great artwork of course, she also noticed the individuality of each drawing. For example Flora being Chinese; drew a Chinese man, David and Charlie being black Both drew a black man. And Tisha's spider on the man's arm no one else had seen that.

Notes for Project. page 1
Joyce Webb
April 14 1990 9:28pm

    I have studied the drawings done by the team of what they've seen, as to be the man inside the tree trunk. It's obvious to me that each one see's a different feature more clearly than another. For example Flora see's his hands clearer while the others just see hands. Charlie see's his face while others just see a face. Andrew-legs, Andrea; The Chest, Janet-the head of hair and beard, And Tisha shows all of these features very clearly but she also see's a spider on his right arm. I don't believe that the spider is some sort of arm bracelet due to the fact that its color is green. A bright green. The spider has a body length of about 1 inch and a width of half a inch. The spider has 3 legs on each side that are long enough to rap around his arm so that the ends of each leg touch each other. I do not know what she means by seeing this spider, I will be sure to ask her about it Monday.

    Another thing about the seeing of the man is that 4 out of 7 saw the man with a beard. Which to me seems to have some sort of significance.

    The title of the piece I've decided is to be "Man Contimplating" which will be sure synonomuse with the other statue titled "The Thinker". I acknowledge my boyfriend with the discovery of this man.

page 2

As I myself contemplate the value that is to become the project in progress, I'm designing the necessary action that needs to be taken in order for the value to occur.

One aspect is to define the contribution for one self that comes from being on a team. The contribution must be on such a broad scope, in order to be value to each individual. For each one has thier own special existence. Be it Race, Religion, Background or culture. Each is rich with distint personalities.

We have approximately a month and a half to complete this project. A moment ago I've decided to let each other carve what they see most. Instead of having each of them work seperatly on the tree trunk, I have them work on it at the same time. That way they're be working as a team.

I will have each of them summarize in the simplest form of thier experience and draw a conclusion to what was the value of being on the team. Like what was empowering. Also what was disempowering. To write the conclusion so that the bottom line with have a result of contribution and discoveries for others. So that way instead of presenting results that has a an effect of momentary satisfaction, The results will provide a contribution to others that may impact them for the rest of thier life's. Providing insights into being in relationship with any human Being no matter the Race, Creed and Color.

page 3

To sum it up. What I've so far designed to be the outline of this project.

1.) For the next 3 to 4 weeks, have a team gathering every Monday and Wednesday after school for aprox. 2 to 2½ hours. And on Saturday a gathering from 1:30 to 4pm.

2.) At this gathering {or coming together, or meeting.} for the next 3 to 4 weeks all they do is work together in my class room with caring thier assigned area of the piece, doing this while accepting constructive criticism from the other teammembers.

note - I'm not sure of a few assignments yet I have to go over thier drawings some more.

3.) Spend the last meeting of the fourth week ~~long~~ ~~the~~ discussing being on the team and what they've discovered about themselves. I'm most play an instrumental role in that ~~is~~ meeting because of thier adolens~~cence~~ scence, they~~'ll~~'ll surely want to withold what they may feel to be embarrassing or unimportant.

4.) During the 1st and maybe the 2nd meeting of the 5th maybe finale week to write thier reports. And the last meeting of the fifth week to read it to the class and after each has read thiers they summarize it and cut out the story and proceed to the heart of the matter which I'm sure will be the essence of the value of being on a team

page 4.

Though I haven't actually looked on the calendar to be specific about the dates of our meetings and how long it is untill June 4th I do know it's on a Monday and there's a sixth week. During that 6th week the team will be off and will gather on the Saturday the 2nd to review and put finishing touches on the "Man Contimplating."

Althoyth also since this is a rough draft of the outline, I'll keep it for reference so that I can come back to it in need of what I basically want this project to be.

Since my team has 5-13 year olds and 1-12 year old and 1-11 yr old I'm sure that this is simply enough for them to handle and with it being so simple and them being so brilliant, they will only take this to possibilities that I can only imagine now.

Joyce Webb
April 14 1990
11:43pm

The next morning which was Sunday, Joyce woke up at 6am as she usually does everyday during the school year. It didn't make a difference wether it was the weekend or not. She jogged 4 to 5 miles during the weekdays. And on weekends since there was no school she jogged 8-10 miles. On Sundays after jog she'll take a shower then prepare for church after a hardy breakfast.

Today she decided to stop by Steven's after the service and discuss with him the project. She arrived around noonish and Steven had just waken up. She seeing that he had a slight hangover, from spending all night partying, decided to make brunch for them.

They ate and enjoyed eachother's company. During the hours they spent together Joyce got clearer about the design of the project; from the coaching that Steven provided.

They went out for dinner that evening. Neither of them considered themselves on a date because of the depth of thier relationship. After Dinner Joyce drove him home and decided to turn in early to do some reading and studying so she will be prepared for the following school week.

She departed for home excited as were she about the unlimited possibilities of the project. She visioned what an impact that this simple tasks to work as a team will have on the kids.

The next day which was Monday, Joyce was surprised by the way she seemed to breeze thru her first 4 classes before lunch. Andrew which was in her 2nd period class knew the reason. But the other 6th graders did not. Janet which was with the 7th graders in her 4th hour class also knew while the others did not.

Instead of Joyce eating lunch in the teacher's lounge she had made her a few sandwichs that morning and brought along a pint of apple juice. She instead went to shop around for a place where she could purchase the tools that was needed to carve the tree trunks. She found a place just on the outskirts of the city limits. After hurrying to get back she breezed thru the next 3 classes that was the eight graders. Joyce usually dreaded Mondays, but she had a Monday with a purpose for being this time so she was excited to say the least.

After school the team met at around 4pm. That gave them enough time to horse around and go to the ~~corner~~ store that was across the street. Everyone from seeing Miss Webb excited during thier class became ethusiastic themselves, and was eager to get to the meeting. Everyone except for Charlie and Janet showed up a quarter to four. When all had arrived Miss Webb passed out thier drawings and ~~of the~~ explained to them how she choose which area of the statue they're be working on

She gave them the assignments as follows. Janet, the head of hair and the beard. Charlie - The facial expression and to help Janet with the head. Andrea - The shoulders and chest area, David the muscular arms and to leave a four inch wide and a one inch thick square on his right muscle of his arm for Tisha. Flora the distinguished hands that has the fingers fold into each other. Andrew the legs and the rest of the lower torsole that Andrea might not can get too. Tisha; she gave her the spider to create and to also write a short story of a few pages about the man contemplating while she's waiting on David to complete his arms. Miss Webb decided to have them all have input on the backs of the man such inputs like how much arch to put in and like that. She told them that when one is stalled by another, they are to work on his back.

Miss Webb then got out the different types of chissels that the team would be using, and the various sized rubber mallets along with some wooden headed ones also. She demonstrated on the 1st tree trunk that Mr. Thurngood had brought in from the pile, and showed them that she wasn't an expert sculptor and said to them that she knew that they would do better than thier best.

Joyce didn't go into the outline of the project that she had designed for them, for she thought it may some how distract them. Instead after her little demonstration she let them choose thier tool and turned them loose on the tree trunks.

429

She was surprised at the immediate harmony for which they worked together. She knew or atleast it seemed to her that it would only take a short time before they would be complete with the sculpture.

Right away they decided to divide the tree trunk into sections and those that worked in a section would position themselves so that it wouldn't get in the way of another. They worked it out like this. Andrew who had the legs would work on the right leg, Andrea would work on the right side of the chest. Which gave them perfect opportunity to use thier brother sister relationship to work together. Flora would work on the left wrist and hand, David would work on the left arm. That way by working together they agree on the strength the size will show. Also Charlie will be working on the Forehead while Janet works first on the lining of the hair. Tisha's job is to be there as a coach and cheer leader.

They only had time to work for an hour and within that hour the tree trunk looked nothing like "Man Contimplating" more like kids that went crazy with chissles and rubber mallets. But the team left that day very exicted, they had actually begun taking action on a project that one of the most orginal contepts that was around. Joyce smiled while they was cleaning up the wood chips. She knew that they would do good. And they would do thier best. That's all she requested.

Monday May 7th they finished the sculpture. It took them 9 meetings to roughly carve out the figure, then to add details like the curls in his hair or viens on his arms etc. Then to sand him down. Everything including Tisha's spider was complete. They had a little completion party with Cool-Aid and cookies. With a little conversational music. Ten minutes before the class ended Miss Webb told them that of carse the job wasn't complete. She told them to be prepared Wenesday to have a conversation about what they've learned and experienced by being on a team and working together.

Wenesday the 9th and Saturday the 12th they spent houres discussing what they've discovered. Mostly in the beggining they were talking about what they've found out about others. But Joyce, through her coaching and by the questions she asked, had them look at what they've found out and discovered about themselves.

At these discussions Tisha verbally participated fully cracking jokes, speaking out of turn, the whole 9 yards. Miss Webb was pleased with this.

She told them that at the next 3 meetings they will be writing down what they've discuss and by the 3d meeting to have it written on just one page. Not to leave anything out, but to bottom line it. Then they would have the following 2 weeks off to enjoy the ending of the school year and meet back on Saturday June 2nd. One day before the Big Event on the 4th. With their assignments done, there's the one page reports.

431

Summary of Discoveries
By Flora Chiu

I've learned a lot that I didn't know about the personalities of my friends. Three fellow team members I've known for years and if you take what I've learned about them, you would think I didn't know them at all.

It baffles me, that when one works as a team, the attitudes of the persons changes. But not really a change. More like they become more themselves, and that may look like to some as to be change. But as I said, I've known these three and the more I look at it, the more I see that at times before they've at one time or another has really been themselves like they've been this time. The only difference is this time it's been for a longer period of time. And I believe that this has helped in sustaining the seeing of the good it is by being themselves.

It has been a honor for me to be a member of this team. I will cherish this for the rest of my life. I don't know, but I think that it has made me more myself also. It's hard to evaluate myself. You have to ask them.

Flora Chiu

Summary of Discoveries
By Janet Greene

I've realized a lot about myself. Some of the things I've discovered is not all that pretty. It doesn't matter because it's still me. I noticed when there was the times when I was working with Charlie on the little things like how long his beard will be and he'll tell me that it'll be too long for his face, How I got my way by using what female perswayision I have acquired from my mother. And how Charlie was so willing to go along with whatever I said only after I through a fit or pouted or something like showed him I was angry. Just a little bit.

The main thing I discovered about myself was when I was using my stuff from my mother, I felt something for Charlie that I had never felt for another boy other than my older brother Rufus. With that feeling I felt like I could do anything. Especially make the Conitimplating man's hair on his head and his beard stand out as a distingushing feature like it does my father.

Oh yea I asked Charlie to be my Boyfriend And he said yes.

Janet Greene

Summary of Discoveries
        By Charlie Dunn

I'm no Artist by Any means, Neither Am I A person who knows or knew how to carve something out of wood. I was surprised when Miss Webb chose me to do his face because the one I drew showed up clearer and distinctive from the rest. She told me something like that I saw the rest of the drawings and it seemed to me that Tisha's face looked better. But I guess she knew what she was doing. I told her when the team 1st began that Janet was putting a beard on this man and I didn't draw one, And I asked Miss Webb how I was suppose to carve out his face when she was going to put a beard on him? And Miss Webb told me to work together with her and compromise. Janet is such a fox that the compromise was that she'll do the beard anyway she wanted and I'll let her. But I noticed that I couldn't let Janet think I was falling for her so I sort of played mean with her. The funny thing is the face came out not looking like the man I drew but it still looked great even with the beard, and Janet asked me to go study with her and I'm no fool I didn't play mean when she asked me that.

                                            Charlie Dunn

Summary of Discoveries
By Andrea Bennidick

I told mommy about our project and she was just as excited as me and Andrew. She called her friend Carol Flagers who as you know or might not know is a world reknown sculptor. Carol came over. She was going to show us some techniques but me and Andrew decided that it would be a dissadvantage for us instead of an advantage. Because we wouldn't have learend the stuff we or atleast I know now by knowing it already we or I would have just been going through the motions. I don't know about Andrew but for me I felt like getting advise from a famouse sculptor would have set me apart from the team. So instead I admire her attitude and brang it with me to the team gatherings and shared it with them. That seemed the approapriate way to take advantage of her greatness. And it was easier for me to convey.

I think I've shared with you my discovery in a round about way. Miss Webb told us to write this in a story style instead of a flat out list of discovery. With one page it's hard to say a lot.

Andrea
Bennidick

304

Summary of Discoveries
By David Bell

This piece we've done titled "Man Contimplating" I say is one of the most impressive works I've seen up to date. I'm not saying that because I haven't seen anything to compare it with as you all may think I've gone in the past few weeks after school to the museum and various Art Gallerys and I've seen some famouse carvings. None may I remind you has been done by any teenagers let alone 7 teenagers. Ladies and Gentleman, Teacher and my teachers Boyfriend, My fellow team members listen and understand "We Kicked But" with this project.

I learned how to share and accept ideals. I learned how to not be selfish in a seeming selfish situatation. Like when I was working on his arms and Tisha suggested a size and then Flora suggest about the same size. but I was going to make them larger. So we compromised and I carved them in the middle to satisfy all.

I can't wait to hear Tisha's story about that spider she saw on the arm where I saw none. I'm sure she's going to tell a great one.

This one page thing is not enough room. I was just getting started.

DAVID BELL

Summary of Discoveries
   By Andrew Bennidick

   It was great working together with the team. But I found it to be most invaluable working on something together with my sister. We had always been arguring about the littleest things but since we've started on this science project we've only had a few dissagreements but not arguments. Mother was very surprise and suggest that we should do more school projects together. I never told Andrea but since I'll be reading this to the team I know she'll hear. But I think that it's not right to be arguring over little things. And I'm sorry for being such a bad little brother to her. And I'm going to beat up Butch for pulling her hair the other day because he don't suppose to treat my sister like that. And I'm sorry for laughing while he was doing it.
   The way I carved his legs eventhough they were in trousers or atleast looks like they were in pants the way I carved them was so you could tell that he had a good foundation to stand on. Sort of like the relationship I have with Andrea is a good one for the rest of my life.
                                  Andrew Bennidick

Sumarry of Discoveries
    By Tisha Simmons

   These past few weeks has been extraodinary. Before I began sculpting the spider my job was to stand with the team and coach and give encouragment which for me has been valuable. By having that assignment I've decided to no longer only speak in sign language. That is Majority of the time. It is not because I couldn't have done it to communicate to the team, but I decided that since the way the team communicated was verbally, That I shouldn't be apart from them, and I should prticpate. So with talking I found it fascinating to find myself surprised to suddenly have my voice back.
   Miss Webb is most pleased with me and she says I have a voice like an Angel. It was my mother once said. Actually I can't wait to read this summary out loud. I know after 4 or so years of persistant silence that it'll take a while to get use to me hearing myself talk for a long period of time, and I'm sure some of the team is already fed up with me calling them and talking thier ear off.
   What I've discovered other than Abe and Spoon Spider, Is my beautiful Voice.

                                    Tisha Simmons

Spoon Spider
Also by Tisha Simmons
page 1

Abe is, a part of this world. The only reason that one would belive otherwise is because one has not the strong trust in the possibility of the story I'm about to share with you, to be true... In other words you might not belive this because it may not fit into youre understanding of how the world works.

Donald, Abe's cousin invited him to a meeting of some kind to be held at the highschool. Abe invited his good friend Susan to acompany him. She met him at his house which was only a block or so away from the highschool.

As they were holding hands crossing the highway they enjoyed each other's smile. Abe thought that today would be the day that he would ask Susan to marry him. Since they've been friends for a long time and really they have passed the level of being boy friend and girlfriend. The only reson he hasn't popped the question before is because Sally was going through a period that seemed like she was going away, but that all seemed to have gone.

Sally senses the same thing. For a while she hope had had visons of going away, not dying or even leaving town just not being there. Today she's comfortable and content because she knows now that no matter what happens Abe will always love her.

page 2

They arrive at the meeting that was being held at a trailer behind the high school. Actually it was a Jr. High school. Steven G. Whelchel Jr. high school. The trailer beside the parking lot behind the cafeteria.

At the meeting which neither of them was sure what it was about, There was a buffet table set up. Instead of finger sandwichs they had it set up for brunch. The main course was spegehtti. Neither of them want to eat so they decidend. Some how Susan was seperated from Abe for just a second or two. She was drawn over to the corner where the Air conditioning vent was. All of a sudden a thousand knats came out of the vent and surrounded her. The incets made like a moving clouds of particals around her. She was ineffected by them. She just stood there. After a moment or two the knats dispersed and Susan was dressed in a costom of a fairy. She had on a diamond studded leator with white stockings and fixed "into" her back was huge transparent wings. Three feet long and two feet wide. They were beautiful. Abe thought so too.

Abe took her by the hand and decided to take her home. None of this is affecting him. As if this happens every day. From the moments of taking her hand and walking outside the door something else occured. When he got to the steps he saw his cousine that had just arrived.

Donald smiles up at him from the bottom step. The stairs was only three steps. And Abe greets him by saying I'm taking home my little genie. Then he opens up the left side of his jacket and there's Susan 2 feet tall grasping on to him and almost crying. She gives a smile to Donald with her black pearl eyes. She looks up to Abe and says in a hurry voice, "Let's Go! Let's Go!" Donald stands on the steps and watches Abe as they walk toward the parking lot. As they're walking Susan explains. "I remember now, I'm not human I'm an insect. Those were apart of my family in there to prepare me for the transformation back. {speaking about the insects.} I don't quite remember what kind but I do remember that I was rare." "You are rare." Abe says. "And I will love you no matter what." Then within moments, while he had just reached the parking lot, Susan shrieks more and more and grows seven legs. She screams not because of the pain of the transformation but because of the pain of going away. Abe tries to comfort her, he thinks of the wild times ahead. The many conversations they're going to have. Then her body shrinks to two inches long and her legs grow out and she turns a color of grass green. A spring grass green. She jumps off his jacket and runs around the parking lot hysterical. A car runs over her leg and she loses one leg.

page 4

leaving her with six. Abe didn't see Susan turn into a spider he just felt her shrieking and felt her jump out from underneath his jacket.

Donald comes running over toward him pointing and screaming, "Hey there's a spoon spider, There's a Spoon Spider." Then Susan crawls up Abe's leg and clings to his arm. Abe had taken off his jacket to look for her. Abe and Susan knew that the devestating blow to their relationship wasn't that she was a spider it was that she could no longer talk.

Abe screams "No! No!" He refused to accept that it was her untill he looked into her big black pearl-eyes and then he knew. He starts crying and Donald walks away not knowing why Abe was crying. The spoon spider crawls down and walks over across the parking lot to the grassy hill.

Abe stands there for a moment and then walks over to the small forest behind the school that's also on the other side of the parking lot. he finds a tree trunk to sit down on and die. He feels like his life is over now. Susan crawls up and hugs his right arm and they both just stay together there.

They stayed there even when the trunk grew around them and enbodied them in the tree. And until now that is where they stayed. We've discovered Abe and Susan the Spoon Spider.

Tisha Simmons

Although maybe to the rest of the world it was just another reagular Saturaday After noon. June 2nd the 1st Saturaday of the month. To Steven it wasn't reagular at all. He sat on the steps of the trailer instead of the hill where was sitting last time he was here. Partly because of the shade from the warm afternoon sunshine. But mostly because the hill was now cement and the new trailers was now set up for the next school year where there had once been a forest.

He, like last time first say Tisha approaching of the classroom. He smiled and waved to her in the distance and she smiled and waved back. He waited until she got up close before he greeted her formally because he remember her style. He jestered with his hands. First he pointed behind her then he rased both hands up in the air and gave a facial expression of confusion. "I'm coming from the store where my folks always drop me off." Tisha replied. Steven was surprised to hear her respond. He asked her "So you'll talking now?" "I've always talked but so little of the time." she replied laughingly.

She reached in her back pack and gave him a Ice cream Sandwich. "It might have melted before I got around to it." she said as she was pulling out a can of grape soda and some BBQ corn chips. She sat next to Steven as he wondered what laid ahead with more surprises for him.

443

As he sat there eating the ice cream and listening to Tisha as she tells him about the many hours they spent carving out "ABE". He was touched that she had named him. Nobody knew he had a name yet because she had just created the story the past week and she was going to read it today at the meeting.

She told him how they would work for the 1st hour and a half then spend the rest of the time talking and cleaning up the wood chips.

Steven hadn't had a chance to see the sculpture yet, but Joyce had told him it looked wonderful. She failed to mention that Tisha was now talking. He guessed that she wanted to surprise him. Which indeed it did.

Flora arrived next and was just as pleased to see Mr. Thorngood. She stood around and also shared with him her excitement from working on the project.

It was now only 1 p.m. and with Flora and Tisha already there Andrew and Andrea arrived. They were brought by their mother in the family Audi station wagon. Steven enjoyed all they were sharing. When Janet and Charlie arrived together. Everyone except for Steven started ahhing and ohhing. They had decided to spend the morning together and walk to school.

Steven knew exactly what they meant. And as soon as they mingled in with them, Joyce arrived with David. She beeped her horn and everyone went to help get the grocery bags out of her car. There was only 3 but everyone wanted to carry them.

444

The bags were filled with party stuff. Joyce had decided to surprise them. After they have read their summary of Discourses and Tisha has read her short story, instead of discussing what they've learned they would celebrate. She knew that they would have all their lives to discuss that with one another and that this was their last official time together.

Steven and Joyce greeted eachother with a gentle kiss with in the lips and the kids started giggling again and Janet and Charlie mocked them as they too kissed eachother. They all laughed as they were entering the classroom.

Of course Steven being the perfect gentleman let everyone enter before him. Then after every one was in the classroom they all sat down and Joyce then unvieled their Sculptors. Steven was in Ahh. This was the first time he ever could remember when the anticipation didn't outlast the outcome. He was speechless, it took his breath away.

The man contimplating was real now. he sat there on the tree trunk with a serious expression on his face. with a big Green Spider. They or Tisha had decided to add color to the spider. It was the most profound time he had experienced. The team was also still amazed at themselves at what they had achieved as a team. Everyone was silent for a moment to enjoy Mr. Thorngood's speech'ess acknowledgement of them.

445

314

While everyone was reading thier pieces and Tisha was reading her tiny short story about Abe. Steven sat on the edge of Joyce's desk with his arms folded and thinking the brilliantlance of these kids.

Tisha read her story last and when she completed it Steven and Joyce gave a standing novation. Then the rest of the team joined in applauding themselves.

They stood in a half circle with the statue of Abe in front of them. Joyce was at one end and Steven at the other so they was facing eachother. He was holding the pitcher in one hand and the other he held the six oz cup of fruit punch that everyone was holding. "Let's have a toast." Joyce suggested then she raised her eye lid to suggest that the floor was open to anyone.

Charlie raised his cup and everyone followed and he said "I toast us. A team, A family, life long friends." "Hear here" they responded and drank the fruit punch. Then held out thier cups and Steven refilled it. There was a moment of silence for just a few. then Janet raised her cup and the others followed. "Here's a toast to my 1st Boyfriend" everyone laughed and drank up. Once again Steven refilled thier cups then he sat the pitcher on Joyce's desk. He put his right hand in his pocket and raised his cup and they followed. He smiled at Joyce then took a minute to smile and be with each and every

446

one there.

"There's a lot I've discovered in my life." he said. Then he ~~raised his cup~~ arm and the rest followed. "I know there's a lot more that I don't know that I don't know. But one thing that I've discovered ~~that~~ today. I know that, my future wife here, Miss Webb's, has choosen a team that has me looking forward to the future. The world will be in you all's generation's hands and I'm confident that with what ingenuety you've shown and the courage you've shown to take on something that you have no knowledge of the "how to" and get it done by pure commitements. I'm sure that this world will be in peace. This is what ABE represents." Steven looks around again then he raises his cup and they followed and he said through his smile. "Here is a toast to the "Peace Makers"."

9-25-40
10:32pm

chapter 11

chapter one
meeting sexy

Chapter One
Meeting Sexy

By Gihoy

Introduction for the oringinal pages.

I haven't written anything a few days shy of 3 months. That has been the longest period that I haven't written any thing in about 9 years. I've decided to have this project be a reentryish kind of piece. As of now, which it shouldn't be a surprise, I haven't decided on a title. Nor have I decided on a subject, nor design, other than a 3 page intro, and a 45 page piece. With this 1st paragraph I welcome myself back. Thank, It's good to be back.

It's reassuring to find myself not lost for words or to find my handwriting in such the same condition which is as you can see "Chicken Scratch." It is also comforting to know that nothing has been taken away as far as the context to the state of mind that I bring to writing. In time to come it will be discovered if any thing was added during my absence.

Figuring out the context is a part of the adventure of writing a project. Over the past few months I've read novels like they was going out of style. It is still my wish to create a short story that's not from a dream. One that's purely from my consciouse. One that is not from memory of some one or some things. One that is truly created. I belive that along with everything I've written that it is time for me to experience that. So the decission is made on this 1st page. This project will be a short story.

Now that the decision has been made, Yet the subject is not yet decided on, I will describe to you how I will go about writing my first extensive short story.

I will first begin by writing and as time goes along so will the plot. As I live, I will provide life for the piece. I could say that I don't know if it'll work or not, like I say, I could say that, but I'm not. Of course it will work.

As in all the projects that I've completed. I will at the completion of this one, be very impressed with myself, then the next moment move on. For I will know that there more to be provided.

I have before outlined a story or two that I was going to write in this way but the time was not right. Now I feel that this is the time. A time for stepping out, A time for going further.

From the previous paragraph to this paragraph things change so quickly, I have decided to use a piece in the book Thinkings as an outline for this. Who knows that's being comfortable. So with that, I of course will not follow that idea.

As long as this story is thought provoking, and contributes, then the prose is served. I will be aware to not overtly state my philisophy in this story but to have it exist within the framework and context.

I've come to realize that in life one can not

live without risk. And so by stepping out and moving further in this way, I believe that this will be very contributional to me as well as to you.

Being a writer has been a privilege, even during the times when it's not a choice. For you always are there during the ends. So at the end of this short story let me know if you can dig the new directions I will. If by chance the story isn't clear, I'll work on that. If by chance you're unable to see what I've worked on in order to be clearer, for possibilities exist that this story won't be clear, then reread this shall it is.

Peace and Love
Obay
November 24, 1991

Prologue

11-25-91

It's a place that he knew well. Since when he was once younger, this place has provided great moments both of joy and anguish. He realized that he hasn't been here for quite some time. The last time he was here, he was with Becky. He smiles as he remembers her and this place, as they co-exist one with the other.

Yet these are not times to smile, not even for a brief moment. Everythought he knows must remain serious and on purpose. A distraction such as a happy memory could prove to be desatorious. So he pushes the memory of Becky aside and returns to the moment. Although it's been a longtime since he's slipped and thought of something joyful, he realizes that only Becky could break his discipline in such a manner.

The place is a simple place, nowhere close to exotic. It's the 5th level of a parking garage on the edge of the city. He and Becky would meet here at 5:30 pm during the weekdays when Becky was getting off of work. She would park her little blue car in the corner facing the city and he would wait for her and they would just sit and talk until it was time to say good night. Their moments of good-byes were never the same. They would depart eachothers company whenever it was right. They were great friends. As he reflects on this, he realizes that Becky has broken in on his thoughts again. He must remain serious!

He stands here in solitude. There's no cars here at 3°Clock in the morning. He's in the same corner, facing the city. This place was choosen for a meeting place many times by him, when there was absolute secrety involved. He has meet many people here. At all times of day and night. This morning was different, he could feel it. Feel it deep within himself. He knew the person, whomever they may be. When he or she arrives with the message, The message will be the end of his life. He has accepted that for thats the way he has choosen it to be.

Acknowledging this truth he allows himself a small smile with his eyes as he looks out onto the city. No one on the street, The messager has probably been in the garage before he arrives. Even though he arrived discreetly at 10 pm when the late employees were driving off for home. He had parked his car 5 blocks away himself. He checks his watch and it's 3:05 am, 5 more minutes to go and he will be aware of the fate of others, for he knows his own.   Sadu, "SA-doje"

His name is Judas, he's 43 ½ years of age. The year is 1999 during the last days of December. And this is a brief tale about him.

***** Chapter one

He was sitting at a table in a lounge. It must have been a lounge because where else would there be for a place with

So many book shelves. Even though there was only 43 books on the shelves, she knows because she counted. The room was huge. She doesn't remember how she got here but somehow knows that this is one of the many rooms of a castle.

She stands and starts to walk to the shelf where the 43 books are. Other than the odd titles of books such as "The Young Ink Pen." She notices that they are all written by the same author. A person with a funny name. She hears a squeaking noise, like door hinges that hasn't been oiled. Then she realizes it's the door, so she turns around and she sees a lion walking through the door.

The lion's mane shone like sunshine, the body was like polished bronze. The loin came walking toward her, looking her in the eyes, and Valisa sensed that the loin would not harm her. She knew the loing was a friend. Suddenly the lion at the shelf of books and to Valisa's Surprise, the loin devoured all the books in a matter of moments.

The loin started roaring wildly, as if in great pain from eating the books. Yet she sensed that it was a pain of joy and satisfaction.

Moments later the loin settled down and said to her "Whew! That was some meal." "You can talk?" She asked. "Yea but I can't read so I had to obtain the knowledge another way." he replied.

She was just recovering from the moment of being baffled when her best friend Becky came in and motioned for the loing to come with her. When they left, Valisa looked at the empty book shelves and then woke up. ✶✶✶✶✶✶✶ 3

"It was 8:15 am on a spring June morning. Valisa rushed out the door toward the busstop around the corner where she lived. She was on a rarely late for school. Not that it really mattered to her now since this was the last week of school and all the important test had already been taken. Yet ~~she~~ was instinctively punctual.

"Hay wait for me!" Becky screamed from her upstairs bedroom window, for she was late too. She just happen to glance out the window during her mad rush to put the last touches of her make-up on, and see Valisa. Only for a moment does Valisa looks toward the busstop and wish to make it. She stopped jogging and started walking back toward Becky's house. She waved at Becky and motioned her to hurry up.

As Valisa sat on the steps that starts the sidewalk that leads up to Becky's front door. She stops her momenta... to take in the beauty of spring. She inhales the sweet smell of the Buttercup flowers that's sprinkled throughout the front yard, as the morning sun beckons them to life.

It amazes her that her friend doesn't damage her hearing, because if she can clearly hear the loud music behind the closed bedroom window from ~~to~~ where she's sitting, Becky can surely surely hear. Valisa remembers the times when it's been like being at a concert while sitting on Becky's bed.

Becky came dancewalking out the front door eating an apple. Of course she lets the ~~cassette~~ run it's full course, Valisa thought. "Good Morning Beautiful." Becky says. "Good Morning Sexy." Valisa replies. That was their ritual each time they spoke their hellos.

As they was walking and enjoying the morning shine, Becky suddenly had a bright ideal, one of many during her moments of brilliantance. "Hay Let's walk to school, and enjoy this beautiful morning." She said. "Becky," Valisa replied "Every morning is great, I don't want to be late to school." "Val baby, we're already late, we'll just be a little later, anyway our morning classes are only scheduled parties anyhow, so just consider our as starting already and enjoy this beautiful morning."

Valisa conceded to Becky's persuasion and they began walking to school. "What are you going to do this summer?" She asked Becky. "I don't know, I think I'm going to work for L.J.'s department store downtown. Malisa's going to talk to her manager and she's sure he'll hire me." "That's great Valisa, what will you be doing?" "Ladies panties department." Valisa roared with laughter. "What's wrong with that?" Becky said a little hurt. "Oh nothing, it's just ladies langerie," Valisa answered patting Becky on her back. "Well smarty pants, what are you doing?" "I have no ideal." "What do you mean? At least I have plans. You got to be planing something. It's not like you to not have plans." "Well, let me put that another way, I have an ideal, only one, but I have no ideal about how to go about planning to make it happen." Becky smiled at Valisa, for she knew exactly what she was talking about. Valisa smiled back and Becky asked "you mean a man right?" "You got it girl. That's all I have planned. And when and if I get one I'll come by your department and help pay your salary." They started laughing, and enjoying the beautiful morning on their way to school. * * * * * *

Judas suddenly became aware of where he was. It was like waking up in a dream from a dream. "Where am I at?" He asked himself. "You're here where you suppose to be." The answer came as a thought. "What is my job this time?" He knew that this question was pointless, still he asked it anyway. And sure enough a thought replied. "Judas you know in time what will be. Don't be concerned with that. Just know that now and what was, is well. I'm sure that you know that question is pointless." Sometimes Judas disliked the way the thoughts replied to him yet he knew that without that inner voice he would be lost. He asked another pointless question, but the answer that came he did not expect. "How long will this job last?" "Until your end here on this planet."

15 years from now. He thinks to himself. This must be one hell of an assignment. The usual ones doesn't last no more than a few months. One or two lasted a year at the most. He knows he'll discover what needs to be done in due time, but the hugeness of it all is a bit overwhelming for the moment.

Judas knows it's the month of June, early June but the exact date escapes at the moment. As always when he starts a new era he doesn't remember how he got here, but he also knows that in a few days, he'll remember where he was at before he got here and how he got here. He knows that knowing that information at the start of an assignment could hamper the beginnings, before one has a sure understanding of the surroundings. He know one must always start fresh, without a past.

6

3 days later Judas became accustom and comfortable with the city that was his new surroundings. He also became that way with the societal culture. Eventhough he found himself with enough money to spend a month or so in an expensive hotel, he choose to stay at a cheap motel because the thoughts haven't revealed to him when his employment for money will started.

The night of that 3rd day he took his 1st field trip. He went to a bar in a middle class neighborhood. Eventhough he was comfortable with all, the "Yuppies" never ceased to amaze him. As always when he goes out, he took very little money. He took just enough for the the transportation and for 2 drinks.

As he stepped in the bar it didn't make him feel uncomfortable knowing that he hadn't decided upon who to be that night, for he knew the thoughts would tell him in due time. As he was headed toward the back it seemed like he was a participant in the ancient ritual of body crunching. Going through the throng of human beings was an act of joy in itself.

He bought a pitcher of beer, which he discovered to his surprise, was the price of what he estimated to be for two drinks. The idea came from the place he was previous before coming to this city. "Obviously" he thought to himself. This is the right city. He found a spot to stand where he could witness the coming and goings of the patronange; and have a place to place his pitcher and mug. He smiled at the thought of how ridicules he would look holding a pitcher of beer and drinking from it like it's a mug. But he knew if that sort of wildness was called for, he would handle the scence like a seasoned wildman.

The women of this city is fascinating. He thought to himself. They are such jolly spirits. Even in the previous one, he could detect a hint of sadness behind the smile, but here, there was no hint of sadness or loneliness, there was just the pure pleasure of enjoying the evening. He notice this girl dancewalking her way through the crowd, she was short and slender with a beautiful smile. When she became in front of him, he leaned quite close to her ear, not only for her to hear him, but also so that others can not. Eventhough the music was loud and people was talking, he could still hear what different conversations was being made. Maybe that was just him, he thought, he still leaned close to her ear anyway, and said "I would like to acknowledge you on your cleavage. It looks very delicious." She blushed and smiled. He knew that she accepted this acknowledgement, not because she hasn't been told this before, but because his was genuine. "Why thank you. That's very kind of you to notice. It took me a half an hour to make it look this good." She responded smiling. "Good evening, my name is Judas." he said as he held her hand, gently kissing it. "Hellee handsome, my name is Marlisa. Pleasure meeting you."

The thought told Judas "I just want to let you know that, you are right on key. Out of all the women in this city, out of all the bars in this city, you had to pick this one, and this young lady. She's a pre-guide to your first assignement at this Era. This is a good-sign." Judas thought back "Well you know, your training has become helpful if not nesseeary for me in perfecting my moments to become perfection, and purposeful to the cause."

8

"You look too young to be here." he said. "I am" she admitted. "I came here with a friend of mine from work. She's somewhere around. But who cares I'm with you now." She said smiling shyishly. "You're such a flirt." "I'm a flirt, you're the one who said I looked delicious." "That's right. How soon do I forget. So ah where do you work?" Judas asked trying to change the subject, because since she admitted to being young he didn't want to get to deeply involved into something that's considered against the law. Malisa paused for a moment, then replied "So, you don't want to pick me up, you're trying to change the subject because you think I'm too young for you, that's cool, I like you already. I could make your wildest dreams come true, but I'm engaged to be marry." This babe is quick, he thought. "Just my luck" he said. "Yea I'm so sorry", she said with a smile. "I'm 19 and I'm a manager trainee for the female clothing department at the L. J. store downtown." Judas jestures that he doesn't know the place, "You see I'm new to town and I don't know where's that located." "Really, that's funny, I was just thinking how funny your accent seems, You're from up north aren't you?" "No not really." "From out west?" "Not really." "Overseas?" "Nope." "You're from this planet?" "Well in a manner of speaking yes." Malisa curiously looks at him for a moment then decides to let it pass. "Anyway # L. J.'s is located on the edge of downtown and I've been working there every since I was in the 9th Grade. At first part-time then full time once I graduated. I think I'm going to go to college. I'm saving up the money now. Either that or a new car. Who knows maybe both."

Milton and Judas had been brainstorming their story for only a few minutes when the friend Matisa came with, walked up to them and told Matisa it's time for them to go. To Judas surprise, they looked so much alike they could have been sisters, but he knew they weren't because Matisa hadn't said so. Judas said jokingly, "But I've only just arrived." Matisa hugged and said to her friend, "Isn't he great? I'd kill a rhino." "A great fan of Matisa," Judas said interrupting Matisa smoothly got the message that Judas didn't want to be known and continued, "Yes he's also crazy, we'll meet him," she said holding out her hand to no's else. "I've seen greater." "It's been real," he replied as he kissed her hand and embracing it with his face. A short moment and with that, they were gone.

"Damn!" Judas thought, "If I was suppose to meet her as he thought, I was suppose to, then why didn't I ask for her address or something or something?" As the thoughts answered, "So did you something more important it was your impression" "What did I get?" "You'll know when the time is right." The thought answered. Judas let it go at that. He checked his watch and noticed that it was 12:15 am and he knew he must be going to catch that last public bus to the subway station so he wouldn't be spending the night in the street. Just as he figured, the crowds started coming in and he was leaving. "What a crowd to go with this crowd" he thought as he was making his way to the door. "I think I'm going to be here often, maybe I'll find a place to live near here, or at least I can bring enough money for cab fare." ✲✲✲✲✲✲✲

463

It's been 15 years since Judas first distinguished between his thoughts that he thinks to himself and the thoughts that came not from him. He was 13 years old. The revelation shocked him but not as much as 8 when he discovered where those other thoughts came from.

One Afternoon, Judas was catching the bus to go home. As he stepped on the bus another kid ran up behind him and when Judas looked around the kid punched him in the nose and then jumped off the bus. The bus driver closed the doors and started driving off. Stunned, Judas heard the bus driver ask, "Are you okay son?" Covering his left eye he looks up at the driver and politely request for him to let him off the fucking bus. "That fucking Neal!" Judas thought, he had no reason to hit him like that. "But I don't want to beat him up." He thought to himself. As if he was arguing with himself, the questionable thought asked "What else is there." "I don't know" he answered. "I know." The other voice said. "What, you better tell me because here he is."

Neal came walking up to Judas. Neal was shorter and skinnier than Judas. "I should tear him apart." He thought. But the other voice said "No. You should Love him." Neal jumped back into a boxing stand as Judas reached out his hand for a handshake, smiling. "I'm sorry Neal. Whatever the fuck I did to you, I'm sorry. Please accept my apology and tell me what I'm apologizing for." Neal looked up at Judas, a little puzzled and a little concerned too. "You told my girlfriend she had big tits." Neal said. "I'm sorry I said that about Debra." Although it's true he thought.

A week later on a Sunday afternoon, as Judas was returning home from church, he remembered suddenly the conversation he had had with himself. Maybe it was the peaceful afternoon that caused that moment of reflection, or it could have been just the right time. He wondered about the voice. Although it sounded like his voice, he knew that it wasn't him. "Maybe" he thought, it could be my conscience. What little he knew of the subject, he thought it was ~~possible~~ Possible.

While walking to the park on that spring afternoon he sat in a garden swing, and decided to get in touch with that voice. Who knows he may be on to something.

"Hello? Is anybody out there? ... I sound like a Pink Floyd Album." He thought to himself. What was he expecting anyway. How would he know which was its voice, and which was his voice, if they both sounded the same? Then he realized the difference in the state of minds. Judas continued to try for at least another hour until he finally got a response.

"You will not be told the unknown until it's time, for reasons that will remain unknown to you. There are secrets in the universe that many have discovered but few have understood. In time it will be known if you are of the few. Even if you are of the few are that not only understands but also accepts without doubts." "Wait a minute!" Judas said, Realizing he ~~spoke~~ spoke a loud he put his hand over his mouth and thought "Wait a minute. Who are you and why are you trying to drive me crazy by using my own voice to speak to me?"

"You didn't let me finish my speech, oh well, I'll have time later I'm sure, first of all let me just say that I chose to use your voice because I didn't want to go crazy. Now as far as who am I am, well sit back and relax, I got some heavy explaining to do."

Judas sat back and swung softly in the afternoon breeze. He was aware of the clouds in the sky, the smell of the dogwood trees in the park, the people that was strolling the park but mostly he was listening to his voice in his head. The voice told him that it spoke to him from another plane of time and space. That it is what Judas would understand as a guardian angel, but not really in the context of Angels, that it wasn't sent by God, it was sent by one of the Supervisors of the universe. The universe as he understands the concept. The voice said that in its time, it has done tours of duty in his reality a few times with only special cases. It had just returned from an Educational vacation and accepted this assignment to be with him with pleasure. "What am I to do?" Judas asked. "There will be some period of training before that's revealed to you." "Let's say all of this is true, and I accept that you are real, and I choose to go along, presuming I have a choice, If I don't know what is expected of me, how am I to train correctly?" "You have done what is expected of you," The voice replied. "You do have a choice up to a point. You see it's like I'm speaking to you through a door while stepping through. You can shut that door, but before long I will be in, and there will be no turning back. So I suggest that you have faith in God and choose soon.

Yes, he thought to himself. That was 15 years ago. Yes he had choosen to go along with the program. And eventually after a couple of years, his immaturity got the got the best of him and after what he thinks, was "The Experience." The voice told him it's real name. The voice revealed to Judas that it was a female name Olivia. She also told him that she was a spiritual personality, and since she was a female, that was another reason why it was choosen to use his voice when she spoke to him instead of her own. Ya. That was 15th years ago. * * * * * * *

Judas had been in the city for a few weeks now. He had gotten a steady job with a moving company and moved a 2nd story of a duplex house. It was in the neighborhood of the one he had visited on his first field trip. He admitted to himself that he was hoping to run into that young lady that Olivia had said to be a prequde to his assignment. But as luck would have it, he didn't see her, even with the frequent trips to the bar, she was nowhere to be found. He didn't worry, He just kept a normal schedule because, he knew that things would work out. Don't they always? He thought. He wondered if since this was going to be such a long assignment, if it took a longer time to prepare one self. Because usually by now something would have occured. And he would be knee deep in contributing. By Now he thought, he would be clear about what to do and whom his contributions would serve. The whole nine yards. All that he was sure of now was that this city was where he was suppose to be.

It was near the end of July in the middle of the week during the early evening while shopping for groceries, in the frozen food aisle, that the next meeting occured. But it wasn't the same young lady of the 1st field trip.

He had noticed her by the vibes that was dripping off her being. Although every female he noticed, This one really stood out. Not because of any unordinary bodily structure, It was her vibes. He also noticed that she was younger than Malisa. This fact disturbed him, Yet he went with it. "That's your Guide." Olivia thought to him. He smiled, and with only a brief moment of wonderment went to meet her.

"May I have this dance?" he asked her. She looked up quizically and he repeated. "May I have this dance?" "But it's that dreadful Muzak." she said with a smile. "Not to the music from the speakers, But from the music of my heart that beats to the rhythm of the excitement you've caused from the sight and feeling of your beauty." "Damn!" she exclaimed. "Who are you the man of my dreams?" "My name is Judas, I'm new in town and You're beautiful." "Thank you, but I'm also 16." "Age doesn't or shouldn't determine one's friendship." "I do agree." "° May I have the pleasure of having the knowledge of your name? "Oh I'm sorry. My Name is Valisa." "Well Valisa, let go my Eggo." Judas said as he took the box of waffles from her hand. And that was the first words shared with Valisa.

They parted their separate ways that night, And Judas neither gave nor requested a phone number because Olivia told him it would be inappropriate. Judas was content is with a smile good-bye. The next day he took a sick leave from his job because he felt it was necessary although his health was fine. He walked around the neighborhood hoping to see Valisa since he felt quite certain that she lived in the area. He walked up and down many streets for hours and still didn't see her. Tired, hot, and sweaty, he decided to go to the ice cream shop that was in a plaza up the street from where he lived.

The plaza consisted of a drug store, a chinese restaurant, a old bistrom theatre (which showed the latest movies.), The ice cream shop, and a record store. After buying a scoop of fudge ripple ice cream on a sugar cone, Judas decided to go home. Hearing music from a small speaker from infront of the record store he decided to buy an album of jazz and listen to it that afternoon. Something to do. He certainly wasn't going out walking the neighborhood anymore. That had proved to be fruitless.

As he walked in the store a familiar voice said "Excuse me sir, you must leave that ice cream cone outside." Judas turned in the direction of the voice and it was Valisa with a big smile on her face. "It might melt." He smilingly said. She walked up to him and took the ice cream cone from his hand and said "Not with me standing gaurd." And walked out the door. Judas watched as Valisa walked out the door and stood infront of the record store holding my ice cream cone. "Some gaurd." Olivia thought to him. "Yea." he replied. "Judas she's a part of the whole scheme of things, yet she's not the whole. I must point that out. You will of course discover later what I mean. Now let's go find a nice jazz album." Olivia said in his head.

with a smile good-bye. The next day he took a sick leave from his job because he felt it was necessary although his health was fine. He walked around the neighborhood hoping to see Valisa since he felt quite certain that she lived in the area. He walked up and down many streets for hours and still didn't see her. Tired, hot, and sweaty, he decided to go to the ice cream shop that was in a plaza up the street from where he lived.

The plaza consisted of a drug store, a chinese restaurant, a old fashion theatre (which showed the latest movies.), the ice cream shop, and a record store. After buying a scoop of fudge ripple ice cream on a sweet cone, Judas decided to go home. Hearing music from a small speaker from infront of the record store he decided to buy an album of jazz and listen to it that afternoon. Something to do. He certainly wasn't going out walking the neighborhood any more. That had proved to be fruitless.

As he walked in the store a familiar voice said "Excuse me sir, you must leave that ice cream cone outside." Judas turned in the direction of the voice and it was Valisa with a big smile on her face. "It might melt." He smilingly said. She walked up to him and took the ice cream cone from his hand and said "Not with me standing guard." And walked out the door. Judas watched as Valisa walked out the door and stood infront of the record store Politicking his ice cream cone. "Some guard." Olivia thought to him. "Yea." he replied. "Judas she's a part of the whole scheme of things, yet she's not the whole. I must point that out. You will of course discover later what I mean. Now let's go find a nice jazz album." Olivia said in his head.

"Some guard you are." he said as he exited the store with a bag containing 3 jazz albums. 2 of them he knew was good, & 1 was of an woman singer he never knew, but Olivia had told him it was good. Valisa looked up at him shyly and said "Well, It was dying and I sort-of saved it." "You started saying it as soon as you walked out the door." Judas said as they started walking together. Changing the subject Valisa asked "What type of music you got there?" "Oh some Jazz, Sade, Rickie Lee Jones, and ah Betty Wright." "So you're a Jazz man. Being a Jazz man is okay I guess." "Why thank you my young music expert. Hay I got an ideal, how would you like to join me for lunch. I make a mean hamburger." "I don't know about that." Judas putting on his politest smile replied "My frozen pizza ain't bad either. We could sit back listen to some Sade, You could tell me all about yourself." Valisa thought for a moment then looked up at him and said "Are you a pervert or something?" Not really surprised by her question Judas said "My dear Perverts don't like Sade." And with that they went over to Judas's apartment.

"Nice place you have here." She said as Judas escorted her way. He felt it would have seemed forward of him to let her come through the door first. "Yea, It's reasonable priced at about a thousand & monthly utilities included, I before I got a great deal." Leading her to the dining room as his TV was busted she noticed that everything seemed new. He told her that what little furniture there was he had bought when he moved to town. He pointed out that there wasn't a television set because he had no need for it, & he didn't watch T.V. that often anyway. He told her whenever he wanted to see sports championship games or a boxing match or something important like that he would go to a bar with a television. Valisa asked him is that the only reasons he goes to bars. Judas told her no, but added that in light of the present signals he wouldn't be going to bars that often anymore for a while. Valisa didn't know what he meant by this so she let it go.

He showed her the rest of the flat, She had seen the living room with a sofa and love seat, and the dining room where Richie Lee Jones' record was playing on the turn table, He respectfully just pointed to his bedroom door, And showed her the other bedroom which he was converting into a study room/library. She noticed that all the books just like the furniture were new. Judas told her that he had 32 more books to buy. He had already bought the 1st Beloven that was on his list of books to read and to study. Valisa thought that seemed some how familiar but couldn't recall how it was familiar to her. So she let it go. They went back into the dining room and spent that afternoon enjoying each others company by getting to know one another. Valisa didn't mind doing the most talking and enjoyed Judas for being such a great listener. He would often crack jokes and there was times when Valisa would laugh tears. Valisa left around 5 that early evening and Judas saw her to the door and discovering that she lived in the neighborhood invited her back anytime during the day. Valisa asked him about his job and he replied that along with deciding on not going to bars so often, he decided to put his job also, so his afternoons would be free. ★★★★★★ 18

It was 8pm and Becky had been waiting for Valisa since supper. She was in her room listening to some music. The music than her mother had told her to turn down twice. Even though it was still too loud, her mother understood what it was to be a teenager. So she put up with a lot of things that other parents probably wouldn't stand for. Becky and her mother had an understanding with each other. She would respect Becky's privacy as long as she doesn't get pregnant.

Valisa arrived around 5 minutes to 8:30. She started telling time that way since she's been hanging around Judas. "Good Morning Sexy," Valisa said. "Good Morning Beautiful," Becky replied. Eventhough as stated it was in the evening, They considered their day beginning when they first saw each other. It was a tradition everysince childhood.

Becky and Valisa made it a promise to see each other everyday of the summer vacation. For no special reasons, it was just they were best friends. The days when they wasn't able to see each other they atleast talked over the phone.

After spending a week or so recuperating from the school year Becky went to work full time during the days at L.J.'s Department store downtown. And Valisa just spent the summer hanging out seeing different guys and going to the movies. Valisa knows that Becky had been concerned a little about her because she hadn't been talking about Jim, or Brain, or any of them. Valisa haven't told her about Judas yet and was trying to find the right words to explain their friendship. Valisa did decide to tell her tonight.

I'm going to meet him. or even him?" Judas knew that she knew everything that he was suppose to do. He even accepted that she knew he was going to ask this question. He also realized that he wasn't going to get a straight answer but whatever she said would be a hint. Olivia although knowing that this confrontation was coming still didn't think her response was going to be adequate but it was the only response she knew that didn't give away anything. "Enjoy your breakfast, Enjoy your music, and go out and search for employment. All is being taken care of. When your guide VALISA, with a little help of your pre-guide MALISA, remember her. When they come together and introduce you to the one, Then you will understand. Of course I know when that will happen, and I tell you, It will happen when you are ready." Olivia answered. "But I'm ready now." Judas responded. "Are you ready for the next 15 years." She asked. Judas thought for a moment, fully contimplating what she was asking and after a few moments he answered that he was. "So" Olivia said. "Go out there and get yourself a g job." *******

Judas showered and shaved and went on his way. It was a beautiful day. or as Judas would put it, It was Another beautiful August day. Because it could be raining sleet and snow in the middle of winter and it still would be a beautiful day for he knows that to have something to show up as beautiful one must have a beautiful state of mind, which he has. The clouds were like white pillow towers spread out through the sky, every now and then providing shade from the blazing sun. Judas wore clean jeans with shirt sleeves, and clean tennis shoes. An attire he always wore when job searching. After all he wasn't going looking to be elected as president or anything. It would have been simple to go to the corner store and buy a newspaper, to look at the Help wanted ads then inquire by phone at home, But Judas knew that when Olivia said or suggested for him to go out searching that means just that. To go out, to get out the house. He decided that he would just go downtown to the library and read the newspaper specially the want ads, or he would get a paper and sit in the city park and too go around looking for a job later on. One thing for sure he's going downtown and he's going to buy a newspaper.

He gave himself at least 30 minutes for the bus, so he had time to stop by the store that's right across the street from the bus stop. He bought himself a brown cow {Ice cream on a stick usually chocolate}. As he was standing at the bus stop licking and enjoying his brown cow, he thought back when the last time he had had an ice cream cone. It was when he was lucky enough to meet Valisa. Then he thought that he had just used the word "Lucky" as if "Luck" was real. While wondering why he thought he was "Lucky" and wondering when had he begun to slip. Or if he was really slipping, a familiar voice from behind said "Excuse me sir, You must have the ice cream outside the bus." He turned around to see Valisa beaming her beautiful smile at him. He felt an odd need to hug her. "How have you been?" she said while taking the brown cow from him. Within the few moments before he spoke Judas not only looked how beautiful she appeared but also felt her powerful vibes. Once again he was amazed at how young in body she was. She was just standing there with the a chocolate on the corner of her smile. ✳✳✳✳✳✳✳

25

president or anything. It would have been simple to go to the corner store and buy a newspaper, to look at the Help Wanted ads then inquire by phone at home. But Judas knew that when Olivia said or suggested for him to go out searching that means just that. To go out, to get out the house. He decided that he would just go downtown to the library and read the newspaper specially the want ads, or he would get a paper and sit in the city park and to go around looking for a job later on. One thing for sure he's going downtown and he's going to buy a newspaper.

He gave himself at least 30 minutes for the bus, so he had time to stop by the store that's right across the street from the bus stop. He bought himself a brown cow {a icecream on a stick usually chocolate} As he was standing at the bustop they said licking and enjoying his brown cow, he thought back when the last time he had had an ice cream cone. It was when he was lucky enough to meet Valisa. Then he thought that he had just used the word "Lucky" as if "Luck" was real. While wondering why he thought he was "Lucky" and wondering when had he begun to slip. Or if he was really slipping, a familiar voice from behind said. "Excuse me sir, You must have the ice cream outside the bus." He turned around to see Valisa beaming her beautiful smile at him. He felt an odd need to hug her. "How have you been?" she said while taking the brown cow from him. Within the few moments before he spoke Judas not only looked how beautiful she appeared but also felt her powerful vibes. Once again he was amazed at how young in body she was. She was just standing there with the chocolate on the corner of her smile. ✳✳✳✳✳✳ 25

"You know the sky never ceases to amaze me!" Judas says. They was on the bus going downtown. He was sitting next to the window and Valisa was sitting next to him. He decided not to overwhelm her this time and instead of getting on the bus first, like a gentleman, And he sat down first. Valisa sort of knew that he was doing this to show her that he was defining their relationship. "Yea," she said taking a look at the cloudless sky. "The sky is to you as you are to me." They both shared smiles with eachother.

Downtown was crowded with people rushing to get one place or another during their lunch breaks. Judas and Valisa casually stroll aimlessly while others rushed pass them. Neither of them leading the way, or so Judas thought. He thought that as soon as they see an agreeable place to eat they would stop and have too lunch. But there had been a few places that was suitable, and they didn't stopped. Finally Judas realized that he's purpose for being downtown was not to look for a job but to be with her. He also realized that she was coming down town for a reason. He asked her, and she told him that she was meeting her best friend for lunch. She said it was a heck of a coincidense that he was with her because she wanted to introduce her to "Becky" (that's her best friend's name). Because she had told Becky all about him. Atleast all she knew about him. Judas felt a tingle travel down his back. He felt that everything was coming together. He asked her where were we suppose to meet Becky and when Valisa told him, Judas smiled because he knew that this was its

"What's wrong?" Valisa asked. She noticed a subtle change in Judas's attitude. He seemed a little withdrawn yet was trying to hide it. This was different from the outgoing Judas that she knew. After getting off the bus, they had rode the subway downtown to meet Becky. It seemed that as soon as they arrived at the crowded subway station he had made this change. But up until now, he had been cool so to speak, but since she was already nervous about introducing him to Becky, she felt that it wouldn't look right if they both showed up withdrawn. "Well," Judas answered. "Belive it or not, I'm not one to go out among society like this. I'm a very private person." Valisa was surprised by this answer, and Judas saw it on her face so he contiued to explain. "I know how it might look, I go out to bars on weekends, I work jobs, and catch public transportation to those jobs when I don't have a car, but that is different. I do those for a reason. I work because I have to pay rent. My jobs are faceless jobs. I work at places where you meet someone once or twice at the most, not everyday. I choose my jobs. The going to the bars on the weekends is my works also, that job is much harder to explain, but to sum it up, I look for folks in need of contributions. Out here (he waved his hands out in front of him) the space and state of mind of society is so plastic I don't like it at all. I go to movies at theatres way out, in the afternoon, in the middle of the week because I don't want to be around society with thier designer clothes, and thier plastic state of mind."

"Wow, that's wild!" Valisa exclaimed. "But if that's true, where was you going?" She thought to herself that if he answered, he was going to the bus stop to meet her or knew that he was going to see her, that he must be crazy. "Well isn't it obvious?" Judas said. "I have to be with you." Valisa started laughing. *******

L. J. Department store from the street looks six stories, but actually it has seven floors counting the basement. Judas was told that the top 2 floors were where the headquarters had offices. So actually from the basement to the fourth floor were actually merchandise. They walked in through the ground floor and once in Judas was barraged by various fragences. Carmel popcorn which was being sold at the candy counter, the sweet smells of sweets, to the discenfetiant smell of the floor wax. Valisa didn't get annoyed at this intrusion of the nostril, actually she seemed like she barely noticed.

Valisa informed Judas that they were to meet Becky at a resturant on the 3rd floor which has sort of a view of the city. During the elevator ride up, Judas made a consciouse effort to relax. He knew that this was important to her and he didn't want to embaress her by seeming anxious. For he also knew that this was actually the beggining of his assignment. Finally, he thought.

When they reached the 3rd floor the aroma of the resturant was everywhere, one could literally follow one's nose to it. It was in a corner of the building, where the walls were windows with a "sort of" view of the city. Since the resturant was on the 3rd floor, and although it was on the edge of downtown, the view was still blocked by huge sky scrapers. Yet it served it's purpose for a pleasant view. To Judas's surprise the restaurant was not crowded as he expected. Even before Valisa started walking in the direction of where Becky was seated. He spotted her with her back to them sitting by the window, looking out at the sort-of view. It seemed that a ray of sunshine was shone just for her, for it beamed at her table and engulfed her with it's glow.

Valisa squeezing his hand nervously, for she had taken it and was walking in Becky's direction. Becky must have sensed her, for she turned around and gave a most perfect smile. At first she only noticed Valisa, which Judas thought was cool, It was a sign of their great friendship. Then when she noticed Judas she stood up slowly with her mouth in an "O" expression and whispered "Oh my God". Judas being totally at ease, replied, "Nope, Not your God, But your new friend." Valisa gave out a genuine laugh at the first words shared between these two most important friends of her young life. Sitting down while her hands on Becky's shoulders easing her down with her, for she was a little stunned. She was still staring at Judas. She said "And your new friend is named Judas.? Judas, This is my best and Dearest friend Becky." Becky looked at Valisa and just burst out laughing, then they both laughed. Judas knew that this is what teen-agers do sometimes. He just sat there and took in Becky's vibes. While they were laughing they paused for enough breath to say "Good-Morning Beautiful" and Valisa replied "Good-Morning Sexy" and Judas thought to himself, So, All this time in this city, I've been preparing myself to meet Sexy. ✳✳✳✳✳✳✳

Becky was sitting in front of the mirror she uses to see when she needs to get her make up straight. Valisa is stretched out on her bed. They're listening to some Rock-N-Roll on her stereo. The odd thing is that Becky isn't using the mirror for make-up purposes, she's looking at her eyes. Judas, a couple of times had mentioned to Valisa about her eyes. It has been about a week or so since their first lunch together and Becky has been (if you're asking Valisa) a different person. She rarely wears make-up, because one time Judas nonchantlantly mentioned that make-up covers her natural beauty. She took this comment to be from one who's experienced with women. Although her father had said that to her many times, she didn't get it. After all it was her father, and she belived he was suppose to say things like that.

"So what do you think he has in plan for us tonight?" She asks, while looking at Valisa's reflection in the mirror. Valisa looks up and replies that she doesn't know. It was Friday night and Judas said he wanted to take them out around 11:30 that night. Luckly for Becky, her parents were out of town for the weekend, and all Valisa had to do was to tell her mom she was spending the weekend at Becky's. "Do you think he'll take us over his house and take advantage of us?" Becky asks with a wicked smile. "Only in your dreams." Valisa says as she sits up on bed. "How did you know about my dreams?" They both laugh at that. "Maybe he take us to the movies, or sneak us in a bar." She tells Valisa. But she knew from the expression on Valisa's face that she was just as confused about where

481

they was going as she was. Valisa said "You know he doesn't like society that much, and he wouldn't break the law just to get us in a bar, or best. Whatever it is, we know it's going to be wild." "Yea" Becky says with a sigh. She looks at her watch and it's 11:15, Judas should be coming any minute. "Can I ask you something?" "Sure anything Beck." "How do you feel about Judas?" "Becky baby, I was just thinking the same thing." "You were?" "Well not exactly, I was thinking about how you felt about him. I think that you suppose to be his friend more than me. I don't know how to explain this, but when I see you two together, although it's because of me you are together, It's like I don't need to be there, or that soon I won't be there." "Val, Are you saying that you're feeling left out because Judas has had all my attention those two times I've seen him." "Of course not, It's just, it's just, ... I don't know." They laugh for a moment, because they both know that Judas has come into both of their lifes in such a way that they can't explain but like anyways.

"So" Becky says, being the first to attempt to be serious. "So what?" "So how do you feel about Judas?" "I feel good about Judas. What about you?" "What you mean what about me?" she asks standing up to go get her purse. As they leave the bedroom and go down stairs, she continues "You still haven't answer my question." "I did, you just didn't like my answer. Now answer my question." Becky looks out the front window to see if Judas is coming and doesn't see him. She was really just stalling for time. She turns and says "Well I like him. And..." Just then the door bell rings.

31

"And saved by the bell." Becky says as she opens the door." I just looked out the window and didn't see you." She says to Judas as he steps in the front hallway." One thing you should know, I'm always here even when you don't see me." Then he greets them "Good Morning Beautiful, Good Morning Sexy." And they in unision greet him "Good Morning Judas." For it had been decided that Judas couldn't be categorized. "So where are we going?" Val asks as she goes gets her purse from the living room. Judas looks at Becky and smile, "We're going to an intellectual gathering, or in other words a poetry reading." "Oh yea, that's next. Where at." Becky says as she cuts out the lights and opens the door for them." This coffee shop up the street on the Bulovard. I went in there one morning and read a poster that they have poetry readings every first fridays of the month. It starts at midnight until." "Until when?" Val asks innocently." They they now have reached the sidewalk and with Judas in the middle was walking down the street. "Until it's over." Judas answers with a smile.

When they arrived at the coffee shop, Val noticed that she always thought this to be a mexican restuarnt. Maybe because of the taco signs on the window, then she decided that that was just a contra the cafe was a medium size. About a hundred people was in there. And Val noticed right away that she and Becky was the youngest ones in there. Over half the heads turned when they walked in, After all she thought, We're two young sexy girls with a guy in his late 20's. This must look odd she thought.

It was a small but crowded cafe. The dining room was of an L shape. Actually a backward L of sorts. Like when they stepped in the door they was at the corner of the L. to their left was the short end of the L and straight ahead was the long end. Booths was along the left side of the long end and tables in the area of the short end. Across from the booths was the serving counter. At the front which was at the beginning of the long end was a spot light with a microphone and a stool. A big black speaker was sat on some milk crates and a young lady who was reading poetry was being heard at the moment. The cafe was crowded and people was standing in the aisle. Judas told them to follow him and they did. To Val's surprise he led them to an empty booth. She shouldn't have really been surprised she thought, after all he is who he is, which she has no idea. People was coming up to the table and speaking to him. They called him Andor. Becky and Val first thought they had made a mistake then when the 3rd and 4th person spoke greetings to him as Andor they knew that he had lied to them. Or maybe, Val thought for just a moment, he had lied to us. Judas like he had become aware of Val's brief doubt in his authenticity explained to her. "You see," he said "last month I came in here to recite some of my poetry and I felt sort of shy about reading my works. That shyness, mixed in with being with a feeling that I feel about hanging out with society, even with a society that's formed outside of your everyday run of the mill 9 to 5 society. I decided to not let these people know my real name so I told them my name is Andrew Horvath. He's a..... What are you laughing about?... He's a character of one of the 43 books I have in my library. What's so funny?" Val said "You shy?" And began to laugh again. Then Becky told him while smiling "It just seems a little too wild that you would have to play this charade." "Yea, Yea I know" Judas conceded. "But it was a spur of the moment thing and I went with it." "Hey you guys want some coffee, I have to sign my name on the list, I'm going to recite some more poems I wrote." "Where's your poetry?" Becky asked, and Judas pointed to his head then his heart, then to the both of them. Then he smiled and asked "Coffee?" While he was gone the only thing that was said was said by Becky. She said "Far Out."

Judas returned to the table with 3 mugs of coffee, he said that they were special mugs. You could get a refill if you wanted. "You know, he said, "The first night I was here I was standing back there by the door and I bought a mug of coffee, and I set it on the counter between sips, I noticed this guy standing off to my right. He just felt like he was up to no good, I didn't think twice about it because most writers give off that vibe, because they're breaking boarders of reality, Anyway after a few moments this guy stands right in front of me and blocks my view of my mug then when he passes he has my mug in his hand. I politely tap him on the shoulder and tell him that that's my mug and you know what he does? He takes a gulp of my coffee and says he's sorry. And offers to buy me another cup. I says okay and he goes and comes back with a smaller cup of coffee. I say to myself what the hell I had a half a cup left. Come to find out later that the cup the coffee came in that he gave me isn't refillable, but the one I first bought was. Isn't that crazy? A tricker got tricked."

Becky discovered that some things that Judas says should be left alone. Like what does he mean when he says he's a tricker? But one thing did catch her attention and she asked him about how this booth was empty when any one of these people that was standing up could have had it. Hold again his answer required another question but she didn't ask about it. He's answer was "I created this empty booth for us, like when I go downtown and it's rush hour, I create an empty parking space for me that's close to the location I'm going to."

They sit back and relax, and listen to the ones who read their poetry. Sometimes Judas would comment like "did you understand that wierd stuff" or "that's crazy" or once he said "it bein read by this pretty woman was good. Sometime around 2:30 am he asked them if they would like to go to the park Sunday late morning and have brunch. Becky said she would love to but Val said she couldn't, she has to go to church. "Oh yea," Becky said. "She has to worship Paul. Not the Paul in the Bible but the Paul who's going to be starting Quarterback and a Senior next year at school." Val blushes and tells Becky to hush. Judas smiles and says "Lucky Paul."

"Speaking of Lucky Paul," Val says "Not trying to change the subject or anything, but is there anyone out there who's lucky because of you?" "Because of me?" Judas says slyly, pointing at his chest. "Yea, Judas Andor Horvath or whatever, is there!" Becky asks resting her face on her hands with her elbows on the table, really interested in the answer. But before Judas has a chance to answer, the guy called out Andor Horvath name as the next poet to read his poems. He looks at Becky and asks "Don't you feel lucky?" then while he gets up to walks to the front of the cafe he winks at Val and smiles at Becky with the look of surprise on her face.

"Thank you." He says in the microphone. "My Name is Andor Horvath. I will recite to you poetry by a writer name Judas, a very close and personal friend of mine. The first is for my two friends.
"Very few comes along
And impact me the way you have
Lonelyness wasn't even a friend like you.
I say things sometimes
Simple answers to questions yet to come
Ah... Let me pause for a moment
And breath the breathe of life you've given me
Not since I was once younger
Did I ever have such true friends.
Beautiful and sexy
Envokes smiles from my thoughts
Catch in this brief moment
Kindness and lasting love
Your friend forever even after I'm gone.

He recited a few more poems. Everyone was quiet. Becky and Valisa both noticed that this was the first time that every one was quiet. Even they had talked during a few poets speakings. When Judas would pause for a breath one could hear the flame on the candle flicker. When he finished by saying thank-you only a few applauded. Becky and Valisa didn't clap because they were still traveling among the words of his poetry. It seemed only when the guy announced the next poet did people stop traveling. By that time Judas had returned to the booth. "That was real cool. That was incredible." Becky said with a big smile across her face. Valisa was wiping tears from her eyes. "I'm sorry" she said. "You, you just said some things that make me cry. I'm not crying because I'm happy or sad, I'm just crying. Isn't that wild?" "Thank-you, I really wanted you all to enjoy yourselves tonight." "It's 3 o'clock in the morning." Becky said looking at her watch. "I'm glad I have the weekend off." "I rather do this than sleep any old day." Valisa said still drying her eyes. "You know," Judas said "There's some people who sleep because they're sleepy. And there's some people who sleep because it's time." I'm not going to ask about that one. Becky thought. Instead she said "Well it's about that time." Valisa laughed and gave her a push on the shoulder. Judas smiled at her wit. He really enjoyed them being with these two beautiful young ladies. 15 years he thought. Imagine. Then he realized he couldn't realize it. "What are you thinking?" Valisa asked. "I was just thinking how you two have made me Lucky Judas. or Lucky Ander tonight." "Well, I'm Lucky Beatiful. Because of you." "And

"I'm Lucky Sexy. Because of you too." "Hay, Hay, none of this mushy stuff." Judas says. "Well okay, one more mushy question then that's it for tonight." He places his hands on the table, looks down at his coffee mug for a moment. Then looks at them with a serious expression and asks "May I have the pleasure of escorting Beautiful and Sexy home this morning?" They started laughing partly because of relief because they expected something else. What they expected they didn't even know, but what they got was so cool. * * * * * *

"This is wild." Olivia thought. She had been trying to get in contact with Judas for at least an hour for no particular reason, other than to conversate for a while. The thing is that Judas unknowingly shut the doorway to his world by being in the state of mind he's in. This perdicament has occurred only after he has transferred. In the early stages of his new Era usually it's not possible to happen after a few weeks into his new Era. But that was when the Era's was expected to be a year or two. Now since this is it. Since this is going to be it for the next 15 years, the possibilities of this blockage occurring is endless. Olivia could close her eyes and an image of what Judas was doing and where Judas was at would appear in her mind. Really the source of this blockage goes deeper than his state of mind. Because now its Saturday afternoon and he's in the backroom E where he's in his study looking out the window as the jazz plays in the background. Judas does this often in the afternoon and a blockage hasn't occurred. Maybe, she thought, It's the thoughts that's he's having while in this state of mind. So

"That's it!" she said to herself. It has to be the thoughts that he's thinking, that's causing the blockage. She knew that at certian levels she couldn't hear or know his thoughts. That's the level that also he's in less control of. After all theses years together he hasn't mastered that level of consciousness. Oh sure there was an emergecy way she could get through but that as she found out once before, would cause a massive head-ache. This wasn't an emegency so she'll have to wait a while untill Judas came back from deep deep thoughts.

Again Judas realized as he sat there looking out the windows that he lived on a planet that was alive. It wasn't the way the branches of the trees swayed in the afternoon breeze, It was the branches themselves. The leafs on them was life it self. They could easily be considered hair, like the bark can been seen as skin. Only in another form. "What is this? What is this?" Judas kept asking himself. Lastnight with Valisa and Becky, or should he say Beautiful and Sexy, Being with them was joyous and sad all at the same time. It reminded him of some great friendships he's had in the past, yet those memories were also what made him sad. For every friendship had to end because he had to go away, he had to move on to the next Era. And now here he is, with great friends at the begining of the last Era, a long Era, And he doesn't know how this friendship will endure in the long run because he's never been in the long run. It's always been a short joy. He feels for the first time every since he was once younger a sense of doubt, a sense of lost confidense. "What is this? What is this?" "This is Life" Olivia answers. "Where have you been?" she asks. "Lost, you could say." Judas sees that his answer although it was his first thought, It was the truth.

"Ya know Olivia I was just thinking." "What was you thinking?" She interrupts. Not just to answer his question but to speak in her voice, which should let Judas know the importance of this conversation. "Well I was just thinking about how involved I get in peoples lives." he contuies. "Like Greg and Gloria, and then I just leave and move on. How I never able to see the result of what I've done. You know I was just thinking about a lot of things like that." Olivia paused for a moment to feel what he's feeling and to also come up with the right comment. "What it sounds like to me Judas, is that you've allowed doubt to creep it's way in your state of mind. If you remember correctly, You gave Greg and Gloria back their marriage, and insight to the possibilities to the power of choices, whether they be wrong or right. You know it wasn't planned for you to spend the rest of your life by their side and make sure everything works out." "I know But," "But nothing" she interupts again. "Even if you were not an employee of the universe you would still meet people, become friends, and say good-by, that's apart of life my friend." "I wonder where would I be now if I wouldn't have discovered you." "Where do you think you'll be?" She was really interested in this for Judas had never ventured in this area of speculation before. He always kept to the now, what was, or what will be, only in the strictest of reality sense. But now he was actually sharing a part of himself that he's kept private from her all these h years, which makes her wonder how much more is in that private sector of his mind that she can not see. That part of mind that when he gets involved with it, She is unable to to get in contact with him. That part she senses stay could be dangerous and create another incident like the one that occured in the beginning of their partnership. "Olivia are you there?" "Yes, I'm here, my mind wondered for a moment." "I was saying that I probably would be a college graduate or working in a computer firm or a world class jewel thief on the run from an international police force. I asked you what you thought of that and you didn't respond, that's why I asked you were you there." "Well I guess we both have a part of our minds that's our own." "What are you talking about." "Never mind. no punn intended, I'll explain later, anyway I think that those two ideals of what you said you'll probably be now is interested. and perfect. Because as you will remember when we met, you was on the border line of Yen and Yang and ofcourse you would have choosen one way or the other. Luckly or Unlurkly whichever way it is at the moment, I came along and unknowingly to you gave you the opportunity to be both. So you see, you got the best of both worlds."

Judas realized what she was saying. He had so far lived a life of both the resposisble man, and the secrective man. The under many aspects of the graduate and thief that he pictured himself he could have been. This doubt that he was feeling was as simple as seeing it as a part of life but it was difficult as hell when feeling it. And easy to say it's a part of life when you're and observer than a paticapant. "I heard that thought Judas. And you seem to forget that when you feel it, I can feel it too." "I wasn't implying You." "Oh Sure." "Really I wasn't." "Wether or not you was implying me is illrelavent, because if one has life within, one can experience the life of others simply by extending a conscious effort to be in touch, after all everyone and everything has the same source of life. I can feel your doubt just like you can feel the warmth of the sunshine on the leafs of the tree outside your window. Dig?" "Ohh, you said Dig? Yea babe I dig?" "Judas I think I've been hanging around you too Long". They laugh at this. "Not long enough." Judas says.

Out of nowhere Olivia says "Judas you need a car. you've no need to use the public transportation any more." "Now Olivia, you know that I can't afford a car right now unless it cost half a thousand. The few thousand that's in the bank is covering the next five months rent. Unless you think I should move to cheaper residence, or buy a plunker. The latter is out of the devil." "Oh yee of little faith. I know that you're not going to buy a horrible car, also, I know you like where you live. It just so happens that this arrived here yesterday who told me he died of old age a couple of weeks ago. He had remained behind to make sure his wife was okay. He was telling me how she put an add in the newspaper to sell her car for 400# because really she didn't need it and it was all she needed. But the problem was that no one called because everyone is thinking it's a joke. Guess what the model of her car is? well it's a Benze Benze. 1978 model. I told the the guy, by the way he was a teenager about time he got here. I told him not to worry I'm working with this fellow who will not only buy her car he will also look in with her from time to time. The guy a was overjoyed. He dissappeared for a while and came back and said everything is fixed. Now Judas all you have to do is make a call here this evening at exactly 5:05. What do you think of that?" Of course Judas wasn't suprised, Olivia had always told him things that wouldn't be normal, but he was accustom to it so he said what he usually said when she revealed something only a privialeged few could handle. "That's some kind of wild inside information." "So you'll do it?" She asked, because sometimes she knew he didn't like knowing what others didn't, or what he wasn't suppose to know. She withheld from him that the guy, when he dissappeared, went over to disconnect her phone untill 5:05 pm, and that at 5:06 a customer was going to offer 2000# dollars, and if Judas was late calling she would sell the car to the other guy. "Of course I'm going to call...... Geuss what Olivia?" "What?" "I think I know what you meant when you said our personal part of our minds." "What do you think I meant." "Well I can't explain it exactly, but I just had a brief glimsp of an experience of yours. When you was just thinking about disconnected phones and 2000# dallers and everything." Olivia was of course not shocked that Judas had actually read her mind, "After all he is a special person." she thought to her self. So she replied "So you in a way got some inside information on the inside information?" "Yea. But I'm sure somewhere in there it wanted to come out so that's how I got it. Dig?" "Yes I think I know." She realized that he was trying to tell her that guilt from withholding whatelse she knew inside her share that information. "Judas you know what?" "What." "You're cooler than an ice cream cone

494

at midnight in the middle of winter at the north pole." "Why thank you my dear," Judas replied with a smile. "So you'll call?" "Yes, I'm still going to call." "Listen..." Olivia said, she was about to say something else when she heard "Simon" another partner of hers, He was calling her. "Listen Judas, I just wanted to check in you know, If you need me just think me and I'm always here. Simon needs me." Judas never heard of Simon before but knew he was another employee she manages. For a brief moment he wondered how many others he's never heard of. But that moment was very brief. "Okay Love, I'll talk to you later. Untill then You'll always be in my mind." And Just like that she was gone.

They never said good by, He knew she was go because whenever she left it always felt like when you closed a window on a windy day. The wind ceases. That's how it felt in his mind.

As he got up to go change the record on the system, he checked to see what time it was. It was only 3 o'clock. Satisfied he went to fridge to retrieve a bottle of beer. He pushed the replay button on the phonograph player. Which would replay the Album as many times as he wished untill he turned it off. It was a classic Billie Holiday so he'll let it play and play again for awhile. He returned to his "study." He selected a book from the shelf, one which he'd only read once and started rereading it at selected places. In between reading he would glance up to see if any of the leafs of the trees had grown since the last time he glanced up. Every so often he would just pause and smile from appreciation of the fact that things were finally coming together. Then he stop smiling because he'll realize how easily everything could fall apart. Doubt once again creeping in. ✳✳✳✳✳✳ 44

chapter 12

yours

truly

steven

Prologue

The stage is my life. The chalk board on the stage is my Being. Gikuyu is the name I gave the chalkboard. The chalk is used to write the necessary state of mind. That's required of any given situation in order for insights and discoveries to occur.

21 days I decided to break down the chalkboard and rebuild it. Then change the name from Gikuyu to Steven. Yet during the tearing down, a source from the stage didn't allow that to happen. So now it's back, strengthen from what was learned from the experience of thought that cause the action of destruction.

THANX

It has just occurred to me. How I was on the brink of a whole new being. (by not being a writer.) I was slowly dismantling all that has been built up to perpetuate the existence of Gikuyu.

I thought that it may had been simpler {for sure borer} If I was only known as Steven Simmons, to go about publishing all that I've written as if the author was dead, which he would have been.

While breaking down the chalkboard I had to experience and then destroy all the insights gained while being Gikuyu. It only took the first insight which I had a long time trying to destroy to discover that-"That way of life is the only way of life." Even though I've come to choose it, it was chosen for me. That fact I cannot escape no matter how I personally feel.

Even now since not writing for three weeks, I've only begun to think about writing within the past few days. It's odd to realize that I'm a writer.

Odd in a sense of appreciation that I've never felt before

For

Something interesting has happened during the writing of these first few pages. A song has "re-popped" in my head. I'm able to star reading another book. As I've done when I've finished one I usually immediately start another one. This morning I finished the last 70 pages of a 572 page novel. The 5th one I've read in about two weeks. The others were no more than 200 pages.

Although there has always been thinking. The thought were more of a general context to prevent contamination from the thoughtlessness of my present atmosphere. Now this book gives me the opportunity to think thoughts that will conclude with having insights occur

Gifts

He was a writer. Being a feast or famine way of life that he lived. Famine often was the way since it was early in his life. The X-mas was occurring and his girl friend was expecting to receive something. He didn't believe in the socialize ritual of giving gifts, but she did. So he gave her what she desired most.. His love.

His job was to transport a prisoner by sea, to a land that would put the prisoner to death. The boat capsized by a tidal wave. He found a piece of boat that he doubled as a raft. He saw the prisoner in the sea and rescued him. They continued their journey. He gave the prisoner a gift... His life.

He saw a world that needed peace. His reality was one of powerlessness. His friends had attitudes of contentment. Yet he saw others that had realities and friends like him, and still lived to make a difference in the world. He saw what it took and that's what he did. He gave up living for....Himself

Received.

    I've had countless conversations where I've given just as much countless examples of how the universe works and serves those who are willing to believe it to be possible. believe it 100%.
    During those conversations I've had insights to occur and I assumed they were occurring for the other party. After all my underlining purpose in many of the conversations is from my commitment to contribute.
    Only recently have I come to realize something. Maybe I've realized it before but not so clearly as I have lately. I think because I was going over the title in my head while having a conversation.
    Then it hit me. I can do all the example giving in the world, and have all the commitment one can have, and still one may not be contributed to if one has chosen to not have the contribution received.

Living

We all know that the season of spring brings various kinds of flowers to life. The main word is life. The flower has life.

It's also a known fact that trees grow and flourish by the process of photosynthesis. A process that can be easily considered to be only done with the presence of life. Dig?

All insects of course has life all animals and mammals. But it seems that only those species are considered to be able to live.

It is my opinion that living isn't just going through the motions, reacting to the circumstance that one finds oneself in during life.

Living is acting to reach a goal set in life. A goal that isn't dictated by the circumstances. A goal that's conceived from a commitment.

Living is also taking a stand and Being that stand when it seems totally crazy Being that stand because the surroundings say so.

Being in life is not living.

Must

    I don't remember which it was, either T.V or in a book, most likely I heard on T.V. Since I was amused by the statement when I was once younger.
    A guy requested another person to do something and the other person (Unaware of the other guy) replied "Is that a Please or Damnit?" I was somewhat struck by the raw authenticity of the persons reply.
    I remember also when I was once younger, seeing photos and hearing about the famine of Ethiopian people. The men, women, and children.
    Although that was only a phase in the media coverage. Many people viewed it as if it was a "should or must" when it came down to a request for their support.
    Now if we're all Human Beings and there are those who are dying a senseless death, while you have the means within your grasp to prevent it. I think it's really absurd to even consider if it's a matter of "Should or Must"

Continue

The chalkboard has been on the stage for so long, countless inscriptions has been written, then erased, then some rewritten. (Only a few has been rewritten.) Still there's been a lot of chalk used over the years.
If the dancing on the edge of sanity caused grief and anguish personally to me, Yet in brings fourth contribution to the world, Should I continue?
If that's the purpose of the chalkboard, should it stay implanted within the structures of the stage?
If while walking along this path, many experiences occur that wouldn't get through without suffering. For example going to jail 4 or 5 times. For weeks to months at a time, and various other experiences like that. Yet also having the exact opposite, like standing in front of a crowd of over a hundred of your friends while they give you a standing ovation for the poetry I had just read to them.
Knowing that I can if I really REALLY wanted to, get off that path..I could. And just leave the world. Should I stop walking and get off. Nope. I think I'll just continue.

After

       If you've only had Joy and Laughter
            When pain comes
            What comes after
         Would you cry tears of joy?

I paraphrased that to consider what does come after. It's from a poem I wrote when I was once younger. I had asserted that one with a state of mind that has always been positive and that that has always believed in possibilities for a breakthrough no matter what happened, if this person is released in the world where society doesn't work like that, and influences them, and they experiences maybe death, persecutions, or incarceration. (Something that is viewed as the taking away of a part of life), may it be life itself, Ones' sense of knowing maybe or even the ideal of freedom.

    Does one reject the influences and realize the awesomeness of their way of being or does one give in into society.

            If you've only had Joy and Laughter
                When pain comes
                What comes After.

All's Gone.

I've not thought much about it anymore. No more than anything else. I've realize that it's only a matter of time that I once again consider to stop being a writer.
Even though I've written a lot about or at least I've referred a lot to the fact, that one shouldn't be I the now with the past as a view shield that'll be used to operate in the future. This book here is written without that "Past viewing shield" so it's truly from the now that from the what will be.
I often think about how will a piece be written when I'm being in the what will Be and All's gone.
I wonder will the words even be the same.

Can I

Can I not Only Love You
And Be myself also
Are you the one for me
I truly would like to know
Time has no say with us
We're forever like the sky
Yet who am I to love
If you would say good-bye
Can I Not Only Love You
And smile at my pain
You left me to wonder
If I'll ever see you again

Become

One would think that at some point in time I have repeated myself, maybe many of times I've said something, then while in the midst of another project years later I say it again unknowingly-{sometimes knowingly) and yet I'm sure you can understand it, when I say that whatever I say. I say it for a reason.

When I'm writing or have written words and you are reading them. {No matter how much I chicken scratch it} The words you are repeating them with the voice in your head. If you're repeating the words I'm writing. I am speaking but only using your voice. Dig?

What is said before and said again is done in a fashion that has it not separated by time and exist as one instead of the same sentence written in two different Eras, for one derives from the first.

It wouldn't take much of a effort to view my words, and the voice within your mind. Both together the Oneness it is to Become.

Insane?

Can one destroy their current reality and replace it with another, and be empowered. If so....does the replacement reality have to have the same surroundings as the previous one. If not does one risk "unnecessarily" the possibility for the opportunity to go insane?

Will You

I'm sure there are many moments in history where a mass exodus has left countless ones with a sense of worthlessness. For those who can afford to leave; do. Which makes the left backs and the want nots disempowered from not having a role model to be an example.

There are those who participate in the exodus, I want to go with my people, not aware that they are only their people through statistics and state of mind. Leaving behind those who truly related by heritage.

I woke up from sleep early in the morning and wrote the previous two paragraphs. The first talks about those who are left behind, the 2nd talks about those who leave. Simply put. If you was living in the ghetto and only by status, or by having money was you able to move to the suburbs, knowing that one's' true essence of life is in that community would you leave? Will You?

Note; Fats Domino with all his fame and riches, stayed in his neighborhood.

Leave Me

Go on and go, and don't leave slow.
Don't look back to watch my frown
for it is needed
So you won't be let down.
Step out and be gone.
With the memory of you
I'll never be alone.
Graduate and proceed.
Complete and be free.
I am no longer what you need.
It's okay to leave me.

Known

When there's no way according to reality, which one can move on onto the next phase, because it's simply accepted to be impossible, given all the facts and evidence that reality provides one with. One chooses to act at this time out of understanding that the actions taken is not those that are considered to be rational if one was paying attention to reality. One chooses to not see reality. When it's like that the danger is known.

People are sometimes taken aback when someone close to them dies. When my grandmother died, or my aunt on my grandmother's side or a close friend of the family, or someone I liked or even loved goes, It amazes me how the folks at the funeral cry and all of that. Every since I was young I've been aware of the fact with Life, just a unexpected it comes, Death is also sometimes somewhat unexpected. This I've always known.

Post script: about eight years after writing this I cried like a baby while carrying my mother's casket to her grave..

Yvonne

Last time I spoke with you, I was in the house next door to your neighbor. I was still overjoyed to just ear your voice. It became obvious to me that I wouldn't be seeing you for a while, even though you agreed to see me that night.

You will not be reading this probably until years after it's written, it doesn't matter. Just letting you know that I've always been cool with the fact that we're great friends.

Also just for the world sake, for this passage is written in the context of a book. Yvonne has an understanding of me that's beyond the surface. We was friends in high school, when I was the guy from New Y. C. and we've remained together throughout my life in public and while I've been a recluse.

Jesse Yvonne Upshaw is a cool woman.

Has Been

One of these days I'm sure I'll be able to say that I was once a writer. I'll be able to brag about those glory days of living life on the edge. Those times when I met hundreds of women.. Friends to most, Lovers of a few. Even Being a Lover to a few of hundreds is a lot.
One of these days I'm sure I'll be able to say, Yea it was the deepest of times, it was the intense of times, there will never be times like those in my life time. Well it may not come down to me saying my lifetime, for I may be dead before I'm able to say I was once a writer.

My friend

Man there sure is that sky
Yonder there above those tress

Find out if you are smart,
Remind me of your thoughts.
I alone live in my world
Even though others are among me.
Notice the freedom
Don't give up my friend!

Through all

Through all of this. This pain, this joy, this celebrating, this suffering, I say to you. Life is Life Babe. Yea once upon a time when there was no knowledge of the purpose for the various experiences, did come to not respect the gifts of life, and to regret the bad times and only cherish the good times. When after all, nothing has to be, before something is to become. This paper must first be clear, before I'm to consider to put this passage here. Dig?
　　Through all those poems, short stories, what not's I've written, there was the moment that I've known what they meant. Those moments were "of course" few and far between. For it is not myself that I should understand them. I write them, you get them. Dig?
　　Through also all of this, it'll be tomorrow that I'll mostly miss.

My Madness

There's a sort of glorified glassy gloss, shone on the new skin covering what I called the tattoos of the moment of sanity. That's on the inside of my forearm. In yet there's nothing glamorous about it. A deception of appearance that's all it is.

The outcome of my life {this life..this time} can not in any way be predicted with a certain degree of accuracy . for it is yet to be determined by me if I should or shall not be in view of the Public.

My simplicity is my own insanity, for how can one maintain knowledge if one is constantly free, it comes and it goes, I'm never quite sure of what I know.

Madness, uh. There's no such fucking thing.

Of Yore.

In these present times of certain confusion, I've stumbled upon the realization that I as a man is even less than flesh as I've considered myself to be.

During these recent moments of grave circumstances I have profoundly discovered the value of this sense of fleshlessness. For if one is more thoughts than emotions, one is able to conquer the space that one's in. Only if one is able to choose the way of thinking.

Now. Everything that is from the substance of the source of my thoughts is purposely in line with inquiring, discovering, and contributing. Now it's necessary. I believe, well I know at some point in the distance future it'll be by choice. Like to be in that existence to get in touch with that power. Like it was in the days of Yore.

It Isn't

I dreamed that I was in school, and this time all the students were all the crazy and mentally ill folks that I've come across, and some were the crazy people I know. People who are totally socialized are the people I considered crazy. Like in life as in my dream, I decided to quit school, in the dream as I was walking up the hallway toward the front door, this kid wearing concrete boxing gloves ran up and punched me in the side and started laughing.

I thought he was just bullshitting around, but when the other students came out wear bigger concrete stuffed boxing gloves, and laughing, I started running for the doors. They caught up with me and formed a semi circle around me. One would punch then another would punch. I thought to myself "If they keep this up, they'll kill me."

I screamed "Hay wait a minute!" They paused. "Do you think this is a fucking punching party?.. Well it isn't!"

As I was waking up I saw myself kicking ass.

For me

It was stated earlier it's you who I'm a writer for. And since I briefly mentioned "true" writer as a description of who I am, that means I'm not part time. Being a writer is my life. So I don't live my life for me.

In conversations it has been asserted if I don't live my life for me, I must not Love myself, so I rationalize that into a purpose which is to love the world.

First let me point out I have to love myself profoundly to give it up for the sake of the world. Secondly when I say the world, as you know (if you know me) I'm not referring to "society". I'm talking about Human Beings. Specifically the Being of Human Beings. Making a difference in their lives. Not the way they go about being individualist, but being more open minded. Somewhat like opening other eyes to not live their lives for them, for I believe that if one truly love themselves they would be willing to give themselves up for the sake of the world.

As usual I'm not sure if that point got across, only through my commitment I'm able to say is has, or it will at some point or another. Just know, I don't live my life for me.

To Send

Now. Of course no one has said, you should go on and go and walk your path, travel your road, take your journey. Yea, no one forced you to choose the way you did. Dig? Yea" one can only accept responsibility in life there's no accidents.

Now of course unless you're unwilling to believe you're even on a path, or journeying through life, well that's just a way to say that life is doing it to you. This by the way is totally false.

Now of course you can step off and die, you can stop moving, you can have life do it to you. But isn't that taking it a little personally.

Now Of course along this path in life we must at some time or another arrive. That's true. You also have that choice to arrive. You have that choice to move. It's up to you. But it's up to God to send.

Wish's

Amy's the type of babe that simply amazes ordinary folks. When I first met her, our eyes met in a crowded cafeteria that faced the lake. We didn't speak much on a vocalized level. Although our conversations varied in length, they were always deep. I met GiGi the same time I met Amy. They were both in the cafeteria facing the lake underneath the clear blue sky. As I've come to know them both, for they are included in novel "the Young Ink Pen" know them both from the impact each has been for me in my life. GiGi I met more frequently, Amy I spoke with more often. GiGi was in school the last time I saw her. Everybody she came in contact with she handed them a smile. She kept them in her pockets. It was her style; Out of nowhere "Here you go." The last time I saw Amy, she was ending her vacation. She needed special time off to continue her style. She needed to refill her pockets with "Wish's".

That's Unpure.

For a devastating phenomenon to occur just when one has successfully, finally overcome a tragic experience which scared one's state of being.

For me and you it might seem like a phenomenon. It may seem like another ordinary thing to happen. But for one, especially one that is very sensitive, the so called ordinary happening could hit one over the head like a baseball bat.   E.G.

Ivy all her life was raised to save herself for this one guy who would come along and marry her. Even in this day and age did not pay any mind to statics about marriage and divorce, or hoe it was for black woman to find a black man. A decent black man. She was raised on a sheltered estate, in a small town, just north of somewhere. The "ordinary thing" which Ivy saw as a devastating phenomenon, it only happened once, but she never was the same since.

She liked a guy that professed a love that was Unpure.

Delightful?

How delightful it is to see you my friend
  I'm glad to be able to give reality the bend
Oh what joy existing on t his spiritual plane
Sweet heart you know I love being insane
How delightful it is to see you my friend
  It's been such a long time to feel you within
Oh how I wish we could soul mix once more
And yet it will never be as it was before
I stood amongst the crowd as they lowered you in the ground

It wasn't you; it was only a skinbag in a box

You my dear, are here, Beside me
                    Infront of me
                    Behind me
                    Within my inner self.
How delightful it is to see you my friend.

Just Ask

Why do you need to know my name? I know who I am. All one has to do is call me and they got my attention.

Why do I need a mirror, I see myself all the time. The mirror will only have a reflection.

Some believe that that has been discovered, and yet to be discovered has already and does exist.

So answers to questions are there.

All you have to do is Just ask.

My Mind.

A collection
A group of cells.
A section of my brain.
A mass of opinions.
A sort of mystery.
The unknown.
A scientific fact.
A myth.
An interpretation.
I just can't make up my mind.

It would

It would
Long ago tomorrow, far away
Say a lot about us, how we was yesterday
Time for reason, non for each other
Sit down and speak, Go a little further

It would
  In the sky below the sea
  Answer the thoughts you have of me
Blue grass, green water, mushroom cloud
Chasing a dream, Because you're Proud

Search for what's clearly seen
Grab hold to a solid mass
If you ever found out, what life was about
Will its' existence ever last
It Would

Think Upon

Dreams- {imaginatively speaking} - may vary in size and scope depending how one's viewing the reality just before sleep. For example, if one is locked up in a little box, but still believes he's on the planet earth, then ones' dreams will reflect that. Also if one is in the world but feels locked up like in a little box, then ones' reflect that also.

OutSide.

A friend named Patrick mentioned in a conversation—My sky has many suns with their fluorescent shines, my clouds of my sky is manmade. There are many rooms in my world, the locks of which can only be opened by the man behind the mirror.

I once mentioned I refuse to see the sky without the trees, Of course one will automatically assume that I think trees grows in the sky. If you think that, well just look at it again.

Whatever I See. Visually is outside. Whatever I imagine is inside. These thoughts are a peak of what was inside. Dig?

Again;

   I live my life again.
     Not as if the statement the "I" can be identified with some solid evidence that would be conclusive as to the fact that some one will know I. For I, am not only who you've known and know, but who has been known by those who are only characters in modern day history books.
   I believe that earlier I spoke on "Living". Well that the context which it exist here.
   My life is one which isn't essentially mine. I live life for life is within me and yet only through an understanding that we all have the same source of life, do I willingly give up my own personal claim and share with others the possibility of getting in touch with the source.
     When one reads "again" one may think I mean "as before" no I don't mean that exactly. To put it simply in a nutshell. I've expired from one skinbag to fill up another.
   I live my life again.

Glitter and Gold

He wanted more than just success. More than just having a comfortable life. He wanted G. and G.

A man that's blind with ambition to only reach his tainted dreams is a man without remorse, for whatever rules that must be broken, or for the ones who's affected by his actions. All he sees is a life of G. and G.

He trims his routines to only be the needed ones that will quickly get him there. He breaks off communications with those that are not there just for him. He doesn't want anyone in his reality that'll slow him from being in G. and G.

He will come to think of fun as only being in the struggle that he'll have. No fun in just having friends and being content in what God has provided. Life, in one can eat, drink, and be merry.

The old saying- G. and G. is all vanity.

Meaningless.

Two days ago was the first time I saw the sky live in over six weeks. Of course I saw it on television, in photos, and through windows,, but in the last four weeks I didn't have the opportunity for the latter. It was without trees and yet I've come a ways since that statement. When I saw it live it was just like as I thought it would be.... Blue.

Earlier today I shaved off my mustache again. The discovery this time is that since I've only had an opportunity to look in a mirror 4 or 5 times in the last seven weeks, I can only go on how I think I look. But that's just it. I just look like me without a mustache. It wasn't premeditated, it was just while I was shaving the little stubbles of my beard then it wasn't. One reason I think is that I was growing attached to it. Twisting the end, imaging I'm a Frenchman. I was giving it too much meaning.

The existences of things become important or unimportant because of the meanings we give them. Their existence are essentially ~~they are~~ meaningless.

Miracles

So far that man on that mountain top hasn't returned. So what does that mean? When he does, after we do what needs to be done, will some call it a miracle? If so who will they be.

Those who all their life had been runned by the circumstances and surroundings, when by chance during some ordinary moment, come across in their mind an original thought or actually find themselves thinking, would that be one.?

Sometimes I've actually realized that some things that has happened to me can be logically explained. But those are the times that can be easily explained. There are many things that has happened which cannot be explained, only accepted. Are they Miracles? If I choose them to be, Will they Become?

Are You.

And she began to seek out
   what she felt was missing
Remaining in touch with that
   which she knew was whole.
Everything that was once with held
   she freely released.
Yearning for a new sense of wholeness
   she searched and searched.
Often she found herself lost
  not knowing what was whole.
Until finally one day
  she just declared it.

Move on

One comes to the point of pure contentment. Satisfied with all that has been done, and where one is at in life.

One has reached that time in life where one realizes this is it. This is where I've wanted to be.

One's reality is splendid, glorious, without problems or conflicts. One's reality could exist forever as it is.

One wish's not to go further, for that will cause change, and change could change the tranquilness that's present.

In order to be joyful with all that has been acquired, One mustn't stand still. For the possessions will just exist. Without comparison, their meaning will only become meaningless. This is the human tendency. So in order to appreciate what and where one is at, One must move on. Dig?

Dreamer

She loved him no matter what. That's what she told him. She knew all the quote "dirty little secrets" and all the crazy things he's done and accepted totally his way of life.

He knew that she really wasn't going to hang around long, although or even still he fully gave his love to her. He has done many times before. He knew that it was all a part of life.

They was and is obvious in Love with each other. And yet one or even both was a dreamer.

Yours

And how it is, depends on how you allow it to be.
How you are willing to accept it to occur within your reality.
Yours. And when it's seen by others, how will they see it?
When other think of it, how will it make them feel?
Yours. And what will you let it be about, with in a context.
What it is, will only be of your choosing. The context that is.
 Yours. When will be the moment to show it.
      When you see the right time.
The "world" is Yours.
Which world do you choose?
The one which I exist in,
Or the world of vanity?
                    It's Yours

Truly

Truly there's no other love than yours
None so wonderful None so pure

   "Truly" is a title also of a poem I wrote when I was once younger. And the above lives are the essence of that piece.
   If I remember correctly it wasn't written for anyone specifically, just like the piece earlier "Can I" and yet any individual can read it as if it was written for them, for the source of the creative substance ifs from a being that's authentic. For I'm committed to Truly Contribute.

Steven

I've come to the last piece of this project. I'm very carefully thinking what to put. For I would like to finish this in the upmost coolest way. The enthusiasm has somewhat deteriorated because of the concern I have about this ending.

It's not necessarily the context of this ending; it's the time frame I'm mostly concerned about. And as you can or will see, I'm accomplishing the completion right on schedule.

When I've completed the many projects I've written, there's a feeling of mild excitement, and bewilderment that it has actually its own existence. It stands on it's on, I need not to be here in order for you to get what it is to get. If it was only half way finished I would need to be around so you could get what's need in order for your message to be whole. Dig?

Here in my surroundings only a few know me as Gikuyu. Most call me Steven, if they know my name at all. {for like I said, I already know who I am.}

The gullibility of the foundation of an insight, comes from your understanding that it is ultimately your choice.

Epilogue

The stage is my life. The chalkboard on the stage is my being. Gikuyu is the name I gave the chalkboard. The chalk is used to write the necessary state of mind that's required of any given situation in order for insights and discoveries to occur.
The pas 30 days I've given the stage a new covering that will have the shine last longer. I've strengthen the foundation so the stage will last longer and I've added various insightive elements to the substance of the chalk board so that its' existence is much more solid. So that when the opportunity of the thought for its destruction arrives, it will not be chosen, unless I'm truly aware of its possibility. And yet it's enviable for it to arrive since I will and always will be living on the edge. Dig?

Contents

     Thanx for gifts received. Living must continue after all's gone. Can I become insane? Will you leave me known?
     Yvonne has been my friend, through my Madness of yore. It isn't for me to send, wish's that's unpure.
   Delightful? Just ask my mind. It would think upon OutSide.
  Again Glitter and Gold - Meaningless!
  Miracles are You.
  Move on Dreamer.

                        Yours
                          Truly
                            Steven

A Finmal Authorz Note

I consider my written pieces as a page that I have turned in the book of life. So my writings are not "non-fiction" neither are they "fiction" my writings are "sort-of" fiction. Everything is from the impact of the momentz of my life lived.

chapter 13

Paths' Way

Speech given to life in November

Thank you. Thank you, Thanx. It's once again as it will always be, a pleasure to speak to here. To be here to speak with you is a request accepted.

One must understand that I do not speak my Thanx in a half hearted manner. My Profound Gratitude is decide from knowing that it's God's will for me to be here in Life, to speak to life. I accept that without question. With all the circum-stances, and all the trials and tribulations, I must say I've survived them well. As well as an insane writer is suppose to.

I've had many opportunities to step off this path of life, and continue living as I've wished. Or to say, to be in life comfortable. That wasn't a wish, more like a choice. Each opportunity that has arise, I've always said to myself, Next time, Next time, I'm going on for now, because I still have life in me. I've often wondered do I have to die to be comfortable. I've just as often discovered the answer to be yes.

As time pass I've noticed memories comes and goes and then only to reappear. I find in those moments of memoires that they come in handy in interpretational dreadful times.

To belong to the universe is of joy and joylessness. Emotions become a choice. Not a reaction. For reacting with emotions to the circumstances will only drive a person sane.

Even though a month is specified in the title of each speech, the underlining context is really like I'm the moment of now in 19**, or whatever the year might be. For as I've said before, while truthing all time is transcended.

To life this speech is given, but of course cannot read this. Yet with that in mind, whom do you think these words are written for. I have no idea,{I admit.} who will be reading these words, when they will be reading these words or what state of mind these words will be read, so one must accept the implications from the interpretations that occurs from the many different human beings. But that's just the point. These words are written for human beings.

It will be a few months shy of a year from now that I will have another scheduled girl friend in my life. I'm sort of looking forward to that. Of course she will love me, yet I once wrote when I was once younger that my next girlfriend must read everything I've written. So she'll be reading this. So I'm letting you know I knew you were coming. It is known. Dig? How can I explain to one who only reads this? Yet I know for one who has read my work no explanation is needed. Destiny is a concept with many different understandings. One can view it as if it was planned, or by accident. My Destiny one must know, is known, it's known. Dig? I discovered that I've known it, and didn't know that I knew that I've known it all my life.

Each moment is like every empty page I encounter. The opportunity to create something from nothing from the commitment on has. I write this in ink. At times you will see some scratched out words, even misspelled words, yet what you see is what you get. The pages are numbered; I must approach the page true to the moment and do my truthing authentically. If not I know the contribution will not be made. For contributing is my commitment.

As I get on in these years a certain kind of certainty occurs within my state of mind. There were times when there was a kind of directionless, even when I jumped off the edge, I wouldn't know if I was going up or down, because I was so open. Now that I've grown accustom to this openness I've acquired, which has allowed me to be able to look upon outside with a perspective as an observer while looking at a participant.

I just happen to be the one participating.

The Decisions I've made in my times, the actions I've taken and not taken, I accept full responsibility for. It is true that everything is perfect all the time, for if what occurred didn't happen then these words would not be here in this way, which is the way they suppose to be.

I search my mind to provoke thoughts so that his state of mind can be expressed in a thought provoking style. Yet the simplicity of the words may not seem thought provoking, it is the easiest way to reach that part of one's' mind where the essential area of the source of life exist.

One must understand that I write for no reasons. I write for cause. I don't write "because" I write "for". It has long been not enough for me to know why I write. The reasons vary at times, but the cause remains the same. The commitment to contribute is the cause for the source of any reasons that may come up with at various times.

One must understand that being a writer is the most dangerous job in the world. For it goes beyond the world and yet includes it simultaneously. I'm talking authentic writers, not your part time society pleasers.

There once was a time when I explained myself to the point that once the explanation was over, I had to rethink what I was getting to. Now I do not let the need to explain, interfere with what I'm saying. It's simple enough.

To Life I speak. To You I write. For the universe I live. Thank you, Thank you, Thanx.

A Ride

This isn't my first ride of a thought, and it definitely will not be my last. I'm sure somewhere within this piece there will be a thought provoked or an insight to occur, for that as you know is my commitment.

Little things could easily be compared to bigger things. For example here in prison one goes to the store once a week. So one has to buy a weeks supply of what one needs. Last week was the first and most likely the only week I'll make store while I'm in prison. I bought two writing pads and three ink pens. I know these last two projects will be enough to gain my release. Other than those items I bought a can of tobacco. Now that can would last me at least three weeks, but I've shared it with a few friends. And now at the start of a day, 6 days later, it won't make it after breakfast. I was just wondering if I had said no to the request for a roll up what would it matter. I discovered that due to my commitment I put somewhat a lot of thought into saying no than I do when I say yes. Can you see the point I'm making. But the original point I wanted to make is that if I refuse to share something that is after all truly meaningless, what will become the habit with the meaningful things that exist, such as viewpoints, and knowledge. More like a way of life than knowledge. Dig?

My Freedom Angel

I remember her at the precise moment
The moment when I need joy
She was so headstrong
She gave me a head rush
With each other a world was shared.
To begin, within the last area of the end
The actions become sure with certainty
Being in the dance with one another
Having faith in setting one free.
Free of the traps
Free of the boundaries
Free of the ideas
All the possessions of societies
She's the dreamers' context of all
She's my view of what will be
I catch myself at midnights' silence
Thinking her and her glorious ways.
Connecting this with that and that with this
Thinking that's what needed
Not even willing to recognize
It will always be forever and forever will Be
One.
She's ah what you call Sunrise Sensation
Her embrace is an edges leap impact
I find myself wondering how to wonder

For when I'm around her I am so sure
Is a question of her really necessary
Do you know who she is
These words are not here to tell you that
Though they do and a lot more
Figuring out the signals
Between the sky and pen
I start to whistle the tune
With a name but harmony escapes me
She appeared in my mindless memory
Just as I stepped from joy
I'm here she said with her arms spread
Just as you've been for me
Along the place where we sit.
The eyes are upon us with wonder
The voices are whispered with discrete regret
And the screams rattle like oceans
Quietly we've come together, as it has been before
We listen to our heart beats
Until mine stops and I join yours
Returning from you   causes anguish and pain
Deeper than why you're here
But the healing becomes with me so insane
I'll gladly invite you again
Would you mind if I invite some one
Within our own private world
They're already here, when I'm speaking to you
Outside looking in, within looking out

She formed a cloud in the cup of her hand
She blew it a breeze from her mind
She sat up straight and touched the sky
Yet she cannot make me sane with all of her powers
We've been fancy in all the ways
We've been rigid in many many ways
All in all it's been our tomorrows
It's been our smiles it's been our sorrows
Oh when I feel for her
Every atom of our existence yearns
She becomes my supplier of life
My source of what's here and now
Shining Suns becomes her eyes
Wisdom is known as her creed
Faith is her being knowledge is known
She brings freedom when you think it's gone
Freedom from reasons
Freedom from thoughts
All the belongings of a world
Since when did I let her go
Was it when I punished myself
She never said good-bye, it was I
That gave giving-up a try
Deep deep further inside the misty confusion
She smiles as she waits for the choice
The choice to have her come back
By willing up the remembrance

She sings to me sometimes
In voices like flowers in a storm
She screams at me at other times
Freezes me like snow so warm
Every time she explodes in my brain
I have no ideas or thoughts
Decisions are not being made
Living goes on by choice
I remembered her at the precise moment
That space in reality
Between Nothing and Joy
She's my angel
My freedom Angel
Whom becomes the factor of living by choice

Innocent witness By the Guilty Bystander

It was a time. Probably before I was here, maybe while I was here. I don't know which because the moments are in a context that has no definite way. The day I' m going to tell you about in other word could have happened during my lifetime this time or before. I don't know for the reason I stated before.

I become conscious of the fact that I'm looking down on a city as if I'm in a helicopter. The air is a little stuffy up here. The top halves of skyscrapers are littered with satellite discs. The big sky scraper looms above me. I can hear the faint noise of the people and car horns. The people look like they are made from Mattel and the trucks look like they're made by Tonka.

I become aware of something else. I don't hear a helicopter's motor that's suppose to work the propellers. At the same time of this realization, I notice the wings stretched out on both sides of me." I'm a bird, I'm a fu**king bird!" I think to myself. "If I'm a bird how can I think to myself?" I think to my self. "Oh f**k it, Just go with it."

One of the skyscrapers I notice is made with mirror glass, so I decide to glide over there to see what kind of bird I am. Maybe I'm a Eagle, or a Hawk, Or a Falcon, some kind of bird of Prey.

To my surprise I instantly dance with the wind toward the building. I'm gliding about 5 feet from side of the about the 60th floor when I look at myself. I actually lose my balance in mid-air when I saw my reflection. But I catch myself. To my disappointment I'm a pigeon... A f**king pigeon; Oh well at least I'm a bird.

I spend the next few minutes checking out the scenery and accustomed to these wings, and this life. Suddenly I feel hungry. I climb higher so I can get a overview of the city and find what I'm looking for. A park where I see my fellow feathered friends around this old lady. Obviously she's feeding the birds.

I swoop down to the park, and there's actually two old ladies feeding the pigeons. As I was landing I suddenly realize that I didn't know how to f**king land. I came down too fast and nearly seriously injured some of my fellow feather friends. And I nearly break my f**king beak in the process. I now found myself embarrassed, hurt but no longer hungry. So I wobble to the side with most of the pigeons looking at me like they was asking "What the f**k was that?"

As I hang out on the sideline watching these birds feast, I for the first time get to witness human beings from a whole new perspective. There are two old ladies sitting at opposite ends of the bench. They look like they're competing for the birds' affection. One is dressed in blue; the other is dressed in blue.

The blue lady is throwing out her crumbs by the handful, the red lady seems like she's more selective. The blue lady has more of the flock. My feather friends aren't that dumb after all. The blue lady runs out of crumbs and then gets up and slowly walks away. The flocks that gathered around her stays and continues to eat the crumbs yet to be eaten. The red lady moves to where the other sat, and her flock joins in the feast. I'm still not hungry; I'm thinking I might have done some major damage, because I'm hurting like hell.

Less than a minute pass when all of a sudden all of the dozens of my feather friends starts to choke and die. They make weird chirps and then just tilt over and die. Before too long all of the pigeons are dead. The red lady sits there stunned. I see policemen running up to her and putting handcuffs on her.

It amazes me the eyesight I have because out of the corner of my beak I see the lady in blue about a block away, and she's smiling. Laughing at the scene of my dear friends. I say to myself f**k this pain and I take awkwardly off toward her. I think to myself "Okay bitch, An eye for an eye, A beak for a beak." I realize there's no way I can kill her but that doesn't stop me. With my little instinct I have of flying and add the hurting received from the landing, which was more like grounding, plus I was mad as hell.

I came at her crazy as f**k. I let out a wild chirp, or better yet a bird yell. She quickly swung her purse and literary knocked the sh*t out of me. Dazed I climbed upward to regroup. I looped through some trees in the park to rethink my next attack. Obviously I wasn't going to do that again. That sh*t hurt. Then an ideal came to me.

I flew like I was retreating. I didn't know if she could see me or not, I wasn't taking any chances, I wanted her to think that. As soon as I felt comfortable, I turned around and came down from above her. I was like a f**king hawk, and she was my prey. When I got ten feet above her, I let out my bird scream again, and she quickly looked up. I realized that she was a younger woman dressed as an elderly lady." So this is how you get your thrills, killing birds. Thrill this you bitch!" I got 1 foot from her face and shat a big drop of white steamy turd. At the speed I was going, if it would have landed in her mouth it would've came out of her toes. It hit her smack in the eyes. About the time I came to her stomach I was already on my way up. I got such a head rush. It was incredible. I looked down and she was staggering around on the side walk.

Maybe it was the effect of the head rush. I was feeling some kind of primitive animal instinct. Something took over and I found myself descending once more. I came down claws first and caught the top of her head. I didn't know what the purpose of that action then, yet I do now.

She reached up and grabbed me off her wig. She started screaming "You f**king free flying bird!" I tried to release myself from her grip, but she only squeezed tighter. All of a sudden she jumped in the street, and the last thing I heard was a horn from one of those Tonka seeming trucks. The last thing I saw was a young lady's' face with white sh*t on it, and a head light one inch from the back of her head.

Then the next moment I was here. It's been a while since then, the moments have been real. I became a innocent witness by the guilty bystander.

Path's Way

The way of the path seems funny
Odd in a way I don't understand
I guess I'll be surprised to become lonely
To dock my boat on dry land
So many dreams are seen by me
It's a wonder I don't live them always
So don't live if you please
For in my time I've seen strange days
She appears at the rightest of times
And smiles a light for me to see
I walk that path as her smile shines
And the flower sings words of praise.
I step off blind folded, carefully
I know time has made space for me
The days won't come unless they're told
They peep around the flowers
                        And wave hello
The kid is dancing to the music of my tears
You know it's been a long time since I had her
                        By my side
It may be too late to accept all of my fears
But you got to know at least I tried
Because the way of the Path sure seems funny

The Point

The importance of my writings Varies with different people. Now, I can honestly say that there's very few who see the importance, and I think they only see it as only to me.

Noticing the underlining scenery of the average reality, and hearing the unsaid words from one's action and responding accordingly, causes the desired effect.

To belong, To not be a part, To send, To be sent, To choose, To be chosen, To understand, To be confused, To all and all see it's ones' destiny.

It's funny that always during the writing of a project Like this, there's a turning point. This is it. dig?

Speech Given To Life In December

Thank you, Thank you, Thanx. Once again I'm here before you speaking, and within this as action there exist an acknowledgement of you.

Through my inquiries in dreams I believe in messages from beyon. Although at times when asking or seeking certain information or answers, it may be given, but I've yet to master how to receive them correctly. For example the numbers 11-15-3 was given to me in response to my request about my release from prison. I've deciphered those numbers in every way I could conceive, and yet the dates I've come up with have yet to produce the predicted results. From which the reason I've concluded to be either, I got the numbers wrong or just haven't figured it out ye. More likely it the latter

In a previous project that I was working on titled "Steel Myself Still" which incidentally was stolen, I wrote down 2 dreams which told of the progress I was making in working in the realm of dreams.

Neither dream had a title, just like the rest of the pieces that I had written in the book.. All was under the context of the title. In a nutshell with just as much detail and comments following, I will share with you the dreams.

I woke up on the sort of like front porch of a huge building. To my right there was a stairway about 12 feet wide with about a hundred or so steps down. To my left was the same. I was in the middle of the porch and was at least 25 feet from the 1st steps on either side. I looked behind me and there was a building at least 2 stories high with doors 10 feet in length , and 3 feet wide. There were at least 8 of them 6 feet behind me. Above me the sky was clear blue with a few birds circling. In front of me there was a wall about 3 feet in height that went the length of the porch and continued on both sides on down the stairway.

Down in front of me was a field the size of a football field. With an oval shaped stadium built around it. Where I stood, it looked like I was at the front end of the oval, for the walls of the stadium stretched all the way to the sides of the building which porch I stood. In the stands of the stadium there was thousands and thousands of people yelling and screaming.

Then I was one of those people in the stands although I wasn't screaming. Its been over 2 months since the dream, so I don't remember the next scene too clearly but what I do remember that some surfs was brought out to the center of the field from a huge garage like door from the bottom of the stairs that was once to my right and they did something like fought lions or something and then was taken back. I don't remember if they won or lost,, but the outcome was that the surfs were to be awarded by the king of the castle upon who's back porch I stood. With a gleeful cheering I can safely assume it meant they were to live.

The next moment I was on the back porch again. Checking out the scenery, I was thinking about what to do next. So my curiosity getting the best of me I decided to enter the castle, so I melted through the doors.

Again this is best as I can recollect. I found myself in what can be called a huge foyer. It was dimly lit by the sunshine beaming thru some windows above the doors that I didn't notice from out side. I f I was facing the doors you could say to my right there were stairs that lead downward toward darkness, and to my left there was a long hall way. Behind me it was huge, empty and dark. One could tell that the ceiling was way up there, although I couldn't actually see it. At the corner of the stairway there was a wall that went further back into the foyers darkness. There was a balcony of sorts a floor above me with a door that led out to a balcony.

Actually I wasn't standing at all, for I don't actually remember a solid floor underneath me. I heard foot steps coming down the hall and I was stuck for a decision of what to do. So I did nothing. Coming up the hall was a gentleman, which I knew had to be the king. As I was facing him I heard foot steps coming from up the stairs. I turned and looked and saw a man in a regal costume. Of what period the king and this man were dressed, I couldn't recall then and I cannot now.

When the king got a few feet in front of me I started floating upward. The king stood in front of me with his back to me and waited for the man. If the king noticed me he gave no reaction what so ever. The man walked up to the king and didn't pay attention to me either. "They have been taken care of Your Majesty." The man said. "Good. It was painless as I ordered? Correct?" The King replied. "That is correct. Your Majesty." the man answered. The King suddenly looked up at the balcony, then the man turned around and looked up. I wondered what was the matter, so I looked up too.

That's when I saw her. She was leaning over the balcony pointing to the king. She was a beautiful young lady. The Princess I assumed. I found out I was right when she screamed out "Father you killed them! They were heroes!" "They why they died painlessly." The king simply said. She looked at the man, she looked at the king, and I thought she looked at me if only for a fleeting second. Then she turned and ran back through the door. It was her bedroom I suspected. The king turned to the man and told him that was all. They both departed for which direction they came. That was when I realized I was in a world.

With that realization I wanted to see outside again, to take in everything before I woke up. I floated through the doors and was on the porch and before there was an empty stadium under the big blue sky. I heard some one say "Pssttt." trying to signal me. I followed the direction of the voice and looked up to my right. Out of a second floor window she was leaning. She whispered "I know no one else can see you, wont you please come up while you got the chance."

I quickly floated back through the door and up and over the balcony. Went through her door. Oddly enough I had to open it. Not really had to, but I chose to. I cold feel the cold gold door knob turn in my hand. The door opened to a huge room which was both a bedroom and living room with a small kitchenette.

The room stood below I was atop of a landing that was steel like which lead downward in spiral stairs that lead to the room. I half floated and half stumbled down the stairs. She was standing looking out the window. She didn't turn around, nor did she speak to me. I didn't mind at all.

I was totally engrossed in the possibility of the moment. I took advantage of the moment to examine the room more closely. I counted how many coins were in the ashtray. There 3 small ones, 2 medium size ones, and 2 large ones. I've never seen coins like that before. I looked at the small photographs that were in the frames placed at places across the rom. I read the titles of some of the many books that was on the book shelves that covered the a half of the wall from the floor to the ceiling. The ceiling was covered in gold leafed designed and white plastic flowers covering the whole ceiling. I noticed the less attention she was paying to me , the more I began to float. I knew that I was invisible.

At this next scene which is the ending, I'm going to share with you some information that wasn't said but just known to me. All of this happened while I also knew that I was invisible. Even to her I was only visible for those few moments.

I saw a scene outside the door between the man and another man. The man was the general that had came and spoke to the king earlier. The guy was his next in charge. The other guy was arguing with the general because he felt the general was incompetent. There was a crowd of a few people around them when the guy struck the general in the jaw. They started tussling with each other. They fell in her bedroom door and down and around the stairs. When they reached the bottom, they both pulled out guns and dove for cover. I looked for the princess, but she was nowhere in sight.

I believe she's upstairs amid the crowd that was staring over the banister in disbelief. I floated over a couch that was by the window where I first saw her standing. As I glanced back at them, they had taken cover five feet from each other. I landed behind the couch and a vase above my head shattered. I looked up over the ledge of the couch just to see what was happening. I saw them and I thought they were in some comedy movie or something. One would stand up and shoot, and the other one would duck then the other would stand up and shoot and one would duck.

When they were all out of bullets they crawled to the middle of the floor, because unlike the movies they both got hit.... The man said to the General "Sir before I go, would you mind telling me one thing?" "Yea soon.. What would you like to know?" The General replied. I expected the man to ask some profound question just before his death and to my surprise, it was very profound.

The man looked at the general and asked "Who the hell is that guy hiding behind the couch?" "I don't know who the motherfucker is." The general replied. Realizing I had never been invisible, that they just didn't pay me any attention. The shock was so profound that I woke up

If you're reading this you probably understand my philosophy {or hearing this.} on dreams, so I won't get into what I meant when I said world. I was in a world and explored it like I've never done before. I had that dream before I was shipped further into the prison system 3 months ago the 8th of September.

Since I have set a page time on this speech I'm not going to get into a dialogue about each dream. I will now tell the dreams and have a summary commentary after I've completed sharing them. The next dream I had about a week or so after I got here.

This is the short version. The events that are told are the major ones that stood out that seemed to me important to point out. I was back in Kingsport at sometime in the future. I was surprised at the atmosphere of the place. The aura of the town seemed very depressing. From my right came this pretty babe, she started walking in front of me. Then a guy came up and started walking next to her. A handle to his gun was protruding out of his back pocket. "This is Kingsport?" I thought to myself. I was shocked that someone would walk around brandishing a gun in public like that. Soon another guy came walking up and the three of them with the girl in the middle was walking in front of me.

The guy with the gun told the girl that she was a bitch, and he'll kill her. She just laughed and they continued walking. I recognized the highway of which edge we was walking. It's the one you're at when one exits the tunnel and goes toward town. I noticed a package store and stopped there to buy a beer.

I ended up buying a six pack, which left me with a dollar and some change. Since I only had 5 dollars had the six pack was on sale I got it. I resumed walking. The 3some was way ahead of me. I down the six pack and immediately became hungry. I was drunk as a skunk. I recognized the corner where I was at. I was at the bottom of the hill at Oak street, but a few things were different.

First there was a red light, then instead of a gas station being on the other side of Oak street it was on the side where I was at. I decided to go inside in it and buy what I could with what little money I had. I stumbled in the store and picked up 2 candy bars and placed them on the cashiers counter. He told me it would cost 4 dollars. I told him something like "Go fuck yourself." Because it was only two candy bars. Then he started piling things on the counter and in my pocket, telling me that either I pay for this or he's calling the cops. There was no need to call the cops because they had just arrived at the gas pumps. When they walked in, I was trying to take the shit out of my pockets, and tell them what happened. They didn't want to hear any of it. They took me outside and started frisking me. When one of them said lets take him out back. There was a black cop and a white cop.
    They got me behind the gas station and with one holding each arm stood me against the wall, and asked me if I wanted an ass whooping or time in jail. Deep deep down inside of me there was fear. I remind you I was drunk. I opted for the ass beating. I began steeling my self actually my body for the beating when the black cop started laughing. That's when I recognized him as the guy with the gun I had saw earlier. He was laughing while taking off his fake police uniform and saying jokingly "You'll really take an ass whooping." He told the whiter guy to go and return the car. Then motioned me over to a corner that was further behind the store.
    In the corner on the ledge of a slopping wall sat the girl, and the other guy I had seen earlier. Plus a few more people. My anger for that prank allowed me to sober up quickly. I was about to ask him what the hell was going on; when in the back ground I hear police sirens.

The guy says to me "You really better decide now, for those are the real cops that's coming to get you." I looked at the people there, then looked up the slopping wall and the darken forest behind it. I quickly steeled my soul as much as my body this time. Then I ran up the slop and through the trees, with the noise of the sirens and cheers behind me. Then I woke up.

I woke up disappointed because of the fear I had. Then after carefully analyzing the dream I realized that in the end my courage won out. The funny thing is that in waking up the fear was felt much stronger than the courage; although the courage was greater than the fear.

My 3rd dream I'm sharing with you, even though dreamt 5 days ago is vaguely remembered. It's important from the psychological training value that I will comment on in the summary at the end of my sharings.

I was walking downtown somewhat like Soho New Y.C. and started floating upwards. I knew this was rare so I paid close attention to the details. The building to my right some 25 yards away was the only one that was apartment'ish, with windows and stuff. So I looked in at each floor. Each had a balcony and sling glass doors. I saw many different people. But now the only that stands out, that stood out then was a guy sitting in front of a huge drawing architect board. He waved to me. I was drawn into the top floor of a building through the window.

Inside was a large narrow room with beds stacked 3 high. I realized it was the dormitory of a prison. Then I realized I was in a world, and that's where I slept when I was in prison, in a dormitory similar to this one. This is one of my sub conscious exercises. I only looked around for a moment and the ideal came to me.

It is often observed by me that an institutionalized person main thing other than the food of prison they enjoyed is a place to sleep comfortable. Since I was in the dorm and not the cafeteria, the ideal was logical.

I found my bed and took the bed frame and as a symbolic gesture not only for me, for the others also I decided to destroy it. There by destroying any connection with that assertion.

The bed frame folded up like a cot. 2 long stems with four legs with 2 at each end. I decided to throw it out of the small window at the end of the dorm. As I was attempting to put the frame out of the window; I found it was awkward. As I put the frame on the ledge the frame turned into a guy. He tried to come back in the window; I pushed him back on the ledge. He sat on the ledge while I grappled with the problem of what to do next. I put my head out the window and saw that it was at least 100 stories down. I now couldn't tell him to jump, although my original idea was to have that be.

A crow flew on the edge on the other side of the small ledge. The guy started talking to the crow. I couldn't see the bird only the guy. He had his head turned and was saying something of his own problem. You see the guy didn't want to jump. He wanted to save my conscious. The crow began to talk. I didn't hear what the crow said, but it was words of wisdom. I wanted to see the crow talk. When I looked out, it looked like I caught it in the middle of a transformation.

It had arms and legs extending to the size of a full grown person, yet its' face still had a beak and the feathers was slowly flying away in the wind. A little while later it came to me that the crow was an oracle in disguise. Through my dream I was suppose to bring that guy to him. The dream didn't have anything to do with me at all. I helped them both in from the ledge and asked the oracle why he was brought here by me. The oracle just smiled. Then I asked that since this dream was a tool to bring this guy here, maybe the oracle could do me a favor by telling me when I was going to be released.

The oracle went into a brief speech with the only sensible thing I could make out was the Saturday. I asked "This Saturday?" {which is today.} The oracle smiled. Then I asked specifically when. The oracle replied "Okay. Okay..." Then as I was being woken up by the guards; the oracle yelled to me "Just when I was about to tell you!" Then I woke up.

The 4th dream, dreamt the day after the 3rd one is even vaguer. All I remember was I was over some guys house eating lunch with his family in Upstate New York. His sister surprised them by arriving. She took a liking to me.

After the meal we became emotionally involved. As she was shyly sitting on my lap she said "I don't even know guys, so I don't gout with guys who wear knockers." I explained that in the south it's culturally acceptable to wear sneakers. Her name is "Jaury" that's all I remember.

In life one must take all the advantages of the opportunities that occurs. Even in my sleep I'm working. I concur with what Seth says when he pointed out that our daily realty is but a dream to the entity, as our dreams are to us.

The expected spiel I was going to give on my dreams is no more. The page time has been used up. I believe that the contributions that will be derived from my sharing are self explanatory. One can reason them out for one self.

I've steeled myself many times in my life. Yet I continue to still steel myself still in the midst of the belief of all steeled up. It's an ongoing process. Just as life; even after my skin bag has long been expired.

Surfacefical

The evening before yesterday, I was watching a football game on television. During the half time show some clowns performed and after half time show the camera was on this one female clown and she jokingly said that the announcer should run for president; that way when he gets in the White House he can draw chalk lines on the blackboard and everyone would understand..

A guy behind me which I refer to as an asshole said "they'll let anybody run for president. They are the ones fucking up the country. I realized that he mustn't have heard the announcer name and realized they were joking, but at least this asshole had an opinion of the political scene in D.C.

Later on inn the 3rd quarter they showed a shot of the Vice President with his wife watching the game. The asshole asked a guy sitting beside him "Who is he, an owner of a football game?" I realized that opinions aren't worth shit if one is dealing with a context that is unknown to oneself.

There's this fellow inmate whom I've coaching on how to see below the surface, when it comes to writing poetry. And I might say he's getting good at it. Yester evening he was requested to sell one of his poems and recited to the guy some of his latest poetry. The guy thought it was okay but not quite what he was looking for. Then my friend went to get his old surface poetry. He read it to him and the guy liked it. By sharing that with me; it somehow hooked up with the previous paragraph which I had planned to write. It also provided for me the insight of a person who's surfacefical.. Dig?

This morning I was awoken during a dream of which I was with Mawakana. It's odd of how I haven't thought of her in years, and she shows up. She was there after I won a Rubik Cubes' contest at the library downtown and I gave her my prize; which was books. She said her daughter would enjoy reading them. This morning the dream started first from the thought of her daughter.

I have decided to have everything I've written while incarcerated to be a book "Prison Memoirs" It will be the largest book I've ever written. Everything except for the part of the series "Written from within, Held from with Outside"
That's apart of the not 2 B printed series. I bought another writing pad today, and I wonder what that means. I'm still trying to figure out the title of this piece.

Post Script- There was one more thing I wanted to mention. It was at times in the morning I would wish that the intercom calling out the names; call mine. Then after a few notice times, I stopped wishing for that was a sign that I beginning to live not in the universe where I know things like that would be taken care of. When my name is called to go home it will be perfect time, and when it's not called it's still perfect.

Truly Yore

    In the histories of a life
      Smiles and sad tears are intwined
      And as I remember
        I take claim to all that is mine
From dreams a spring breeze tosses a world
I present one a gift from with
So who's to say the past will last
Those who listen to the summer wind
      I wish, I invision, I pray, I make
      Doing it all from a knowledge untold
      I mix, I rip, I breakdown, I create
      The rain becomes drops of gold
In the histories of a life
My quest is well defined
Only in the here and now
Do I need to become blinded
      My words become what has to be
      I am mixed up in the whole
I know I won't be free
Until I become a total soul
In the histories of a life
Who is becomes a choice

To Complete With You

In truth my responsibility stems from a choice, or better yet a discovery I made when I first wrote my first poem about a black woman who worked with a under ground movement to free slaves. Although this was an assignment it was; it was also a contest. A chance to show my fellow seventh graders (all 30 of them) that I had an understanding. I realized in order to do that, I had to understand myself. Then write the poem in such a way that all would understand, even though each was different. I did lose the contest, but I walked away with the experience of the task, and discovered the power of words. Over the years as I get older I continue to write and continue to share what others may not be in the position to have a chance to learn. So I'm strict with myself because I placed a responsibility on myself to have human beings understand. I go searching for new insights to share. With that come wild circumstances and great opportunities.

Yes. I care about the outcome of my insights, I don't let that concern influence in a negative manner what I'm doing; for as I've said many times before " As long as I'm committed to making a contribution, Then my actions; whatever they may be, will make a contribution."

I've come to the next to the last piece in this project, and I'm making my closing statement now. Instead of waiting to the final page to do so. Although it was 3 months of not writing before I started this project, one can still detect the shift in my writing. This period of not writing in my opinion did not disempower me. To use an old cliché it's like riding a bike; once you know how to tap into the universe and return with pieces that's profound and contributing, and then you always will, if that's your commitment.

I don't know if I'll finish it or not I do believe I'll start another project while incarcerated. What I'm saying is I don't know if I'll finish the other project while I'm in prison. I don't know if I'll finish the other project I'm working on incarcerated, and I'm halfway finished with that one. I have five more pages to the end of this and I know I'll finish it tomorrow; if not tonight.

There have been occurrences that have happened that afterwards I've been known to say that I knew it would happen. There have also been times like now when I now when I know, but still say I don't know. For no other reason than to have a little drama for latter on. I just thought about saying that that was the only kind of manipulation although mild; it was the only kind I was allowed to do. I thought about saying that, but I'm not.

The other day I mentioned to a friend that for the 1st time in a long time I wrote "trying" or I've tried purposely down in a piece. I figured if you are reading this you've read my concept of trying which I think of as meaningless and that's he context I've used it in a normal statement that's not manipulation, it's a word used that has deeper meaning than the surfacefical definition that one usually applies to it.

Through the journey of this book, I've regained myself and more. As you should know that it wasn't for you there would be no me. Therefore I acknowledge you. For allowing me to be here, and allowing these words to be here, and I request of you to be contributed to. The contributions are there. It's your choice to have them received. At least the obvious ones. There are many that are not so obvious. Dig? Thanks. Thank you. Thanx.

Hidden For A Cause

Younger than I'm now old
Other than before I was born
Until a time that is unknown
Remains who I am to be.
Stronger in a sense of understanding,
The secrets remain hidden for a cause.
Remaining what has yet to be
Until a time that's unknown.
Lying here watching the clouds dance
You can't see that they're not here,
Still it's a belief, it's a reality,
Everyone that knows me feels me.
Visions steps in at unknown times
Everyone that knows me thinks me.
Never have I've been more than an ideal
Obtained Beauty can not be seen in the mirror.
New Illusions becomes the only reflections.
Love and death nay be one in the same,
Your state of mind has the connections.
Interested in only a pebble of sand.

Know this my friend, as you know the sky.
   I see a star that's not there now
   Now becomes the next moments' wish
   Gone are the days when I couldn't see
   Seeing things with only my eyes
Lost as an ideal, found as fact
Inside the mind of a Goddess of the past.
Noticed as the space, between the words of a song.
Gifttalizing the thoughts that's provoked in that joy.
   The secrets remain hidden for a cause
   However the cause will occur in my life afterwards
   One has chosen to believe that I am to live
   Until the secrets are revealed.
Gone are five lines that were just noticed missed.
Having mistakes become perfect.
Thought of you, me, that and this
Surely becomes a mind involved moment
By and By, frown to smile then back again
Easy as a cup of water, harder that happyness
Angels of freedom has one withheld
Sweet sweet agony, Sweet sweet pain
The poetry, the poem, pieces, the speeches

The cause as an answer remains elusive
Other than I was born is all that is known.
Dangling between various reality spheres
I tend to lend toward many othersides
 Seeing me when I'm elsewhere, has confusion to come
 I'm silenced by the ones who wish to remain unknown
 Places that are new, I visit in my dreams
 Love yet to shared exist as seeds
I'm claiming responsibilities that's impossible to accept
 Never has it been easier to live after death.
 Enlighten by the funnyness of the way of the Path.

"You think Patricia will remember me?" D-Dawn turned to me and smiled and grabbed my hand reassuringly. "Don't worry Samuel, How long has it been, 6-7 years?" "A little over 7 years." I said. "Well even though she was 4 when you last seen her, But from one and half, up till then you rubbed off on her in such a way that even the years, he does things, or says something that definitely reminds me of you."

I grinned at that. Ohh boy, walking in the shade of trees holding her hand, and knowing that she really thinks my name is Samuel, yet also knowing that she knows me. She knows my being which is nameless, Therefore it was cool with me that she calls me Samuel.

"What do you mean she reminds you of me? I mean How can a little beautiful girl remind you of a tall dark and handsome stranger?"

"Stranger my foot... Like that question about the rainbow and stuff. I bet if you asked her, she would be able to answer Better. Her mind is very analytical. You shaped her pattern of thoughts. More so than I did. She would out of the blue ask me questions that would leave me flabbergasted. One of the first times I really noticed your influence, was about two or so years after you left, and we was walking home from school and Patricia asked me if, All humans are apart of the same family. And you are my family And you are my friend, who are these strangers you tell me not to speak to? 'Can you believe that? A six year old asking me that?'"

I laughed a brief moment then I stopped because I was pleasantly shocked, for it was something I would have certainly asked. "So how did you answer her?" I asked her, I was really interested in seeing if I had enlighten (b-dan) as well.

"I told her that it's true, we are all one big family. Yet some do not know themselves, therefore they do not know each other. Same is true if they do not love themselves, therefore was able to harm others. When she gets older and know who she really is, she'll be able to tell the difference a little better than she's able to do now because some people can fool you. Patricia was quiet for a minute or so then she stopped and turn me with her face frowned up in thought and said that she could see how that can be, and all, but she's sure that no one could tell her, but she'll do as I say."

Then I inwardly laughed. because of the pleasure I felt knowing that Patricia was a student of life. and not a slave to life. Which was what I wished to instill in her. Having her thinking to be independent from anyone around her- In a way having her be as I wished my daughter to be. THAT IS if I had a daughter. I asked D-Dawn if Patricia ever asked about me, that she had about 2 months after I left and didn't come back... You see I disappeared twice for about a month without a word, but the last time I'd seen D-Dawn I told her that I wouldn't be back for a while. And 7 years is a long while, or a brief moment depending on how one's reality is. Her reality had been measured by the growing up of her daughter, mine had been measured by the growth of the freedom of my soul. While 7 years to D-Dawn may have seemed like 7 years, it seemed no less than a thousand to me. D-Dawn said that she told Patricia that I had gone traveling and I would be back soon, And Patricia had said that she wished I'd hurry up. And that was the only time she had asked about me.

D-Dawn stopped and let go of my hand and sat down on this little wall that was the bottom of a hill that was the front yard of this huge ugly house. We was about a block away from the school and we could see about a dozen yellow buses starting up their engines. I sat down beside her. She was looking at the ground all gloomy like and looked up at me with peaceful expression on her face. I guess she's always have had a life of peacefulness, at this moment it was of ultimate peace, like there was no conflict, yet she asked me "Why are you back Samuel?" I mean you came back after seven years, just 30 minutes ago, and already it seems like only yesterday we said good-bye or that you said "See you later Babe!" I'm sure Patricia thinks about you a lot and even with our openness, she doesn't bring you up in conversation, maybe because of the times she has caught me by myself crying, and suspecting that I was thinking of you. Half of those times it was because of you, the other half, it was because of her. Showing up with no bags is a dead give away as to how long you plan to be around, so tell me why have you come back.

"I've returned because I missed you and her."

"Ohh... Hogwash!" she said and started wiping away the small tears that began to roll down her cheeks. She started giggling and smiling and told me that "this situation is just like you. It's so crazy and unreal, that it can only be real." She got up and grabbed my hand and we proceeded to the school.

As we walked toward the front of the school we passed women who D-Dawn said hellos to and was answered by a curious glance directed toward me. She just smiled them off and coived walking holding my hand, and this one guy looked at me hard and even though I didn't notice D-Dawn look his way, she squeezed my hand a little tighter, which I took to meant, don't ask me about him. So he could have been an old boyfriend or something.

We stood in the middle between the bottom of the front stairs and the school buses. The school bell rang and about 10 seconds later all hell broke loose. About 500 kids came screaming and running out the school as if it was on fire. I actually looked for smoke, because there was none. This seemed to be a school for only hyper-assed kids. I bent down to D-Dawn's ear so she could hear me and asked her "If a butterfly sees that a caterpillar is about to fall off a branch do you think it would have the instinct to try and save it's fellow brethren?" She said "What? I didn't catch that last part, could the butterfly have what?" So I repeated to her "Would the butterfly have a memory of where it came from and reflect and help one who doesn't appear to be like him and yet is an essential part of his family?" She smiled and put her hand on her chin and had that far-out, yo'd stare in her eyes. As I was watching her think, I didn't get her answer right then. I became acutely aware of the sound of a little girl's screams of "Dad, Dad" and I thought this kid is trying to get his attention. Yet I recognized some joy in that voice. You know how you can answer some one when they say "Hey You" and you're in a crowd and yet you knew that that person was calling you. That's how this girl's voice was possessing itself in my mind. It became the only clear voice above the many children. I searched for the owner of that voice and I saw her, Patricia Gray Dawn, pushing her way through the throng of kids with tears in her eyes and a big smile on her face. I glanced at D-Dawn and she also had tears flowing from her eyes. Patricia crashed into me and hugged and

Peace and love

www.ingramcontent.com/pod-product-compliance
Lightning Source LLC
Chambersburg PA
CBHW021756220426
43662CB00006B/78